Structural Design and Crashworthiness of Automobiles

Editors:
T.K.S. Murthy
C.A. Brebbia

A Computational Mechanics Publication

Springer-Verlag Berlin Heidelberg New York
London Paris Tokyo

T.K.S. MURTHY
Consultant
Computational Mechanics Institute
52 Henstead Road
Southampton
SO1 2DD
U.K.

C.A. BREBBIA
Computational Mechanics Institute
52 Henstead Road
Southampton
SO1 2DD
U.K.

Sub-editors: C.M. Mellors and J. Knudsen

 British Library Cataloguing in Publication Data

    Structural design and crashworthiness of automobiles.
      1. Automobiles — Bodies — Data processing
      2. Automobiles — Bodies — Mathematical models
    I. Murthy, T.K.S. II. Brebbia, C.A.
    629.2'6 TL255

    ISBN 0-905451-45-7

ISBN 0-905451-45-7 Computational Mechanics Publications Southampton
ISBN 0-931215-21-8 Computational Mechanics Publications Boston Los Angeles
ISBN 3-540-17504-0 Springer-Verlag Berlin Heidelberg New York London Paris Tokyo
ISBN 0-387-17504-0 Springer-Verlag New York Heidelberg Berlin London Paris Tokyo

This work is subject to copyright. All rights are reserved, whether the whole or part of the material is concerned, specifically those of translation, reprinting, re-use of illustrations, broadcasting, reproduction by photocopying machine or similar means, and storage in data banks. Under §54 of the German Copyright Law where copies are made for other than private use, a fee is payable to 'Verwertungsgesellschaft Wort', Munich.

© Computational Mechanics Publications 1987
   Springer-Verlag Berlin, Heidelberg
   Printed in Great Britain.

The use of registered names trademarks etc. in this publication does not imply, even in the absence of a specific statement, that such names are exempt from the relevant protective laws and regulations and therefore free for general use.

PREFACE

This book contains valuable contributions on the design of automobile structure, particularly from the viewpoint of its crashworthiness, which is an essential feature for the safety of passengers and other road users.

The first chapter deals with the modelling and numerical simulation of car structures under crash conditions. The next contribution describes the methodology behind the analysis system for predicting the effect of impact. This is followed by a chapter on the collapse of the driveshaft during frontal and rear impact.

Other chapters in this book deal with the problems of structural analysis, mainly using finite and boundary element techniques. The last contributions in this volume discuss in particular the potential of supercomputers for the analysis of automotive structures.

The book provides a work of reference on the design of automobile structures and the papers included are the edited versions of some of the papers presented at the 1st International Conference on Computer Aided Design, Manufacture and Operation in the Automotive Industries (COMPAUTO 87) organised by the Computational Mechanics Institute of Southampton, England and held in Geneva from March 10-12, 1987.

Other papers presented at the meeting are published simultaneously in the companion volume entitled "Computers in Design, Construction and Operation of Automobiles".

T.K.S. Murthy
C.A. Brebbia

CONTENTS

Numerical Simulation and Experimental Validation in Crashworthiness Applications
W. Jarzab, G. Bretz and R. Schwarz ... 1

Structural Impact Analysis in Design for Safety
G.H. Tidbury ... 17

Driveshaft Collapse Study
Kin S. Yeung, Fu S. Chang and Heng Yee Chen ... 35

Design Optimization using the Finite Element Program ANSYS^R
G. Müller, B-P. Walter ... 51

Program 'BEAST' for the Analysis of Beam/Membrane Assemblies on a Desktop Computer
D. Kecman, I. Kecman, V. Bulat ... 63

Program 'WEST-EX' for the Optimisation of the Rectangular Section Tubes Meeting Safety Requirements
D. Kecman ... 71

Torsional Rigidity of a Racing Car Frame
J.R. Banerjee ... 91

Thermal and Mechanical Analyses of Resistance Spot Welding: A Review of Existing Work
S.D. Sheppard ... 101

Applications of the 'BEASY' Boundary Element Code for Thermal and Stress Analysis within the Automotive Industry
J. Trevelyan, C.A. Brebbia and A. Mercy ... 121

Hot Spot Stress Concept for Spot-Welded Joints
D. Radaj ... 149

Efficient Computer Optimisation of Vehicle Structures within the Constraints of a Limited Time and Budget Allowance
L.M. Hall ... 171

The P-Version of the Finite Element Method in Gear Teeth Stress Analysis
A. Pidello, F.A. Raffa, P.P. Strona ... 193

The Integrated use of Supercomputers and Engineering Workstations to Maximise Productivity
R.A. Parris ... 213

The NISA II Family of Finite Element Programs for Linear and Non-linear Analysis on PC, Mini, Supermini, Mainframe and Supercomputers
K.S. Kothawala ... 229

Numerical Simulation and Experimental Validation in Crashworthiness Applications

W. Jarzab, G. Bretz and R. Schwarz
Industrieanlagen-Betriebsgesellschaft mbH, 8012 Ottobrun, Federal Republic of Germany

INTRODUCTION

For the automotive industry, safety of a car's passenger cabin gains increasing importance. Especially for prototypes crash experiments are very expensive. Therefore the Finite Element Method has become an indispensable and powerful tool in structural design. The modeling of metallic structures under crash resp. impact conditions requires adequate constitutive equations of nonlinear field theories and also sophisticated formulations of the arising contact problems. The numerical realization of all these models has to take into account recent advances in hardware development (ref./1/).

This paper deals with the numerical simulation of the frontal crash of a car with rear drive. One consequence concerning the contact modeling of rear drive is an additional generation of specific contact zones. The used finite element model consists of 2800 elements and 2604 nodes. The impact velocity is 12.5 m/s.

The numerical simulation of a frontal car crash with an impact velocity of 12.5 m/s has to be made by using a lagrangian code with explicit time integration considering physical shock wave dispersion in the structure. For some crashworthiness applications with sufficient small impact velocities, e.g. the bumper crash with 1 m/s, the use of implicit procedures is possible and much more efficient. An implicit procedure is characterized by an unconditionally stable time step and dynamic phenomena like the shock wave dispersion have no relevance.

2 NUMERICAL SIMULATION AND EXPERIMENTAL VALIDATION

Crashworthiness simulation does not replace experiments but provides a more detailed analysis of crash in connection with experiments. The time history of all interesting physical variables can be described and effects like energy absorption which are not measurable by experiments can be analysed. Also predictions concerning structural modifications of the car can be made.

ADVANCED NUMERICAL CRASH SIMULATION

The mathematical modeling of metallic structures under crash conditions requires the use of nonlinear constitutive equations. Of main interest are adequate material models of finite elasticity and dynamic plasticity (ref./1/). Most of the crashworthiness applications are characterized by finite element models with more than 5000 elements. For these applications the use of vector computers is indispensable. Therefore beside the crash code CRASHMAS which is able to handle models with a problem size of maximal 5000 elements the code Advanced Numerical Crash Simulation (ANCS) was developed. ANCS is an explicit lagrangian code with a linear and sequential program structure. There are the following main features:

- keyword directed input;
- explicit time integration;
- direct element formulations;
- nonlinear material modeling;
- material failure package;
- contact processor;
- adapted postprocessing;

The explicit time integration uses the central difference operator in connection with the lumped mass model. For many applications in the short time range (e.g. impact dynamics, penetration analysis) this form of explicit time integration has proved a powerful tool (ref./2/,/3/). The direct element formulations are based on certain assumptions concerning the local transformation behavior of the deformation gradient. All relevant strain tensors (e.g. GREEN-LAGRANGE, ALMANSI-EULER) can be expressed by means of the deformation gradient (ref./1/). Most of the nonlinear material models are given in a real stress formulation (CAUCHY stress) and an engineering stress formulation (PIOLA-KIRCHHOFF stress) as well. Concerning finite elasticity isotropic and anisotropic constitutive laws are implemented. In dynamic plasticity with finite strain the following options are available:

- generalized flow rule with isotropic work hardening containing the PRANDTL-REUSZ law as a special case;
- kinematic hardening with strain rate dependency;
- DRYSDALE's model for impact applications;
- PERZYNA's over stress theory / viscoplasticity;

The material failure package contains the following options:

- local material failure models (stress resp. strain criteria, specific energy criteria);
- stress intensity factors for different failure modes;
- delamination model especially for crashworthiness analysis of composite structures;
- crack opening model with dynamic crack propagation;
- erosion model;
- statistical models (shear band model);

The implemented contact processor (ref./2/, /3/) is based on a generalized master/slave concept which allows the modeling of arbitrary 2D and 3D contact problems.

The main structure of ANCS is shown in the following Figure 1. After input and logical input check, the geometry of the undeformed reference state is evaluated. The required geometrical information for direct element formulations, nonlinear strain analysis and material modeling is calculated and stored up. Afterwards the mass distribution due to the lumped mass model is done. For given node forces the central difference operator calculates the new positions of all nodal points taking into account the defined boundary conditions. In the finite element part the deformation of all elements is calculated and in consequence via the material constitutive model the stress and the internal forces are known. Specific algorithms compatible with the lumped mass model provide the nodal forces. If an element has failed, the chosen failure model is activated and the belonging nodal forces are modified. The contact processor redefines the geometry in contact zones and calculates the contact forces. After this procedure all nodal forces are known and for the following time step the central difference operator calculates the new positions of all nodal points. If the given final time is not reached the described procedure will be repeated again. At each moment all nodal and element informations are known. Therefore the history of all interesting physical state variables can be evaluated.

4 NUMERICAL SIMULATION AND EXPERIMENTAL VALIDATION

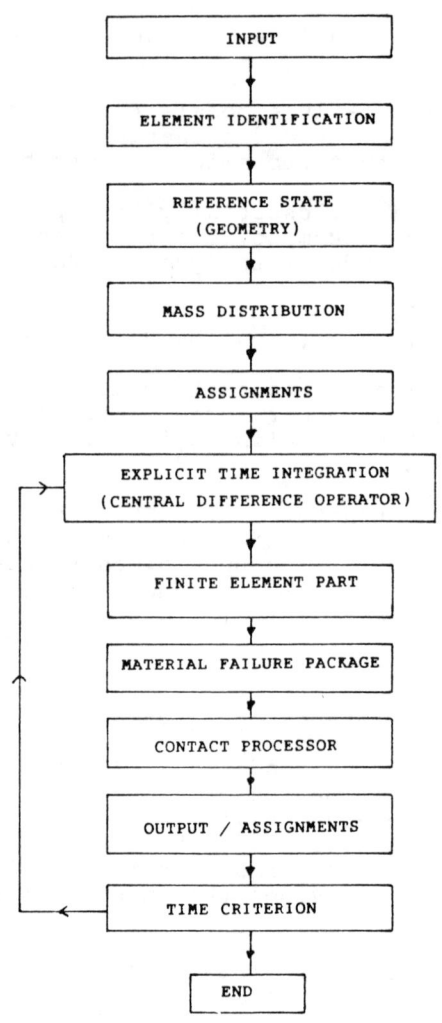

FIGURE 1. MAIN PROGRAM ANCS.

Figure 2 shows the cross-sectional failure of a box beam calculated with resp. without contact processor. The surfaces of all crashing substructures are defined as master planes and slave points as well. Simultaneously with explicit time integration the contact geometry has to be cleared up automatically. The nodal velocities in new contact are modified in relation to the assumption of fully plastic collision. The calculation of contact forces in normal resp. tangential direction is made due to dynamic equilibrium. The calculation without contact processor shows an overrunning of structural points in the contact zone. The same example calculated with contact processor prevents that overrunning.

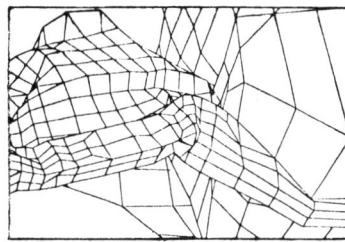 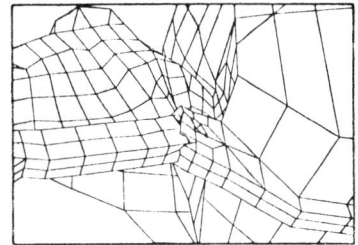

FIGURE 2. CROSS-SECTIONAL FAILURE OF A BOX BEAM CALC. WITH RESP. WITHOUT CONTACT PROCESSOR

The assumption of a fully plastic collision has to be modified for crashworthiness applications for nonmetallic structures, e.g. composite materials. The matrix material of carbon fibre reinforced composites is characterized by dissipative phenomena like creeping, relaxation and retardation. Of main importance for the material modeling are constitutive equations of anisotropic viscoelasticity. The epoxy resin is nearly incompressible and in consequence an additional lagrangian parameter representing the internal constraint has to be taken into account. The lagrangian parameter cannot be determined from a knowledge of the deformation history alone but has to be determined with the aid of Cauchy's law of motion and the imposed boundary conditions. The post failure behavior of composite structures is influenced by the viscoelastic material properties. Only under impact resp. crash loadings the dissipative phenomena are negligible and the material can be considered as anisotropic elastic (ref./1/).

6 NUMERICAL SIMULATION AND EXPERIMENTAL VALIDATION

FRONTAL CRASH OF A CAR WITH REAR DRIVE

For the front half of a car structure without engine and wheels in the undeformed and deformed state, a drop test with an impact velocity of 14.6 m/s has been simulated. This test should show the applicability of the lagrangian code CRASHMAS (ref./1/,/4/). Therefore only a small finite element model with 768 nodes and 797 elements was used (Figure 4). Figure 5 shows the deformed structure at t = 42 ms when 98.5% of the kinetic energy are transformed into work of deformation. The obtained numerical results have been compared with experiments. In Figure 5 the comparison between measured and calculated contact forces is plotted. The calculation was compared with two experiments because the experimental values are influenced and perturbated by external conditions like the transmission characteristics of the measuring apparatus. The correlation between experimental and numerical data is, even in detail , clearly visible.

A more complex finite element model with 2800 elements and 2604 nodes was used for the numerical simulation of the frontal crash of a car with rear drive (Figure 6). The impact velocity was 12.5 m/s. The rear part of the car was modeled as a rigid structure. One consequence concerning the contact modeling of rear drive is an additional generation of specific contact zones. The complete contact problem with 1342 slave points, 1045 master planes and 8 contact spaces is shown in Figure 7 (ref./5/).

The deformation of the car structure at t = 52 resp. 60 ms is plotted in Figure 8 resp. 9. The deformation of the car body is shown in Figure 10 and Figure 11. Of main importance for the comparison between calculation and experiment are displacements, velocities and accelerations. The related variables (normed time axis) for a structural point in the rear part are plotted in Figure 12.

The energy balance (Figure 13) is showing a sufficient numerical stability during simulation. The energy absorption (Figure 15) of the side member is 57%, of the car body 24% and of the engine 14% of the total work of deformation. This effect which is not measurable by experiments gives valuable information concerning the structural design of components and enables the engineer to optimize the safety of a car's passenger cabin. In Table 1 the whole deformation process is evaluated comparing calculated and measured data.

NUMERICAL SIMULATION AND EXPERIMENTAL VALIDATION 7

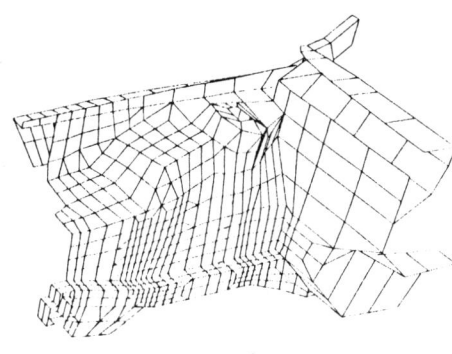

FIGURE 3.
FINITE ELEMENT MODEL

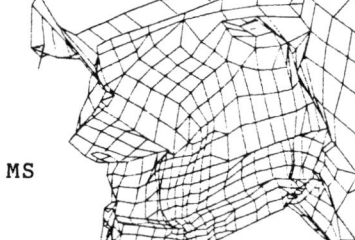

FIGURE 4.
DEFORMATION OF
STRUCTURE T = 42 MS

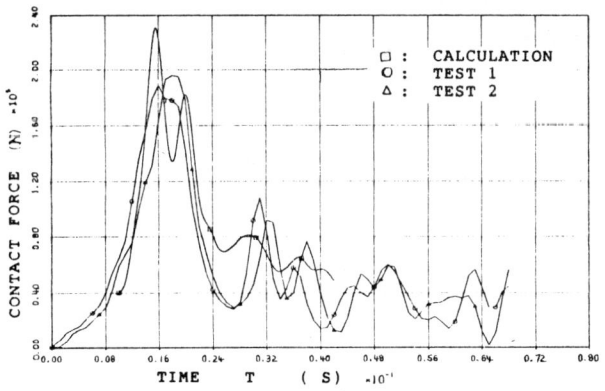

FIGURE 5.   CONTACT FORCE

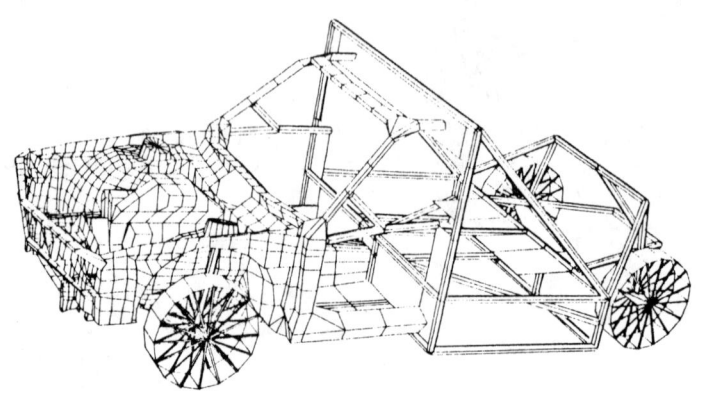

FIGURE 6. FINITE ELEMENT MODEL

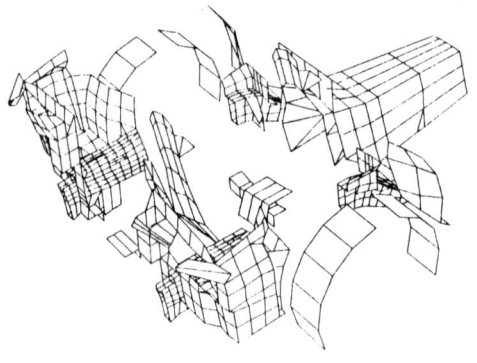

FIGURE 7. CONTACT REGION

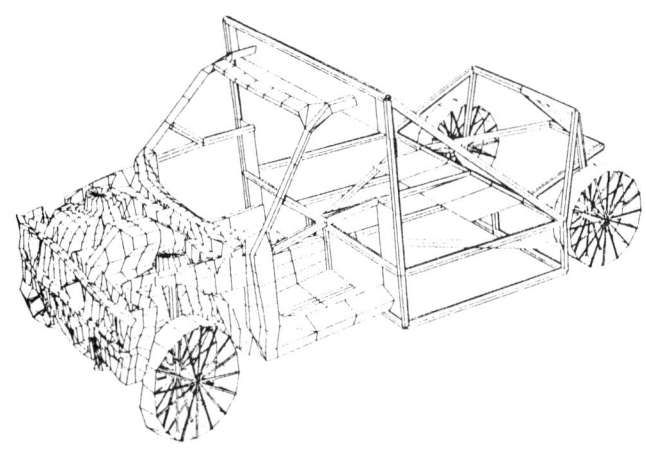

FIGURE 8. DEFORMATION OF STRUCTURE   T = 52 MS

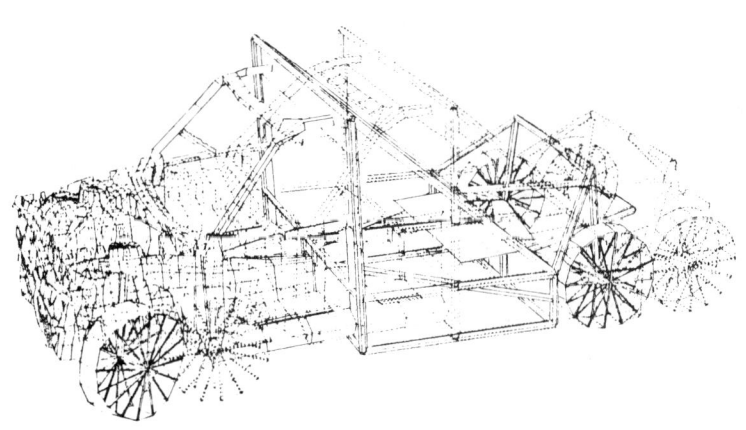

FIGURE 9. DEFORMATION OF STRUCTURE   T = 60 MS

10 NUMERICAL SIMULATION AND EXPERIMENTAL VALIDATION

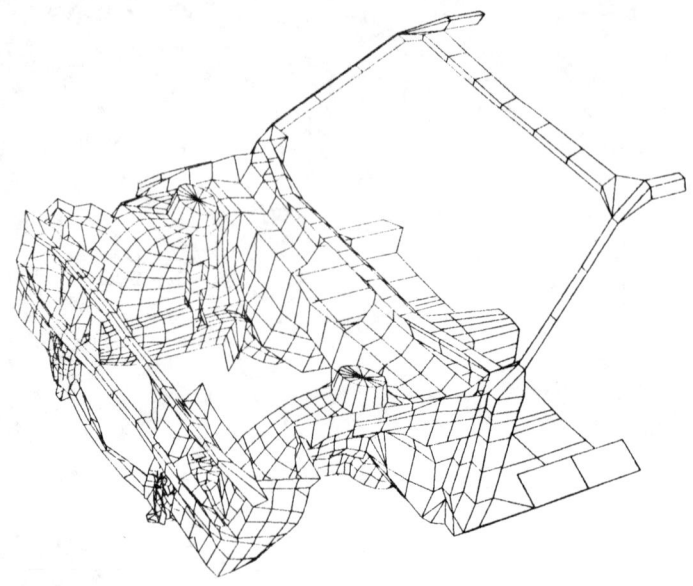

FIGURE 10.   DEFORMATION OF CAR BODY   T = 30 MS

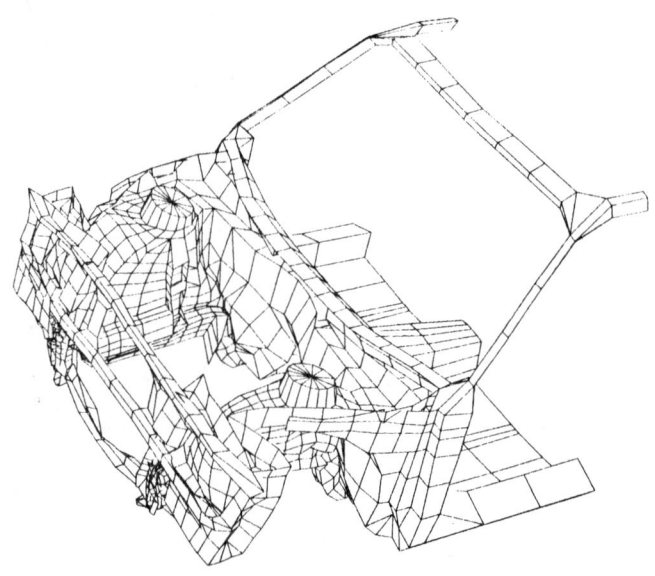

FIGURE 11.   DEFORMATION OF CAR BODY   T = 60 MS

NUMERICAL SIMULATION AND EXPERIMENTAL VALIDATION 11

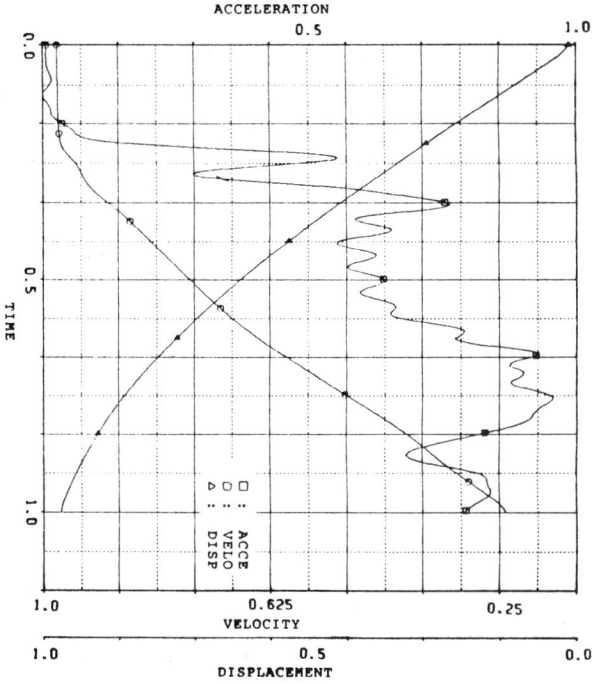

FIGURE 12.   REAR: DISPLACEMENT, VELOCITY, ACCELERATION

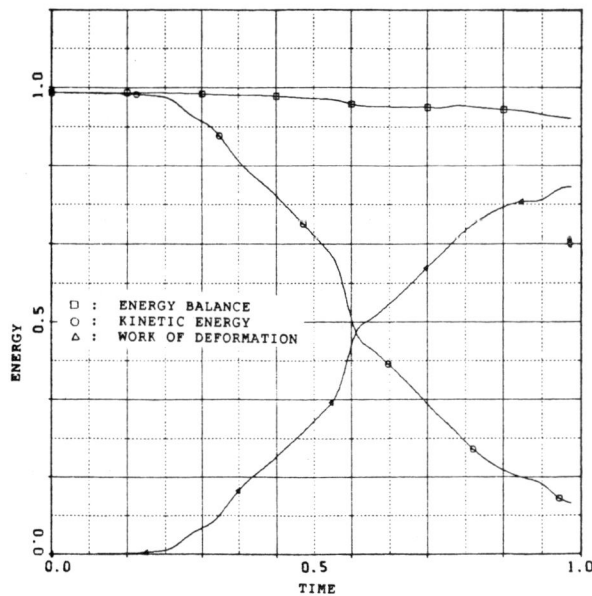

FIGURE 13.   ENERGY BALANCE

12 NUMERICAL SIMULATION AND EXPERIMENTAL VALIDATION

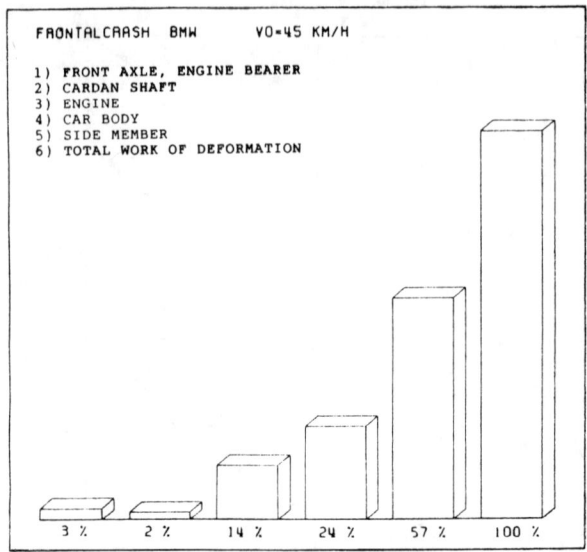

FIGURE 15. ENERGY ABSORPTION

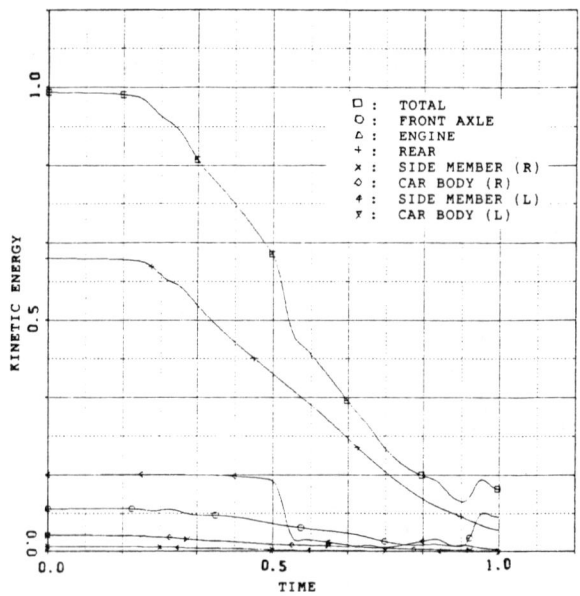

FIGURE 14. KINETIC ENERGY DISTRIBUTION

EVENT	TIME	
	(a)	(b)
CONTACT AND PUSH TOGETHER OF THE FRONTAL PLATES	0.0 - 0.17	0.0 - 0.23
CONTACT OF THE ENGINE MOUNTINGS	0.17	0.10
BUCKLING AND DEFORMATON OF THE ENGINE MOUNTING NEAR THE WEB PLATE	0.17 - 0.40	0.13 - 0.17
CRACKING OF THE RIGHT ENGINE MOUNTING NEAR THE FRONT AXLE BEAM	0.47	0.43
TEAR OFF / TRANSMISSION BRIDGE	---	0.73
CRACKING OF THE FLANGE NEAR THE SIDE PANEL IN FRONT OF THE PADDLE BOX	0.40 - 0.50	0.37 - 0.40
CONTACT WHEEL WITH PADDLE BOX	0.47	0.43 - 0.47
IMPACT OF THE MOTOR ON THE DEFLECTING PLATE	0.53	0.57
CONTACT OF THE FRONT AXLE BEAM WITH THE OIL PAN	0.73	0.83
CONTACT OF THE MOTOR WITH THE DEFLECTOR PLATE	0.80	0.93 - 1.00

TABLE 1. DEFORMATION PROCESS - CALCULATION (a) EXPERIMENT (b).

The correlation between calculation and experiment is quite good until the motor impacts on the deflecting plate. After t = 0.53 s there is no good correlation because the motor was modeled as a nearly rigid structure. Therefore further crashworthiness applications will use a more detailed finite element model of the motor (ref./2/,/5/).

DYNAMIC BEHAVIOR OF STRUCTURAL COMPONENTS

The modeling of energy absorption effects of crushing structures depends on an adequate description of the basic folding and collapse mechanisms. The crushing behaviour of plate intersections was investigated in detail by T.WIERZBICKI (ref./6/). Using the introduced kinematic method of plasticity, suitably generalized to nonlinear strain, the study of collapse modes and the associated crushing resistance of thin-walled structures consisting of a system of two or more intersecting plates is possible. The solutions are correlating well with the existing empirical formulae and the known experimental data. Of main interest in crashworthiness analysis is the determination of the contact force level and the energy absorption capabilities of thin-walled structures.

An explicit lagrangian code allows only the simulation of folding and buckling mechanisms for structures with certain geometrical imperfections. The buckling of ideal structures mathematically described by an eigenvalue resp. bifurcation problem can be modeled only using an implicit code. For many applications in structural design the interesting box beam girders are pre-deformed in order to get an a priori chosen deformed configuration.

Figure 16 shows the buckling and folding mechanism of a box beam with a geometrical imperfection in the undeformed reference state. The plotted structure was modeled by a simple finite element model consisting of plate elements with four integration points in each layer. The basic aim of that simulation was to prove the applicability of CRASH-MAS to the description of folding mechanisms. Further investigations will be concentrated on real thin-walled structures which are of importance in crashworthiness analysis of aircraft and car structures (ref./7/).

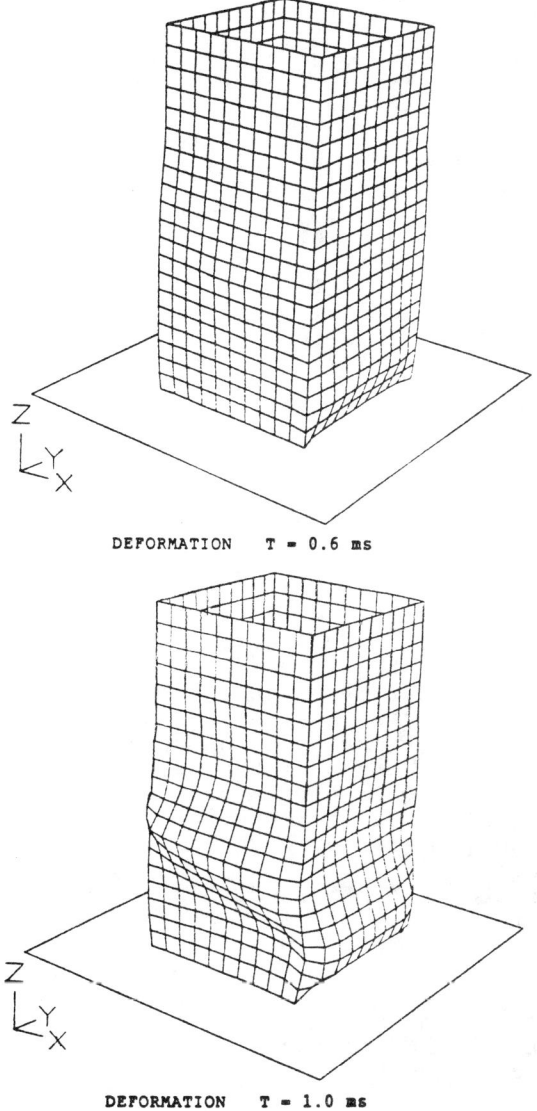

FIGURE 16. BUCKLING AND FOLD OVER OF A BOX BEAM.

CONCLUSIONS

Modern analytical models and their numerical realizations have become powerful tools in crashworthiness simulation. The explicit lagrangian codes CRASHMAS and ANCS allow detailed simulations prior to many experimental tests. The dynamic behaviour of structural components and the involved mechanisms like folding and energy absorption can be described in detail. For most of the interesting applications the use of vector computers is indispensable because the problem size of the finite element models is greater than 5000 elements. New fields of application of ANCS will be the crashworthiness of composite structures in aircraft and spacecraft industries (ref./7/).

LITERATURE

1. Jarzab W. (1986). Mathematical Modeling and Applications in Crash Analysis, in Supercomputer Applications in Automotive Research and Engineering Development / Suppl. (Ed. Marino C.), Proceedings of the International Conference of Supercomputer Applications in the Automotive Industry, Zurich, Switzerland, October 1986. Computational Mechanics Publications, Southampton.
2. Bretz G. Jarzab W. and Raasch I. (1986). Berechnung eines frontalen Crashvorganges bei einer heckangetriebenen Limousine, in VDI-Berichte 613 (Ed. Radaj D.), pp.507-525, Proceedings of the VDI-Conference "Berechnung im Automobilbau", Würzburg, Germany, November 1986. VDI-Verlag, Düsseldorf.
3. Giavotto V. (1986). Crash Simulation Models and Interactions with Experiments. AGARD-report No.737, pp. 3.1-3.10.
4. Bretz G. et al. (1984). Experimentelle Untersuchung des Deformationsverhaltens eines PKW-Vorderwagens unter Crash-Bedingungen. IABG-report B-TF-1576. Ottobrunn.
5. Bretz G. and Schwarz R. (1986). Berechnung eines PKW-Frontalcrash für ein Fahrzeug mit längsliegendem Aggregat und Standardantrieb. IABG-report B-TF-2015. Ottobrunn.
6. Wierzbicki T. (1983), Crushing Behavior of Plate Intersections. Chapter 3, Structural Crashworthiness, (Ed. Jones N., Wierzbicki T.), pp.66-95, Butterworths, London.
7. Jarzab W. and Schwarz R. (1987). Crashworthiness of Aircraft Structures, (paper to be presented at the AGARD-Conference 1987).

Structural Impact Analysis in Design for Safety

G.H. Tidbury

Consultant to the Cranfield Impact Centre, Cranfield, Beds. MK43 0AL, U.K.

INTRODUCTION

The simulation of impacts on structures of all kinds is receiving considerable attention under the general heading of design for crashworthiness. The main impetus for this new technology has come from the automotive industry where the introduction of crash testing as a legal requirement for passenger cars led to the setting up by the large companies of elaborate test facilities. The extensive testing programmes led to the successful design of cars able to pass the test by empirical modifications based on the experience gained from close examination of the results.

It was clear from the start of this activity that it would be a great benefit to designers, both in time saving and in cost, if computer simulation could be used to supplement and eventually take the place of testing. The first stage in this process was the development of spring/mass/damper models of the front end of cars, mainly associated with Kamal[1], the non-linear spring characteristics were originally found by quasi-static crush testing of a prototype front structure of the car. This basic method has proved to be invaluable in modifying designs to improve their crashworthiness since the effect of changes to the stiffness of different parts of the structure can be assessed rapidly. As computing power increases it has become possible to predict the crush characteristics of different elements of the structure and incorporate the results in the simulation.

The Cranfield Impact Centre and its predecessor, the Structural Design Group of the then School of Automotive Studies, adopted a different approach to the simulation of crashworthiness based on the use of static non-linear finite element programs. This was made possible by the assumption that the mass of the crushing sheet metal or other deforming part of the structure is likely to be small compared with the total mass of the whole vehicle. This work started with the writing of a large deflection non-linear program, CRASH-D[2], which has since been substantially developed by other members of the centre. As is shown in the

paper the sophistication of the simulation has developed to
include dynamic programs so that the effect of impacts on the
occupants of cars can be assessed at the design stage. The
development of the method will be illustrated by reference to
projects undertaken by the Centre and the integrated method as
currently applied will be described.

FIRE ENGINE CAB DESIGN

A fire engine cab was designed in conjunction with the
manufacturer to meet hitherto unattempted safety standards. The
preferred method of manufacture of the basic structure was by
welding square or rectangular tubes to form a framework to
withstand roof crush loads and local frontal impacts at the level
of the drivers knee. The complete framework was first analysed
by a standard finite element program, Stardyne, using the model
shown in Figure 1. This was used to isolate the members in the
framework with the highest loads so that a more simple model
could be used for the CRASH-D analysis, Figure 2. The non-linear
bending characteristics of the tubing to be used were first found
by testing samples beyond the elastic limit. The results of the
analysis indicated changes in the design which were incorporated
in the first prototype which was tested and shown to meet the
requirements. Further improvements were then made to prepare the
design for production and after further computer checks this
structure also passed the tests at the first attempt. This
example of collaboration between industry and an academic
institution has been documented (Miles & Wardill[3] and Rose[4]).

AGRICULTURAL TRACTOR CAB DESIGN

An international standard for the pendulum testing of tractor cabs
has been in force for some time and since most of these are
designed as tubular frameworks they have been a natural choice
for the use of the Cranfield method. As in the case of the fire
engine cab the quasi-static approach to the calculation of the
structural deformation caused by dynamic impact was shown to be
adequate for design purposes (Hardy[5]). The computer model used
is shown in Figure 3.

BUS STRUCTURAL DESIGN

The Structural Design Group was involved from the beginning in
the investigation of bus rollover accidents for the UK Department
of Transport and in the formulation of superstructure strength
requirements which were to be submitted to the E.C.E. These
regulations will probably be the first to include calculation as a
method of satisfying type test requirements. In the course of
this work many examples of the accuracy of the simulation by the
use of CRASH-D were encountered and the Department commissioned
the writing of a user manual so that the program would be
available for use on bureau by companies and regulating bodies.

In the course of this work a method of calculating the collapse behaviour of square and rectangular tubes was developed by Kecman[6]. Since the superstructure of buses must be frameworks (window frames) the way was open to calculate the behaviour of a bus structure during a rollover from the drawings of the structure. This was done for a bus a full year before the structure was built and tested, Figure 4 indicates the deformation obtained with the CRASH-D program. The results of the prediction and the test showed good agreement (Kecman & Tidbury[7]) so that the method can be confidently used in the design of buses to meet the regulations and, with some experience of the strength of joints etc., by the regulating authorities.

PASSENGER CAR SIDE IMPACTS

The CRASH-D program was originally written as an attempt to simulate the large deflection of a car side frame under the loading expected during a side impact so it is not surprising that this type of impact has formed the basis of a complete design method developed by the Centre. Known as the 'test aided computer prediction method' (Sadeghi & Suthurst[e]) it allows the analyst to predict the deformation of the structure using the very simple structural idealisation shown in Figure 5. By computing the motion of the impacted vehicle the lateral velocity of the side frame can be found and compared with the test result, Figure 6. The motion of the occupants and their injury levels can also be computed. This allows the design of a car side structure to be modified until the desired safety level has been achieved without expensive full scale impact testing. The 'test' part of the method only involves static testing of the joints and beams in the side frame of the car. The dynamic section of the program used in this simulation is a fairly simple version of the vehicle dynamics programs developed for other purposes, although it does allow for the rolling of the vehicle during the impact in order to assess whether the car is rolling towards or away from the occupant when he strikes the deforming structure. A version of the Crash Victim Simulation (CVS) program developed by the Calspan Corporation is used to model the occupant motion. It has been found necessary to measure the characteristics of the dummy used in the test if the correlation of the measured and computed velocities of the occupant to the levels illustrated in Figures 7 & 8 is required. An indication of the improvement in design achievable with this method is given in Figures 9 & 10 where the lateral deformation and velocity of the sideframe of a 'baseline' vehicle and a vehicle built incorporating improvements to the structure suggested by the analysis are compared.

SAFETY BARRIER DESIGN

In the development of road safety barriers it is usual to test various designs by running different types of vehicles into prototype barriers. This is both time consuming and expensive and the Impact Centre was asked to investigate the possibility of extending the range of tests by theoretical methods using the results of some tests already completed as a baseline. The collapse behaviour of the barrier was expected to be sufficiently low speed to be predicted by CRASH-D and the load carrying capability shown in Figure 11 was obtained. It was realised that it would not be possible to use this quasi-static program to represent the vehicle as the object of the new barrier design was to prevent laden trucks from crossing from one lane to the other so that a dynamic program was required. A program developed for NASA to model light aircraft crashes called KRASH used the same type of collapsing framework model as CRASH-D but included the dynamic effect of lumped masses at each node. This program satisfactorily modelled the path of a laden truck after the impact with the barrier (Sadeghi & Blake[9]) using the idealisation of the truck shown in Figure 12, with the result shown in Figure 13 for an 80 km/hr impact at 15° to the barrier. Figure 14 indicated that the agreement, although not absolute, was good enough to be used for barrier design purposes. The effect on the truck driver could also be predicted using the CVS code as illustrated by the graphical output of Figure 15. Incidentally it was shown that the proposed stake spacing for the barrier could be reduced as a result of the analysis with a large possible saving in cost. It will be realised that the vehicle to barrier impact takes place over a very much longer time period than car to car impacts and this caused some new problems which had to be overcome in this analysis.

CAR TO TRUCK FRONTAL IMPACTS

In all frontal impacts involving front engined cars the mass of the engine is moved rearwards relative to the overall centre of gravity of the car. This means that the CRASH-D program is not likely to be applicable and again it was thought that the KRASH code would be suitable. The program was, however, written for the impact of an aircraft with the ground which was represented by a stiffness and although it dealt satisfactorily with the barrier impact where the barrier could also be represented by a stiffness there was no facility to model another vehicle which could also move. This allowed the adoption of a device whereby the two vehicles could be treated as one during the simulation of the deformation, as illustrated in Figure 16. The large difference in mass between the two vehicles also means that the truck can be treated as a rigid body, further simplifying the analysis. However the car has to be modelled in greater structural detail than for side impact analysis and the collapse behaviour of many parts of the front structure is required for the simulation. Where possible these parts should be tested statically but there are usually many elements whose characteristics have to be estimated by experience. The results have been good enough for the optimum parameters of front underrun bumpers to be obtained, (Walton[10]).

PEDESTRIAN IMPACTS

The CVS program has been developed by other design groups to model passenger car impacts with pedestrians so that the facility that the Centre had built up with the program could be used to model this type of impact. In order to obtain accurate data for the simulation a special pendulum rig was built to measure the dynamic stiffness of parts of the dummy used and the front of the car under consideration. The results of the simulation, Figure 17, were then found to be in good agreement with full scale tests carried out at the company's own facility. The program was then used to improve the shape of the front of the car to minimise pedestrian injuries.

RACING CAR FRONT IMPACTS

When the Formula 1 regulating body (FISA) introduced a safety requirement restricting the deformation of the nose cone of the cars to the area in front of the drivers feet it was found that a pendulum rig existing at the Centre could be simply modified to meet the speed and impact mass requirements. Because this rig, after approval by FISA, proved to be a cheap facility for developing and approving the design it was, and is, used by many of the racing teams. As usual when a regulation has to be met quickly there was no time to develop a computer simulation and the teams managed to meet the requirements by a mixture of test and modification, sometimes with advice based on the experience of the Centre. As many of the teams are using sandwich structures with composite skins of carbon or Kevlar fibres an attempt was made in a student project to use the finite element program LUSAS in conjunction with a preprocessor written at Cranfield called LAMANAL to model the dynamic crush of these composites. This exercise was successful in showing that the combination could deal with this complex problem although more work is needed before it can be used for design purposes (Beermann, Thum & Tidbury").

INTEGRATED CRASHWORTHINESS ANALYSIS TECHNIQUE

The analysis technique that has been developed from the experience gained from the examples given above has led to an approach to the design of vehicles for crashworthiness which is summarised in Figure 18. The numbered steps in the flow chart can be described as follows:-

1. Component Data Base, This consists of the bending collapse characteristics of beams and joints. Most of the data has been obtained from cantilever testing of automotive beam sections, eg. window pillars, B-posts, roof to post joints etc. The more simple shapes are amenable to calculation and the necessary formulae are included in the data base. It will be realised from the number of examples quoted above that a considerable data base already

exists and efforts are now concentrated on classifying this data and extending it by developing empirical formulae to deal with similar cross sections. The data base is also being extended to include the axial collapse characteristics of beams of various cross sections.

2. Acquisition of Component Data. Ideally this step should be the transfer of data from the data base to the finite element structural program to be used in the particular analysis. If the data is not available for the particular design being analysed the individual component must be manufactured and tested. During the test the collapse mechanism and sequence of the collapse is noted so that modification of the cross section to delay or prevent collapse will be made possible by stabilising the areas where fold lines or fractures are initiated. All new data is, of course, added to the data base.

3. Overall Collapse Analysis. This is defined as a non-linear quasi-static finite element analysis normally made with CRASH-D or one of its derivatives. The analysis yields non-linear curves of the load carrying capacity of the structure at selected nodes and in selected directions. The sequence in which the joints collapse and the strength and energy absorbed by each individual component is also output by the program to be used in the next step.

4. Structural Optimisation. The aim of the optimisation is to spread the energy absorption as evenly as possible among the deforming elements of the structure. The information obtained from the previous section enables the designer to single out those joints and elements which require redesign to achieve this compatibility. At the present stage of the system no attempt has been made to automate this optimisation and considerable engineering skill and experience is required to achieve a structure with compatible strength and energy absorption among all the elements being deformed in the impact. If step 3 cannot be carried out it is still possible to achieve some measure of optimisation by comparing the general load carrying capacity of the elements and ensuring that these are compatible.

5. Improvement in the Strength and Energy Absorption of Components. This step and the following two steps are really part of the optimisation process already described but the loop involves the choice of the properties to be improved (bending, compression etc.) and the percentage increase required in each property.

6. Bending Collapse Calculation. At this stage a calculation is made to find the simplified overall dimensions and thickness required for the component to reach the increased structural properties called for by the previous section.

7. Component and Joint Design. The simplified section sizes arrived at in step 6 are generally sufficient to act as guidelines in the initial design or concept stage of the vehicle. In the case of passenger cars these simplified sections are turned into complex shapes due to the design requirements other than crashworthiness and the evolving shapes have to be checked by reference to steps 2 and 6 where appropriate. As indicated in the flow chart it is often necessary to repeat the overall collapse analysis to determine the effect of the new section or joint on the behaviour of the whole structure.

8. Dynamic Analysis. The dynamic analysis may be carried out in two ways depending on the type of collapse analysis used. If the normal quasi-static (CRASH-D) type of analysis is used because the mass of the collapsing structure is small compared with the vehicle mass a simplified vehicle dynamics program is used. The vehicle is considered rigid with the suspension and tyre characteristics either measured or, more often, estimated, for the particular vehicle. The mass and inertia values are also assumed to be constant and similarly taken from measurements or estimated from those of similar vehicles. Since it is usually difficult to obtain measured values for the actual vehicle it is fortunate that the computed motion of the struck car, for instance, is not very sensitive to the values assumed in this calculation. In particular it is almost impossible to obtain accurate tyre force values for a wheel being pushed laterally from a stationary position which is the condition for side impacts. In this analysis the non-linear load carrying capacity of the structure is used as a non-linear spring in the dynamic equations of the car motion. Since the motion of the structure relative to the car's centre of gravity is also known the program can compute the speed of the collapsing structure relative to the rest of the vehicle as shown in Figure 6, referred to in the section on side impacts.

If the major masses of the vehicle are involved in the deformation a dynamic structural collapse program (KRASH) is used the dynamics of the vehicle are usally included so that some of the steps listed can be combined in this analysis. In either case the output is sufficient for the next step in the sequence.

9. Occupant Simulation. This separate program (CVS) calculates the speed of the occupant either with or without a restraint relative to the collapsing structure and times the impact of various parts of the occupant with the structure as well as computing the impact forces. The relevant injury indices can also be output.

10. Dynamic Optimisation. If the results of step 9 show that the severity indices are too high the complete analysis system is repeated, modifying the structural compponents until acceptable levels are obtained.

CONCLUSIONS

The method by which a design can progress from the concept stage to a structure suitable for production is indicated in the chart of Figure 19. It will be noted that in this method design for crashworthiness is included at the heart of the early stages of the system. In actual design situations the method is proving very cost effective as it reduces the number of prototypes needed for crash testing and the consequent late design changes. The ability of the Impact Centre to apply the method to a variety of problems and to introduce new codes where necessary has been well established by the range of automotive examples quoted. The general method is now also being applied to other structural impact problems.

REFERENCES

1 Kamal M.M. (1970), Analysis and Simulation of Vehicle Barrier Impact. SAE Paper No. 700414.

2 Miles J.C. (1977), The Application of Finite Element Methods to Vehicle Collapse Analysis. PhD Thesis, Cranfield Institute of Technology.

3 Miles J.C. and Wardill G.A. (1977), Analysis and Design of a Fire Engine Safety Cab using Finite Element Methods. I.Mech.E. Paper No. 19129/77.

4 Rose R.A.L. (1977), The Evolution of the CVS Water Tender and its Safety Cab. I.Mech.E. Paper No. 19135/77.

5 Hardy R.N. (1983), Analytical and Experimental Investigations of a Tractor Cab. Proceedings of the International Journal of Vehicle Design, London, June 1983.

6 Kecman D. (1979), Bending Collapse of Rectangular and Square Tubes in Relation to the Bus Roll Over Problem. PhD Thesis, Cranfield Institute of Technology.

7 Kecman D. and Tidbury G.H. (1982), Theoretical Prediction of the Complete Behaviour of a Coach Subject to the Proposed Standard Rollover Test. Proceedings of the FISITA Congress, Melbourne, 1982.

8 Sadeghi M.M. and Suthurst G.D. (1982), Test Aided Computer Prediction of Passenger Car Side Impact. Proceedings of the ISATA Conference, Wolfsburg, 1982.

9   Sadeghi M.M. and Blake M.P. (1986), Vehicle to Safety Fence Impact Studies. 65th Annual Meeting, Transportation Research Board, Washington, 1986.

10 Walton A.C. (1986), The Simulation of a Lorry-Mounted Anti-underrun Device in Frontal Collisions between a Car and a Heavy Lorry. PhD Thesis, Cranfield Institute of Technology.

11 Beermann H.J. Thum H-M. and Tidbury G.H. (1986), The Prediction of the Energy Absorbtion of Composite Structural Materials. Proceedings of the Second International Conference on Fibre Reinforced Composites, I.Mech.E. Liverpool, 1986.

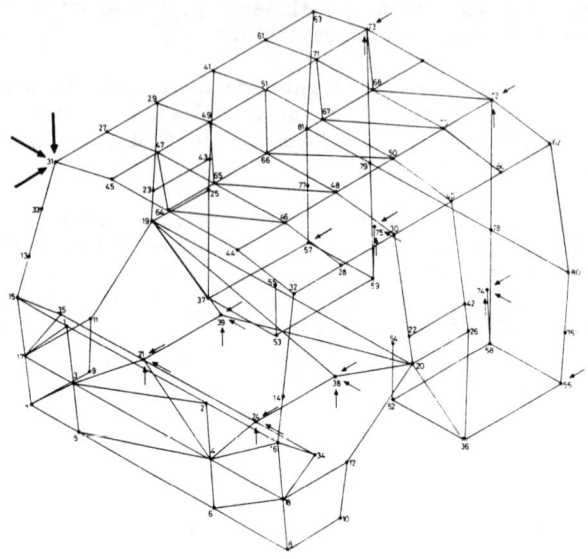

Figure 1. Elastic finite element model of Fire Engine Cab.

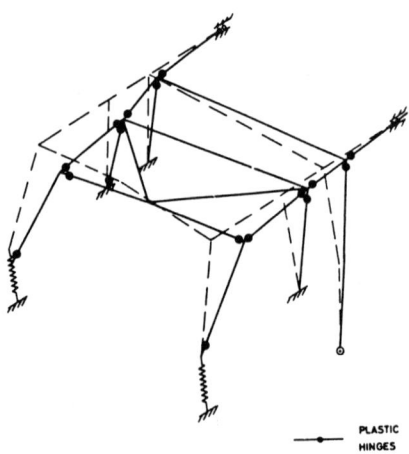

Figure 2. CRASH-D model of Fire Engine Cab, computed deformed shape shown by dashed lines.

STRUCTURAL IMPACT ANALYSIS IN DESIGN FOR SAFETY

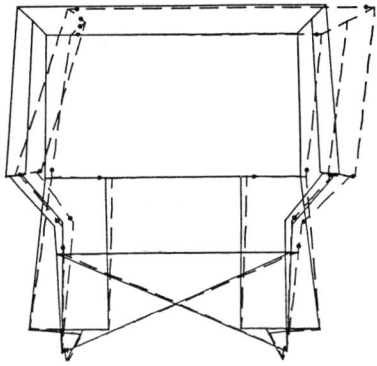

Figure 3. Front view of computer model of Agricultural Tractor Cab, deflection for side impact at roof level shown by dashed lines.

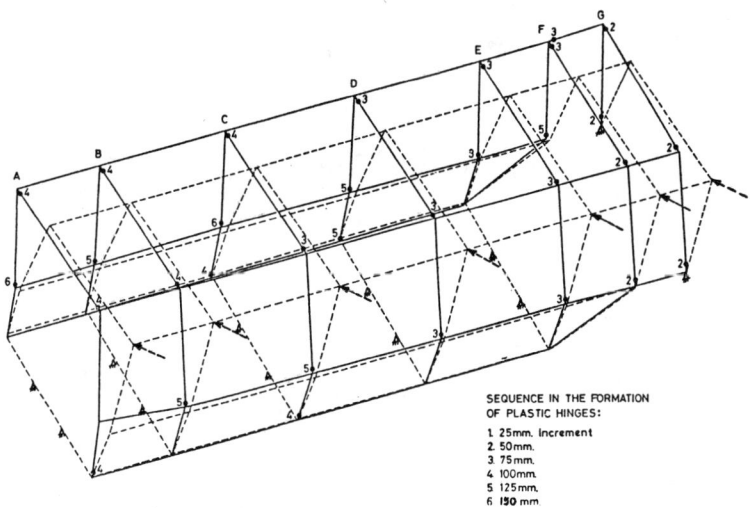

Figure 4. CRASH-D model of complete Bus Structure showing the deformed shape (full lines). Sequence of the formation of the plastic hinges also shown.

28 STRUCTURAL IMPACT ANALYSIS IN DESIGN FOR SAFETY

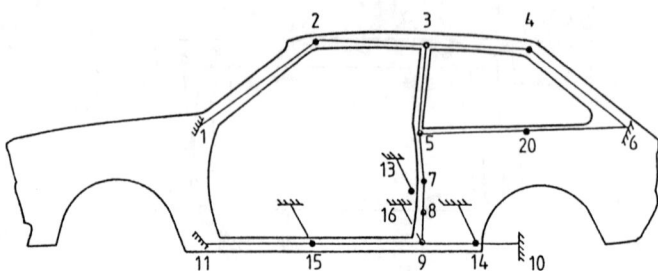

Figure 5. Typical structural idealisation for a Two Door Car side impact analysis.

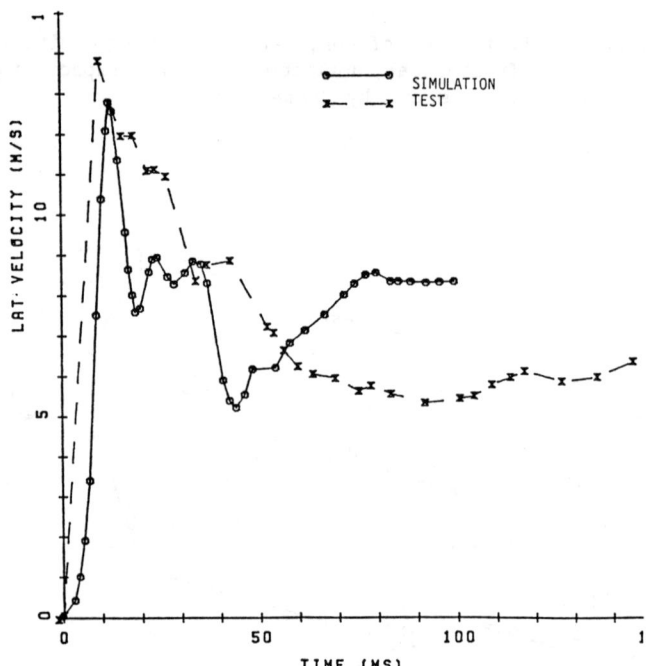

Figure 6. Comparison of test and simulated lateral velocity of the side frame of the target car during side impact.

STRUCTURAL IMPACT ANALYSIS IN DESIGN FOR SAFETY 29

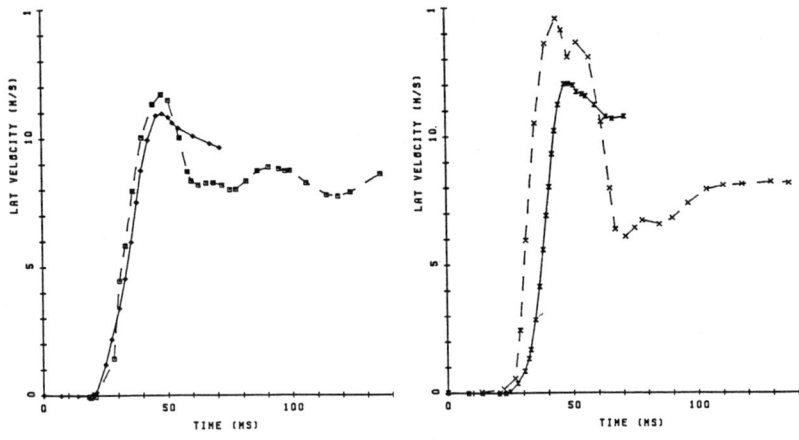

Figure 7. Chest velocity.   Figure 8. Pelvis velocity.

Comparison of the velocities of parts of the occupant during side impact; solid line from theory, dashed line measured from full scale crash test.

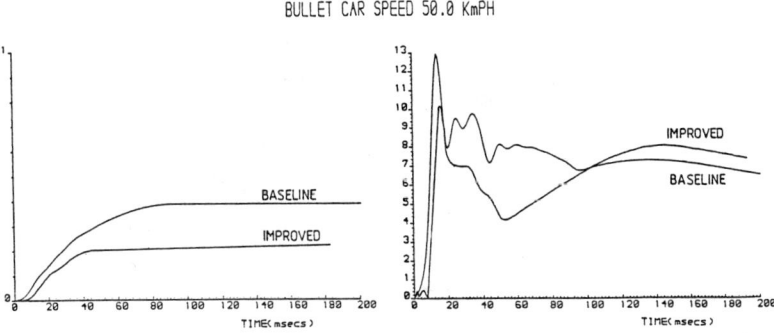

Figure 9. Deformation.   Figure 10. Velocity.

Comparison of the behaviour of a node in the sideframe of a baseline vehicle and a modified vehicle during a side impact.

30 STRUCTURAL IMPACT ANALYSIS IN DESIGN FOR SAFETY

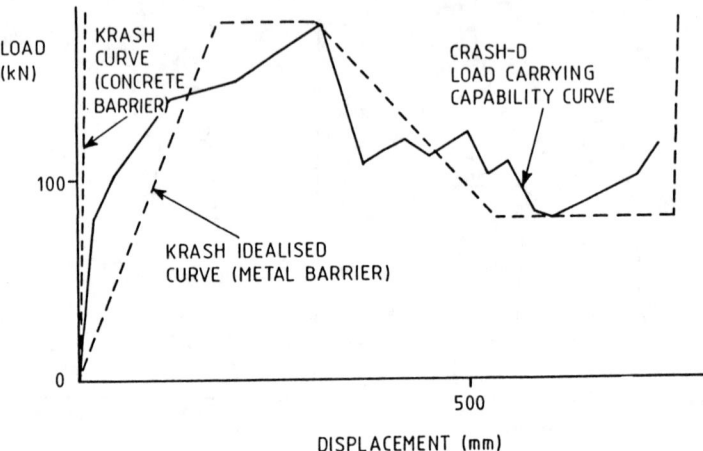

Figure 11. Load displacement curve for safety barrier. Full line CRASH-D result, dotted line is the approximation input to KRASH code.

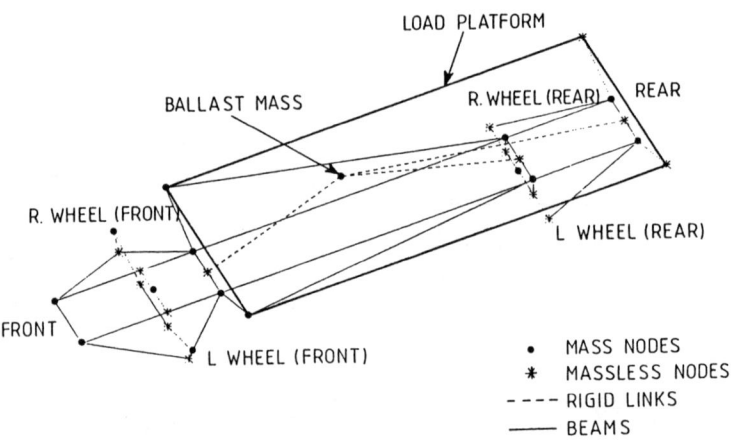

Figure 12. Idealisation of truck for safety barrier impact simulation using KRASH.

STRUCTURAL IMPACT ANALYSIS IN DESIGN FOR SAFETY 31

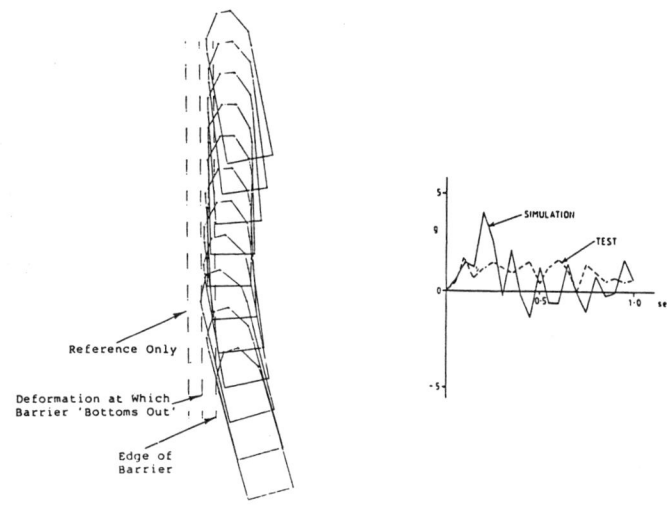

Figure 13. Truck trajectory after striking barrier. (Simulated)

Figure 14. Lateral acceleration of the truck. Comparison of test and simulation.

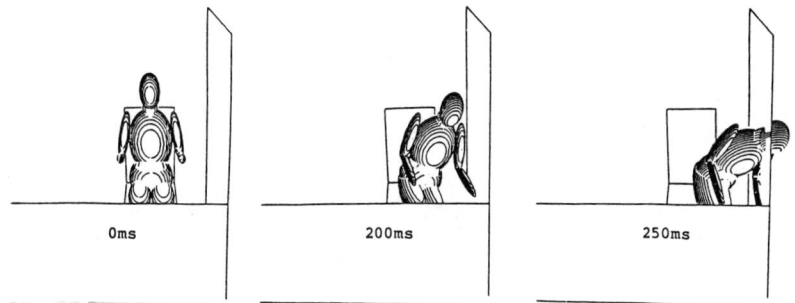

Figure 15. Simulated sequence of the driver motion relative to the cab after striking barrier

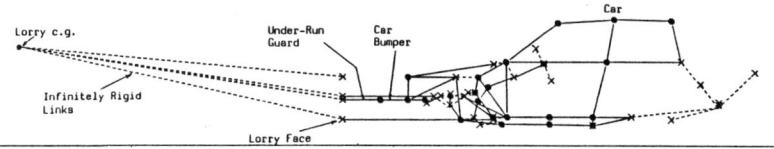

Figure 16. Idealisation of car and truck as one system for KRASH simulation of front impact.

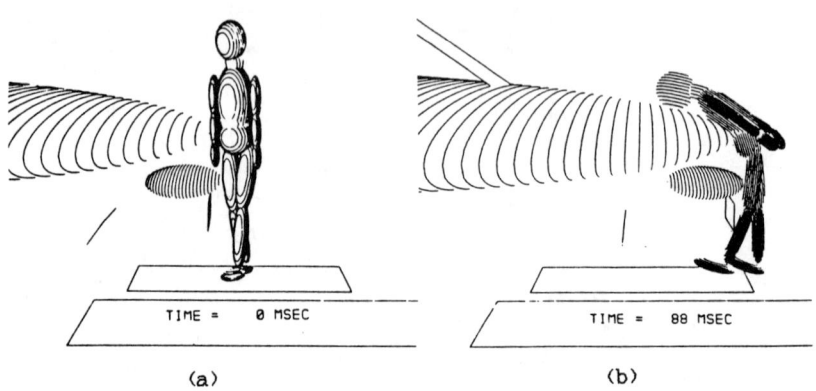

Figure 17. Simulation of a child pedestrian impact by the CVS code. (a) Position of child at the point of impact. (b) Position 88 ms after impact.

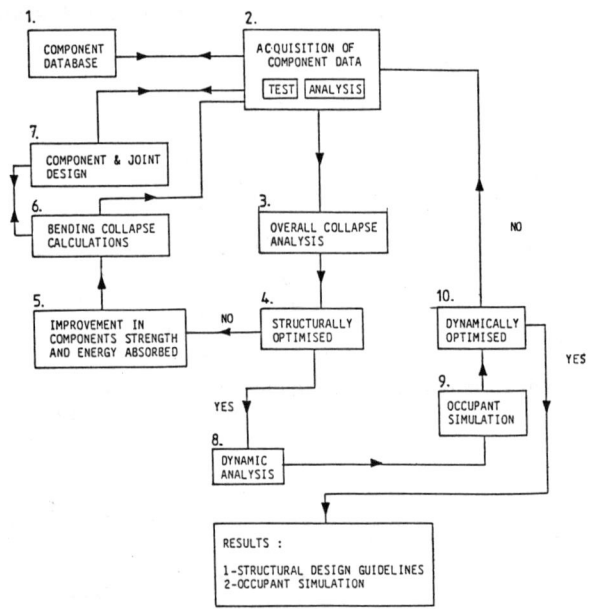

Figure 18. Block diagram of the method of design of vehicle structures for crashworthiness.

STRUCTURAL IMPACT ANALYSIS IN DESIGN FOR SAFETY 33

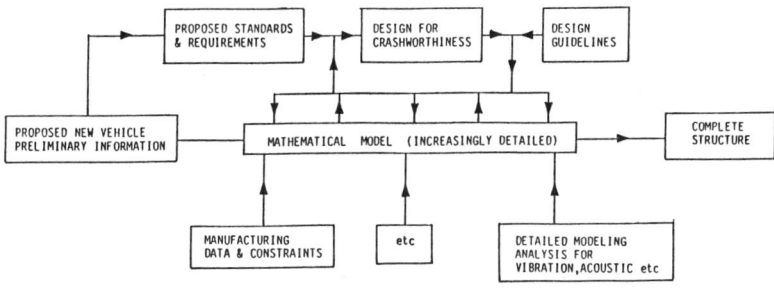

Figure 19. Block diagram of an overall vehicle design system which includes crashworthiness at the concept stage.

Driveshaft Collapse Study
Kin S. Yeung, Fu S. Chang and Heng Yee Chen
Ford Motor Company, Dearborn, Michigan, U.S.A.

INTRODUCTION

Federal Motor Vehicle Safety Standard 301 (FMVSS 301) for passenger vehicles mandates that test vehicles under frontal, rear and side barrier impact must satisfy certain fuel system integrity requirements. It is important to protect the fuel tank from puncture by neighboring components during crash. As shown in Figure 1, in some designs such neighboring components include the driveshaft. This paper is concerned with the behavior of the driveshaft during FMVSS 301 barrier crashes.

The driveshaft system, as shown in Figure 1, consists of two main parts, A and B, connected by a universal joint (U-joint). During FMVSS 301 barrier crashes, there are two types of driveshaft system deformations which should be controlled in order to prevent damage to the fuel tank: 1) the fracture of the U-joint allowing movement of "A" toward the fuel tank; 2) buckling or bending in "B" sufficient to cause "B" to contact the fuel tank.

To help prevent such occurrences a mechanism can be built into "A", forcing "A" to collapse prior to the fracture of the U-joint or the above-described bending or buckling in "B". To achieve this objective the load carrying capacity of "A" must be less than that of the U-joint or "B" and the collapse of "A" must be gradual. It is well known that global bending causes sudden collapse of a structure while collapse through global axial folding is gradual and more efficient for energy absorption. Based on these considerations, part "A" of the driveshaft is made of a tube of two different diameters with a necked-down portion. This necked-down region serves as an energy absorption mechanism, and is used to control the collapse of the driveshaft system.

Traditionally, the collapse load of a proposed driveshaft design has been determined by prototype or full-scale experiments, which are expensive and time consuming. Computer simulation is being used increasingly to complement or partially replace full-size testing in order to reduce cost and shorten the lead time between design and production.

In this study a Ford program named WRECKER-F was used to estimate the collapse load and the mode of collapse for a proposed driveshaft design. WRECKER-F is an enhanced version of WRECKER-II [1,2], a nonlinear finite element program for automobile crashworthiness studies developed under U.S. Department of Transportation funding. In the following sections, an overview of the WRECKER-F program, a simulation of the proposed driveshaft, and the corresponding test data are given. A comparison between the simulation and test results, and the limitations of the WRECKER-F program are also described.

THE WRECKER-F COMPUTER PROGRAM

WRECKER-F (copyright, 1986, 1985, 1984, 1983, Ford Motor Company) has been developed by Ford Motor Company for use in automobile structural analysis in a crash situation. The program has the capability of analyzing structures with geometric nonlinearity due to large deflections and rotations, and with material nonlinearity due to plasticity with strain-hardening. The element library includes three dimensional beam, nonlinear spring, membrane and plate/shell elements, as well as a rigid link element. Rigid links can be used as a means of introducing rigid body masses into a structural model to simulate items such as vehicle center of mass, engine block, wheel suspension, etc. Both the explicit and implicit time integration schemes are available. The program can be used for static or dynamic transient analysis. The program also has graphic packages to be used on display devices employed by Ford Motor Company such as CALCOMP, GERBER, MICROFILM, TEKTRONIX or LUNDY.

A complete development of the theoretical formulation and the computational methods of WRECKER-F is beyond the scope of this paper; instead, a brief description of the methods used is given. The interested reader can find details in the appropriate references [1 to 5].

<u>Reference Coordinate Systems</u>
WRECKER-F uses three different coordinate systems to describe the configuration of a body in space: global, element, and nodal. The global coordinate system is fixed in space and serves as a frame of reference for the three translational motions. The element coordinate system is embedded in each element, and is used to define the rigid body motion of an element and to serve as a reference for element distortions

and forces. The nodal axes are, however, attached to each node. These axes initially coincide with the global axes, but subsequently rotate with the node to which they are attached. This system is, therefore, used to track the rotational motion of each node.

Geometrical Nonlinearity

In WRECKER-F, the treatment of large displacements and rotations employs a decomposition of the element displacement field into a rigid body rotation and translation, and a remaining displacement field. The rigid body rotations and translations are associated with the element coordinate system which is moving with the element. The remaining displacement field describes the deformation of the element relative to the current position of the element axes. This transformation, in effect, removes the average rigid body rotations of the element. In this manner, extremely large rotations and deflections can be accommodated by the analysis with accuracy depending primarily on the size of the elements relative to the curvature of the structure.

Material Nonlinearity

WRECKER-F makes use of simple elastic-plastic stress-strain laws; a uniaxial relation for beam and nonlinear spring elements and a biaxial relation for plate elements. The plastic flow formulation is based on the von Mises yield criterion with isotropic strain hardening. Element forces and bending moments for the given strain field are calculated by a piece-wise linear numerical integration of the stress field at selected points in the cross-section.

IMPLICIT AND EXPLICIT TIME INTEGRATION PROCEDURES

The equations of motion derivable from the principle of virtual work are numerically solved by the direct time integration methods of either the implicit scheme or the explicit scheme at user's option.

In the implicit scheme, displacement increments are directly solved at the end of each time step; velocities and accelerations are predicted by the finite difference method. This scheme requires formation and inversion of a global stiffness matrix. The choice of this procedure results in a program requiring considerably more computer storage because of the global stiffness matrix, and performing more numerical calculations as a result of inversion of the global stiffness matrix. This procedure is, however, unconditionally stable for "arbitrarily large" time steps.

In the explicit method, the accelerations are computed first from the equations of motion (similar to those derived from Newton's Second Law of motion). The accelerations are then numerically integrated in time to obtain velocities and displacements. In WRECKER-F the explicit procedure is exploited throughout the analysis by using a "lumped mass" approach and by calculating the internal forces at nodes from direct integration of the element stress field without reference to element or assembled stiffness matrices of the structure. In WRECKER-F, it is also tacitly assumed that the center of mass is chosen as the reference point for the motion; therefore the translational and rotational equations of motion are decoupled. As a result, the solution of a large set of simultaneous equations is not required in the explicit method. The choice of an explicit integration procedure and a direct calculation of nodal forces results in a program with minimum (but still substantial) computer storage requirements. This, in turn, is equivalent to the capability of processing reasonably detailed and extensive structural models with relative ease.

The principal shortcomings of the explicit integration procedure are the use of a relatively small time increment as compared with the implicit one, and the difficulty of obtaining results for static or quasi-static situations in which loading and response vary slowly with time. Use of the implicit method with large time step or negligible inertia allows quasi-static analyses. However, for impulsive loads or impact loading, a path-dependent material and a rapid change of geometry, the use of a small time increment is mandatory in order to obtain a reasonable solution. Then the explicit scheme appears much more suitable since it generally requires fewer computations for a given time step. In conclusion [6], the extreme simplicity of the equations of motion in the explicit method and the high cost of the reads and writes to disk necessary for solving the banded equations in the implicit method (which allows a large time step) make the explicit method the practical approach for large dynamic-transient problems. When hundreds of millions of words of real memory become available, however, the implicit method may be faster than the explicit method.

<u>Updated Lagrangian and Convected Formulation</u>
In WRECKER-F two approaches have been used to formulate geometric nonlinearity: the updated Lagrangian and convected formulations.

The updated Lagrangian or incremental moving coordinate formulation divides the loading and deformation of the continua into a finite number of steps. In each step the deformation is assumed to be infinitesimal; hence, a linear relation can be used within each step. The geometry is then updated in each step. Implicit time integration is used in conjunction with this formulation.

The convected formulation used to solve transient dynamic problems is developed from the polar decomposition theorem of nonlinear mechanics. The coordinate used in this formulation only rotates and translates with the continua but does not deform with it; hence, it always forms a rectilinear orthogonal system. The large displacement (not rotation) effects are treated entirely by transformations of displacement and force components between global and convected coordinates. Explicit time integration is exploited with the convected coordinate system.

EVALUATIONS

Experimental Evaluation
The driveshaft test specimen shown in Figure 2d is made of two concentric cylindrical tubes. The smaller tube is 160.00 mm. (6.30 in.) long and its radius is 29.00 mm. (1.41 in.). The length of the bigger tube is 120.00 mm. (4.72 in.) with a radius of 37.63 mm. (1.48 in.). The necked-down region is 17.25 mm. (0.68 in.) long. The detailed geometry of the entire test specimen is shown in Figure 3. The driveshaft is made of cold rolled carbon steel with an average wall thickness of 1.89 mm. (0.07 in.) for the larger section and 1.54 mm. (0.06 in.) for the smaller section.

In the test, a load was applied at the top of the specimen (Figure 2d) in the longitudinal direction by means of a displacement controlled device. The load-deflection is shown in Figure 4. It can be seen from Figure 4 that the maximum load the specimen could carry was 110,000 newtons (24,750 lb.) at a deflection of 6.40 mm. (0.25 in.); thereafter the load dropped to a minimum of 30,000 newtons (6,750 lb.) at a deflection of 19.10 mm. (0.75 in.). The load then again rose to 61,000 newtons (13,800 lb.) before the test specimen fractured at 114.30 mm. (450 in.). The deformed specimens are depicted in Figures 2b and 2c; a cut-off specimen is shown in Figure 2a. This form of quasi-static testing is useful in providing a history of the deformed shapes during collapse. However, it does not simulate the rapid collapse of the driveshaft in an actual crash event.

Finite Element Evaluation
In order to perform the simulation, it was necessary to choose the integration scheme and the extent of modeling:

1) Implicit vs Explicit Integration As noted, the test was quasi-static, which would suggest use of the implicit integration scheme. However, due to a lack of cylindrical shell elements in the WRECKER-F computer program, it was anticipated that a substantial number of plate elements would be required to capture the essential features or geometry of the specimen. As mentioned in the introduction, the use of the implicit method requires formation and inversion of the global structural stiffness matrix. Due to the high cost of the reads and writes to disk and forming and solving this

matrix, the implicit method was not considered practical. Thus, it was necessary to use the explicit method, recognizing that this does not represent the quasi-static nature of the test as well. On the other hand, it is a better representation of the dynamic nature of a real crash event.

2) **Size of the Finite Element Model** Previous experience indicated that it would not be necessary to model the entire specimen in the simulation. To determine the extent the specimen needed to be modeled, several very coarse finite element models with different lengths of the specimen were simulated. Based on the deformed shapes and the load carrying capacities of these models, it was decided that a length of 297.25 mm. (11.70 in.) could be successfully used in subsequent simulation.

Due to symmetry, only a quarter of the driveshaft was modeled in the analysis as shown in Figures 3 and 5. This quarter model has 590 nodes and 1092 triangular plate elements with the end C'-D' of the larger tube being fixed. A displacement field with a constant rate of 5.0×10^4 mm./sec. (196.85 in./sec.) is prescribed in the longitudinal direction at the end A'-B' of the smaller tube. A time step size of 10^{-7} sec. was used. The entire simulation was carried out for a total of 7,600 time steps, up to a maximum of 38.00 mm. (1.50 in.). The sequence of the deformed shapes is depicted from Figure 5 to Figure 10. To show the extent of the distortion of the driveshaft at the final stage of the simulation, the deformed configuration is superimposed on the undeformed one in Figure 11. The solid line curve in Figure 12 is the load-deflection curve of the driveshaft for the entire simulation, while the same curve for the first 0.08 mm. is shown in Figure 13. It can be seen from Figure 13 that the peak load of 220,000 newtons (49,500 lb.) occurred at a deflection of 0.03 mm. (10^{-4} in.). Furthermore in the simulation there was no significant increase of load after the load decreased to its minimum at about 12.0 mm. (0.47 in.), see Figure 12. No numerical difficulty was encountered during the simulation.

Comparisons of the Experimental and Finite Element Evaluations
In the process of testing it was observed that the region of transition in tube diameter ("E" in Figure 2) underwent two distinct modes of deformation. In the first stage of deformation, this region appeared to expand in the radial direction, as shown by "E" in Figure 2c. As the smaller tube penetrated deeper into the larger one the same region tended to revert to its original shape, see "E" in Figure 2b. The finite element simulation accurately predicted this sequence. A gradual bulging of the region in question is apparent in E-F from Figure 6 through Figure 8 as obtained from the simulation. It can be seen from Figures 9 and 10 of the

finite element result that the same region (E-F) tended to reduce in size.

Correlation of force levels is not as favorable, and two possible contributors to the differences in force levels have been identified. First, the peak load predicted by the current model was 220,000 newtons (49,500 lb.), while the peak load obtained from test was 110,000 newtons (24,750 lb.), see Figure 12. The main reason for this difference is that the simulation is dynamic, while the test was quasi-static. Second, lack of correlation of minimum load is probably due to the fact that the frictional forces between the contact surfaces were not accounted for in the model. Examination of the deformed test specimen in Figure 2a shows that the contact interaction (frictional force) between the inner face of the larger tube and the outer face of the deformed smaller tube probably plays a role in determining the load capacity of the driveshaft. Since the finite element simulation did not take the contact interaction into consideration, it is to be expected that the load prediction after deep penetration of the smaller tube will be in error.

SUMMARY AND CONCLUSIONS

This study serves as a starting point for the prediction of the collapse load and the collapse mode of a proposed driveshaft design with a built-in collapsing mechanism. Such a mechanism can eliminate the chance of the driveshaft puncturing the neighboring fuel tank in FMVSS 301 barrier crashes.

The current investigation suggests that the deformed shape and the collapse mode can be realistically predicted. Correlation of the first peak load with the particular test result is not conclusive because the test was quasi-static and the simulation was dynamic. The simulation failed to predict accurately the minimum and the subsequent peak loads. It is felt that the main contributing factor to this lack of correlation was the failure to account for the frictional force between the contact surfaces of the smaller and the larger tubes. A frictional contact capability needs to be implemented into the current version of the WRECKER-F program, in order to improve prediction of the load carrying capacity of the driveshaft.

REFERENCES

1. K. S. Yeung and R. E. Welch, "Refinement of Finite Element Analysis of Automobile Structures Under Crash Loading," DOT HS-803 466, October, 1977.

2. K. S. Yeung and T. Hollowell, "Large Displacement, Nonlinear Static and Dynamic Analysis of Automobile Sheet Metal Structure," SAE Paper No. 780367.

3. S. C. Tang, K. S. Yeung and C. T. Chon, "On Tangent Stiffness Matrix in Convected Coordinate System," Computer and Structure, Vol. 12, pp. 849-856, 1980.

4. K. S. Yeung, "WRECKER-F General Purpose Nonlinear Finite Element Computer Program For Use in Automobile Crashworthiness Analysis Part II: Three-Dimensional Plate/Shell Element-Static," Proceedings of the International Conference on Finite Element Methods, Vol. 2, pp. 116-124, Shanghai, China, 1982.

5. K. S. Yeung, "WRECKER-F Theoretical Manual," Ford Motor Company Internal Report, 1983.

6. D. J. Benson, J. O. Hallquist and D. W. Stillman, "DANA3D, INGRID, and TAURUS - An Integrated, Interactive, Software System for Crashworthiness Engineering," 1985 ASME Computers in Engineering Conference, Boston, MA., Aug. 4-8, 1985.

DRIVESHAFT COLLAPSE STUDY 43

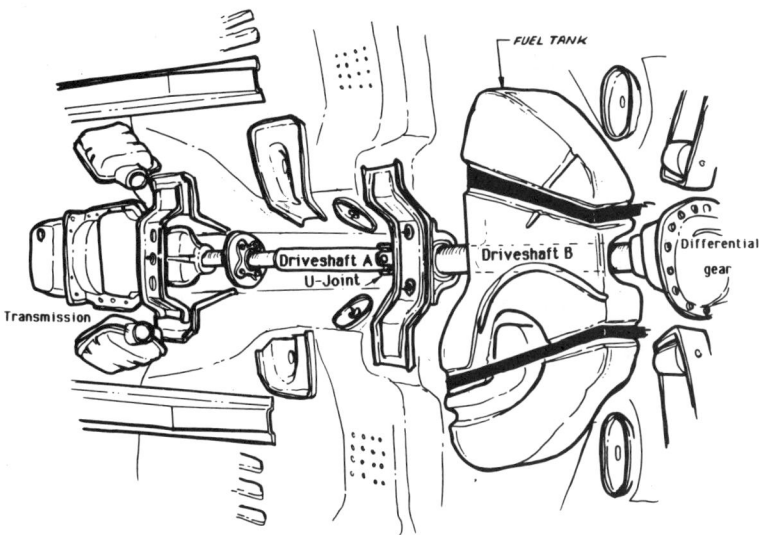

Figure 1 Driveshaft and Fuel Tank

Figure 2 Test Specimen

44 DRIVESHAFT COLLAPSE STUDY

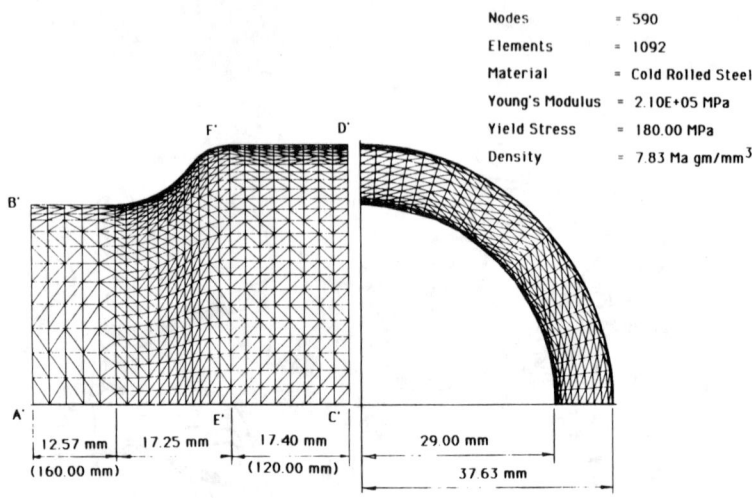

Figure 3 Finite Element Model
(Numbers in Parenthesis are Test Specimen Dimensions)

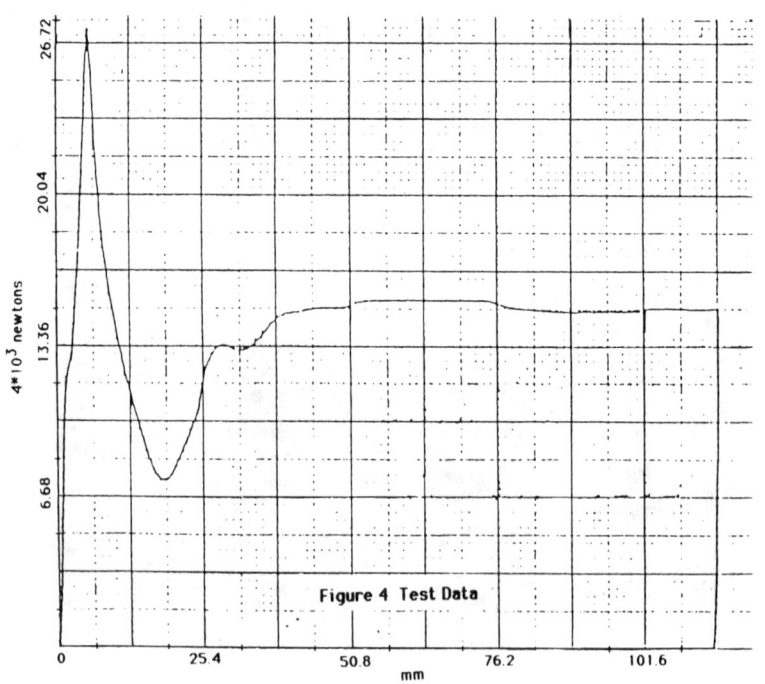

Figure 4 Test Data

DRIVESHAFT COLLAPSE STUDY 45

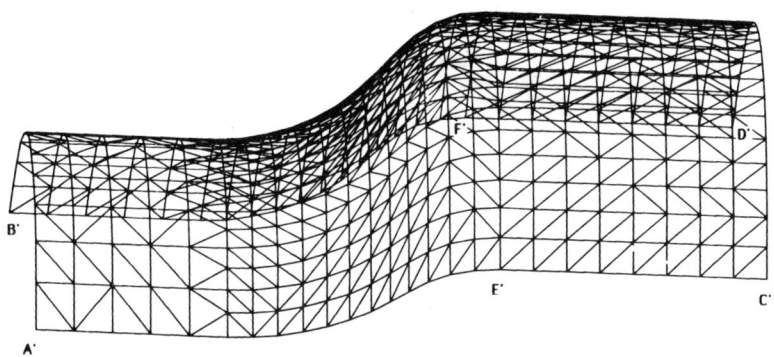

Figure 5 Undeformed Shape

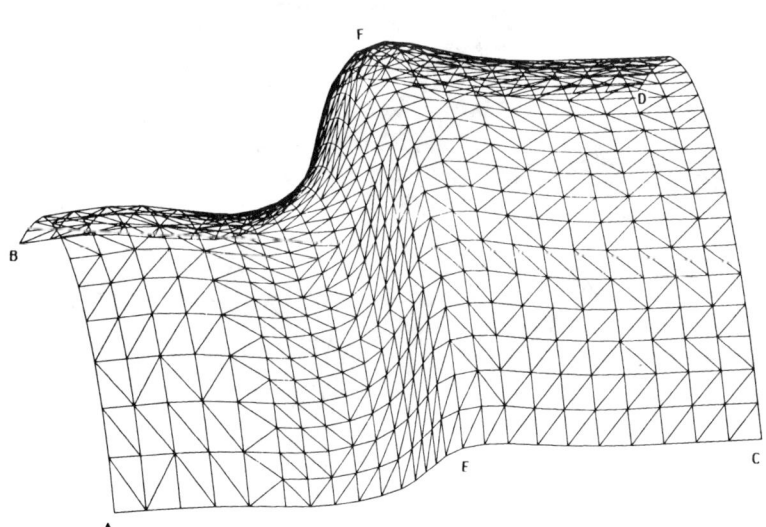

Figure 6 Deformed Shape at Deflection = 5.00 mm

46 DRIVESHAFT COLLAPSE STUDY

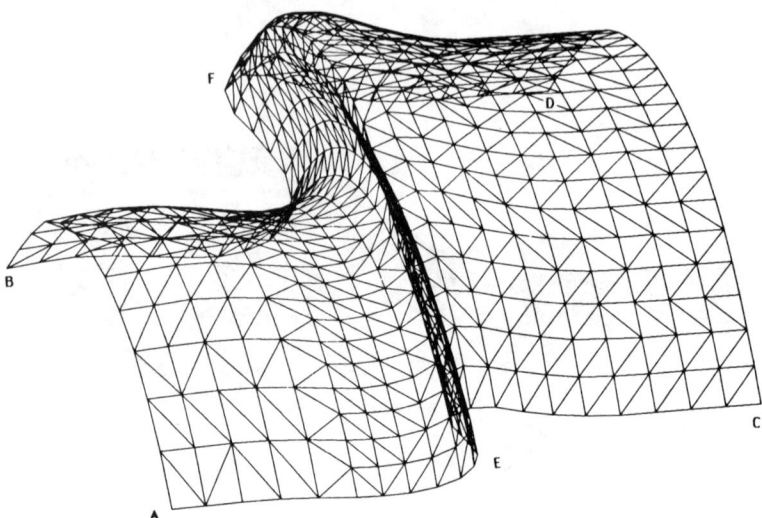

Figure 7 Deformed Shape at Deflection = 12.50 mm

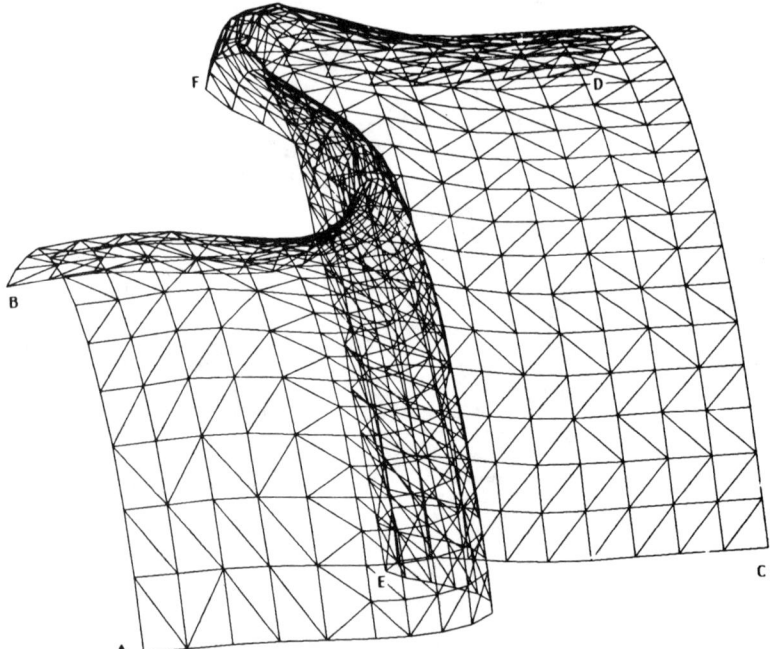

Figure 8 Deformed Shape at Deflection = 17.50 mm

DRIVESHAFT COLLAPSE STUDY 47

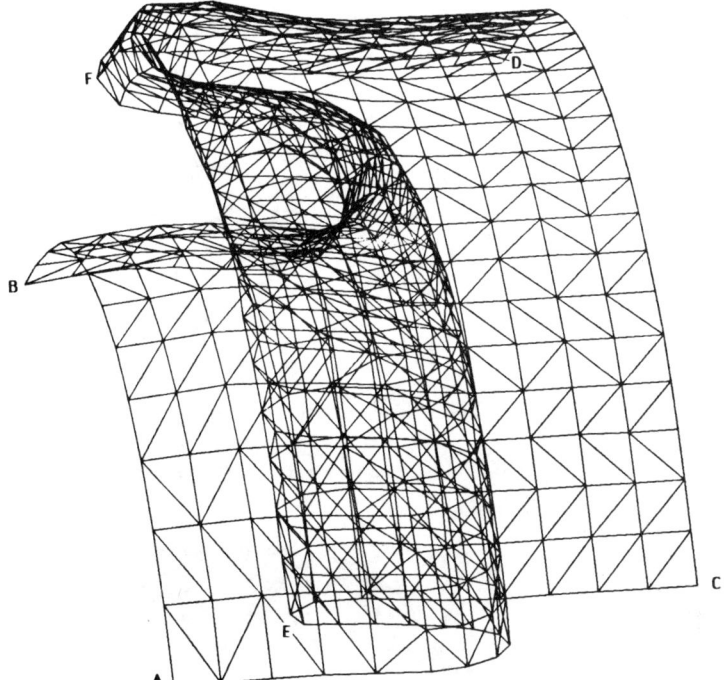

Figure 9 Deformed Shape at Deflection = 25.00 mm

48 DRIVESHAFT COLLAPSE STUDY

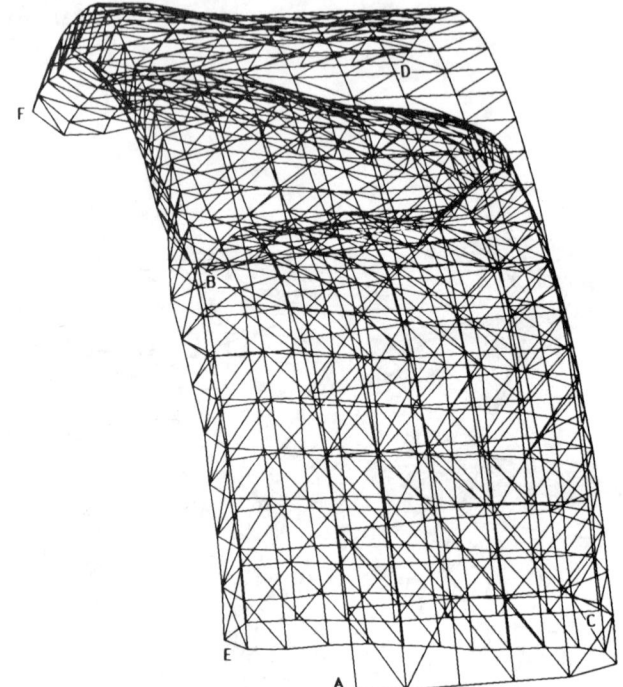

Figure 10 Deformed Shape at Deflection = 38.00 mm

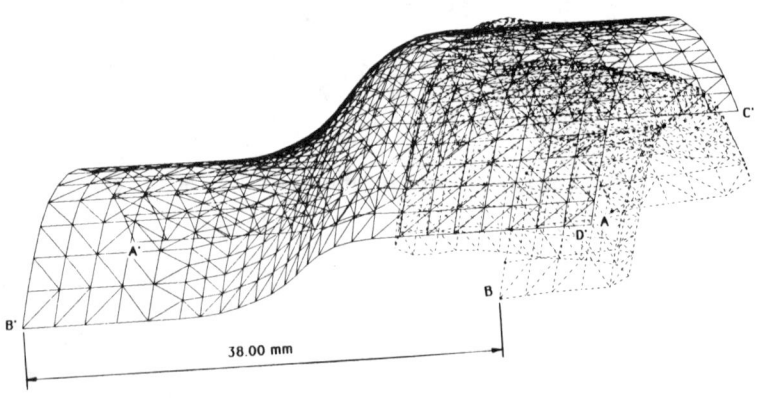

Figure 11 Undeformed (Solid Lines) and Deformed
(Dotted Lines) Shapes at Deflection = 38.00 mm

DRIVESHAFT COLLAPSE STUDY   49

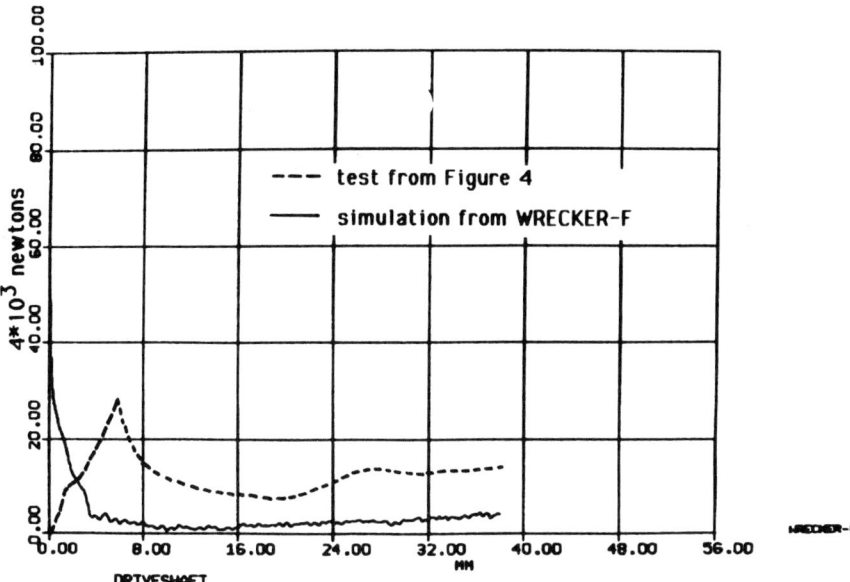

Figure 12 Load-Deflection Curve

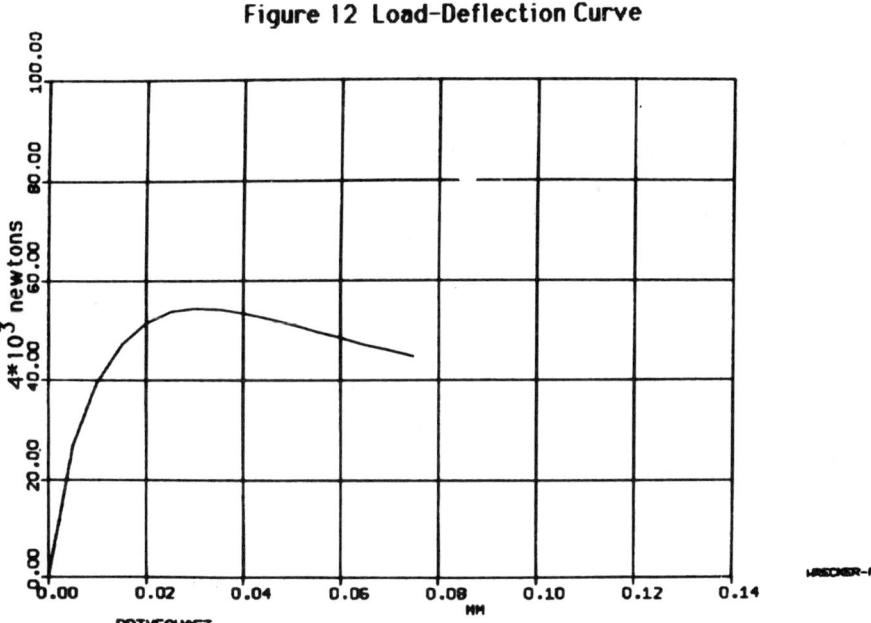

Figure 13 Simulation Load-Deflection Curve

Design Optimisation using the Finite Element Program ANSYS^R
G. Müller, B-P. Walter
CAD-FEM GmbH, D-8017 Ebersberg/Munchen

INTRODUCTION

Finite element analysis has been employed by practising engineers since the late 1960's. The method was used for examples for the analysis of critical components when destructive testing was impossible and for prototype testing to reduce the number of costly experiments. By help of the analysis it was possible to reduce the long lead time to get a product to market with lower design costs. The weakness of this approach is that it still relies on the accumulated knowledge of the designer to propose a good design. And still the method requires significant engineering man time to evaluate results, adjust models and run several iterations until a feasible design is found.

To simplify the tedious revision of analytical models development is going on to incorporate design criteria and optimization strategies into the finite element programs. The potential advantage in using this technology will be: 1. Faster response to design change requirements and "What if?" scenarios, 2. Reduced costs and time for design and analysis, and 3. Lower costs for material and manufacturing of final design.

ANSYS, one of the world's most widely used finite element programs, has recently implemented the ability to link its structural, heat transfer and electro-mechanical analysis options with classical optimization theory (Swanson[1,2]). To provide true design optimization, however, other features like solid modeling, parametric language and data base management have been added to the program and are integral parts of the optimization module. The

following presentation will describe the capabilities
of the ANSYS program in this context. The information
is compiled from various publications of members of
Swanson Analysis Systems, Inc., the developers of the
program (Swanson[1,2]; Imgrund[3,4]; and Ostergaard[5]).

SOLID MODELING AND FINITE ELEMENT MESHING

Finite element analysis requires the creation of a
geometric model which is the mathematical representation of an object. Four types of geometric models
are typically used: direct finite element model, wire
frame model, surface model and solid model. For the
latter three approaches a two step procedure is
necessary: 1. Generation of the geometric model and
2. Finite element meshing.

Direct finite element models consist solely of
finite elements. No geometry data exists exept for
the location of the nodes. Wire frame models are made
up of lines which represent the delineating edges of
an object. No information exists for surfaces or
interior portions of the model. Surface models
describe an object by completely defining the surfaces which compose it. Solid models provide more
information than the wire frame or surface models.
They describe completely the interior as well as the
surfaces and edges of an object. These characteristics make the solid model best suited to finite
element meshing and optimization. Two basic methods
exist for constructing solid models: constructive
solid geometry (CSG) and boundary representation
(B-rep). The CSG approach builds the geometry using
basic shapes, called primitives, such as spheres,
cones, blocks and cylinders. The B-rep method stores
the faces, edges, and vertices of the object. The
interior volumes, faces, edges and vertices are represented by polynomials. For finite element analysis
and optimization the B-rep method is superior to CSG
in that general shapes can be easily modeled and
there is no need for an exact description of the geometry. ANSYS uses the B-rep approach for construction
of the geometric model. A region concept is used to
identify a portion of a structure. Regions may consists of three basic components: line segments,
areas, and volumes.

Once the geometric model is created, powerful
mesh generation algorithms generate node points and
elements on and/or interior of the geometric boundaries. The size and shape of the finite element mesh,
although automatically generated by the program, is

guided by the user. An element type must be selected.
Line segments must have a user prescribed number of
element edges. The intelligence that is built in will
review the region shape, try to generate quads or
bricks, assuming the element type has that shape, or
generate triangles or tetrahedrons if resulting elements are too distorted for accurate results. It
should be emphasized that solid modeling and automatic triangular and tetrahedron meshing are important features in conjunction with shape optimization
because regions to be meshed may get considerably
distorted during the design loops.

PARAMETRIC LANGUAGE

Solid modeling becomes even more advantageous when it
can be defined in a parametric language. A parameter
is an user-named variable which can be used to supply
data to the program either interactively at the
terminal or by way of a file. ANSYS allows basic
mathematical or logical operations with these parameters, so the parameters may depend on each other by
user-defined expressions. A parameter, once defined,
may be used anywhere within the ANSYS input. When the
input is being read in , any command field that requires numeric input is evaluated to determine if it
contains a parametric expression. If it does, the
expression is evaluated and used for the item defined
by that field.

In the model generation parameters may be used
for example for material properties, node locations,
boundary conditions, mesh density, load intensity
and/or location, load duration, and any other commands
that accept numerical data. Parameters may also be
used within a macro, where a macro is a sequence of
commands which is saved for repeated use or they may
be used in user files to pass data into the files. In
the results evaluation phase parameters can be used
to retrieve data from the solution. Some are directly
accessible such as displacements, stresses, frequencies, temperatures, voltages or flux densities,
others result from postprocessing operations, like
max or min of any item, sum, derivatives or integrals
of items.

In conjunction with design optimization, parameters are used to define a design and to define
design response. These parameters are passed back and
forth between the optimization module and solution
module.

DESIGN OPTIMIZATION

The typical optimization process seeks to minimize (or maximize) a set of values by changing some attributes of the design, while maintaining other attributes within specified limits. The function to be minimized is defined as the objective function (OBJ). Some typical objective functions are weight and cost. The items which are varied during the process are defined as design variables (DV). These parameters represent the part's geometry. Some typical DV's are thickness, area, and fillet radius. A DV is specified by its initial value and the range that the final value must fall within. Those variables which constrain the feasible design space are defined as state variables (SV). These parameters represent the part's response. Examples are maximum stress, or minimum heat flow, temperature or natural frequency. The SV's are required to lie within certain specified criterion.

Various optimization techniques have been developed over the past twenty years. Overviews are given by Kanarchos[6]; Stadler[7] and Vanderplaats[8]. In Rouse[9] the optimization capabilities of general purpose finite element programs are discussed. In this paper the various methods will not be discussed, only the approach followed in ANSYS will be presented.

The ANSYS design optimization basically involves two steps which are looped through until convergence is reached: 1. The global optimization problem is reduced to an approximate subproblem. 2. The approximate subproblem minimized using the Sequential Unconstrained Minimization Technique (SUMT). The solution sequence is shown in Fig. 1. The analysis starts with a set of initial design variables which may be random or may be specified by the user. First a minimum of four finite element analyses are done. Then the objective function and the state variables are approximated as quadratic functions of the design variables (Fig. 2). The coefficients for the equations are calculated using standard multiple regression techniques. Once the equations defining the approximate subproblem are determined, they define the constrained minimization problem. This minimization is carried out by changing the constrained problem into an unconstrained minimization problem, using increasingly stronger penalty functions to enforce design and state variable constraints. The minimum of each response surface is found by a series of undirectional searches in the design space, starting at the previous best design. The search consists of minimizations in the following directions: 1. directions along each design variable, 2. directions tangent to each state variable constraint, 3. direction of steepest descent of the objective function. When the minimum has been determined from the approximate subproblem new design variables are calculated based on a linear combination of the best previous feasible design and the new minimum, and are passed on to the next design loop. The loops are stopped when convergence is reached. The designer may control convergence by defining tolerances and/or specifying a maximum of iterations.

Thus the optimization process involves evaluating different finite element models to see which proposed design yields the smallest objective function value in the feasible range. As data is gathered, relationships begin to develop between the objective function, design variables, and state variables, so that future design evaluations are based on the accumulated knowledge.

The main strengths of the ANSYS optimization approach are:
1. Its flexibility available in choice of design variables, constraints and objective function.
2. Discontinuous functions may be approximated by the quadratics if local behavior near the discontinuity is not important.
3. Different analysis types such as structural, heat transfer or even coupled analyses(e. g. structural-thermal) can be addressed.
4. Ease of use, i. e., it does not require in-depth knowledge of the theory and user effort is minimal beyond original analysis.
5. Can be interfaced with external optimizers.
6. Can be extended and updated as more experience is gained and other algorithms have proved to be superior.

Solving a nonlinear constrained optimization problem is still an "art". So we have to admit, there are weaknesses and limitations. The weaknesses of the ANSYS optimization approach are:
1. Global minimum is not guaranteed.
2. Possibilities for poor function representation exist.
3. Design variables and objective function must be positive and equality constraints are not supported.
4. Cannot maximize directly.
5. More efficient (but less flexible) algorithms exist for some applications.

6. Limitation to generally 10 design variables. More need too much computer time.

The weaknesses are more of academic nature and are less stringent for the engineering praxis: ANSYS will perhaps not find the mathematical optimum, however, the solution will always result in an improved design. The approximate functions may be enhanced in future versions, point 3 and 4 can be worked around, other algorithms can be included and computer time will play a minor role with more powerful supercomputers coming up.

EXAMPLES

The ANSYS optimization module being relatively new, not too many application examples exist. Applications to structural, heat transfer and electrostatic field problems are described by Imgrund[3,4] and Ostergaard[5]. In the paper of Johnson[12], it is reported that the weight of a truck frame could be reduced by approximately 25 % while limiting the maximum combined stress level and torsional stress level in any beam element. The finite element model consisting of three-dimensional tapered beams and linear spring elements needed 40 loops for convergence. The computer resources to handle such a problem everybody can afford: The problem was solved on an IBM-PC/AT personal computer in 510 minutes.

To illustrate the solution procedure an example is depicted in Figure 3 to 5. Figure 3 describes the problem. The total volume is to be minimized under certain restrictions. The parameters i. e. design variables, state variables, and the objective function are defined in figure 4. Also a flow chart for the analysis steps is depicted. Note that a structural analysis as well as a heat transfer analysis have to be done, because state variables have been defined both for stress and displacement constraints and total heat flow from convection. Graphs showing the situations along the iterations are given in figure 5. The volume of the structure could be reduced to less than one-third of the original volume.

CONCLUSIONS

A first step in application of optimization techniques is done in engineering. The technique offered in the ANSYS program combining finite element and optimization technology has been presented. The technique first reduces the global problem to a set of relationships between the objective functions, design variables, and state variables. The reduced problem is then minimized using the Sequential Unconstrained Minimization Technique (SUMT). The advantage of this approach is that it is not limited to any particular class of problem and that it does not require derivative information. The optimization module is implemented so that engineers who have no in-depth knowledge of this technique may easily apply it. Though the application is still limited to a small number of parameters due to high computing times, the algorithms are available to allow more parameters as more powerful computers come up. It should be emphasized that optimization requires one common database, solid modeling and parametric language. Finite element programs must provide these features and/or must allow a tight coupling to CAD-packages if solid modeling should be done there.

REFERENCES

1. Swanson, J. A., Marx, F. J. (1985) Design Optimization Including Integrated Solid Modeling Using the Finite Element program ANSYS. OEM Design '85 Conference, September 9-11.

2. Swanson, J. A., Batt, S. C. (1986) Design Optimization. Swanson Analysis Systems, Inc., Houston, Pennsylvania. To be published.

3. Imgrund, M. C., Wheeler, M. J. (1986) Reducing Design Costs by Integrating Finite Element and Optimization Techniques. Swanson Analysis Systems, Inc., Houston, Pennsylvania.

4. Imgrund, M. C. (1986) Applying a New Numerical Technique to the Solution of Optimum Convective Surfaces and Associated Thermal Design Problems. Swanson Analysis Systems, Inc., Houston, Pennsylvania.

5. Ostergaard, D. F. (1985) Adapting Available Finite Element Heat Transfer Programs to Solve 2-D and 3-D Electrostatic Field problems. IEEE-IAS Society Meeting, Toronto, Canada.

6. Kanarchos, A. (1979) Rechnergestütztes Entwickeln und Konstruieren. Fachgebiete in Jahresübersichten. Strukturoptimierung. VDI-Z (1979) Nr. 23/24 - Dez. (I/II).

7. Stadler, W. (1984) Multicriterion Optimization in Mechanics (a Survey). Appl. Mech. Review 37 (1984), pp. 277-286.

8. Vanderplaats, G. N. (1984) Numerical Optimization Techniques for Engineering design. Mc Graw-Hill, New York, 1984.

9. Rouse, N. E. (1986) Design Optimization Goes Commercial. Machine design, October 23, 1986.

10. Johnson, D. H. (1986) Finite Element Optimization of the WABCO 170 Ton Haulpack Truck Frame. Swanson Analysis Systems, Inc., Houston, Pennsylvania. Paper presented at the Earthmoving Industry Conference April 8-10, 1986, Peoria, Illinois.

Overview of Theory

Solution Sequence

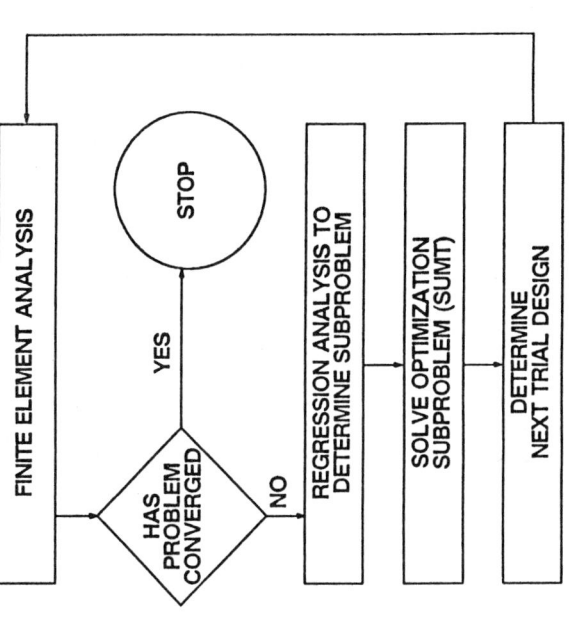

Fig. 2: The Solution Sequence

Overview of Theory

The Approximate Subproblem Definition

Minimize $F = a_0 + \sum_{i=1}^{n} a_{1I} x_i + a_{2I} x_i^2$ (1)

Subject to $\underline{x_i} < x_i < \overline{x_i}$ (I = 1 to N_d)

and $\underline{G_j} < G_j < \overline{G_j}$ (J = 1 to N_g)

Where $G_j = b_{0j} + \sum_{i=1}^{n} b_{1ij} x_i + b_{2ij} x_i^2$ (2)

x_i = ith design variable

G_j = jth constraint function (state variable)

N_d = number of design variables

N_g = number of state variable constraints

$\underline{x_i}, \overline{x_i}$ = lower and upper bounds on design space for variable x_i

$\underline{G_j}, \overline{G_j}$ = lower and upper bounds on state variable constraint G_j

Fig. 1: The Approximate Subproblem Definition

60 DESIGN OPTIMIZATION USING FE PROGRAM ANSYS[R]

Problem: Optimize the design of a pipe with cooling fins by minimizing the total volume. The design requires a thermal analysis to determine the heat loss due to convection. A structural (linear static) analysis is also required with the temperature distribution and an internal pressure as loads. The maximum displacement and equivalent stress are constraints on the design.

An axisymmetric model is used. One half fin thickness and distance between fins is modeled due to vertical symmetry.

Boundary conditions and material properties.

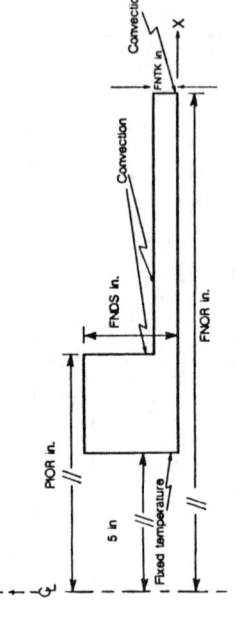

GIVEN: Material properties – stainless steel
Conductivity (KXX) = 1.25 BTU/hr-in-°F
Young's Modulus (EX) = 28.0E6 lb/in²
Coefficient of thermal expansion (ALPX) = 0.9E-5 in/in-°F
Poisson's ratio (NUXY) = 0.3

Loads
Temperature inside pipe wall = 450°F
Convection outside
Film coefficient = .25 BTU/hr-in²-°F
Fluid temperature (air) = 70.0°F
Pressure = 1000 lb/in²

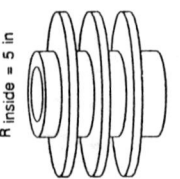

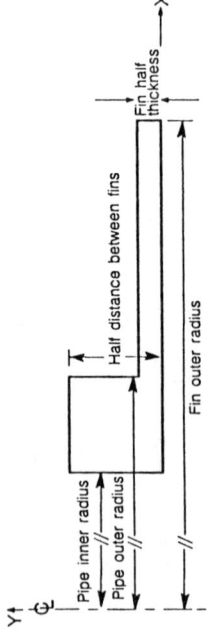

Fig. 3: Optimization of a Pipe With Cooling Fins – Problem

DESIGN OPTIMIZATION USING FE PROGRAM ANSYS[R]

Parameters for Optimization

Design Variables (DV)

		Range
Fin-outer radius	(FNOR)	8 in. to 12 in.
Pipe-outer radius	(PIOR)	5.5 in. to 6.5 in.
Fin-thickness	(FNTK)	0.15 in. to 0.3 in.
Distance between fins	(FNDS)	0.31 in. to 1.0 in.

State Variables (SV)

	Limits
Total heat flow from convection surfaces (HFLW)	$760 \frac{BTU}{hr-in^2-°F}$ to $770 \frac{BTU}{hr-in^2-°F}$
Maximum displacement (DSMX)	0.0 in. to 0.019 in.
Maximum equivalent stress (ESMX)	0 psi to 45000 psi

Objective (OBJ)

Minimize total volume (TVOL)

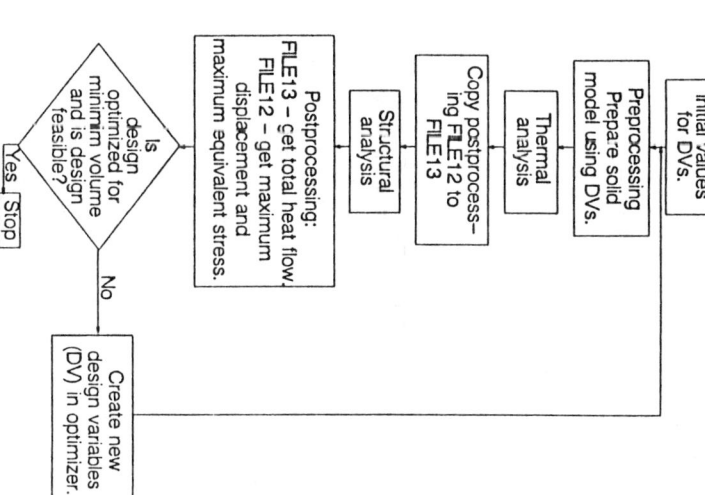

Fig. 4: Optimization of a Pipe with Cooling Fins – Solution

62 DESIGN OPTIMIZATION USING FE PROGRAM ANSYS[R]

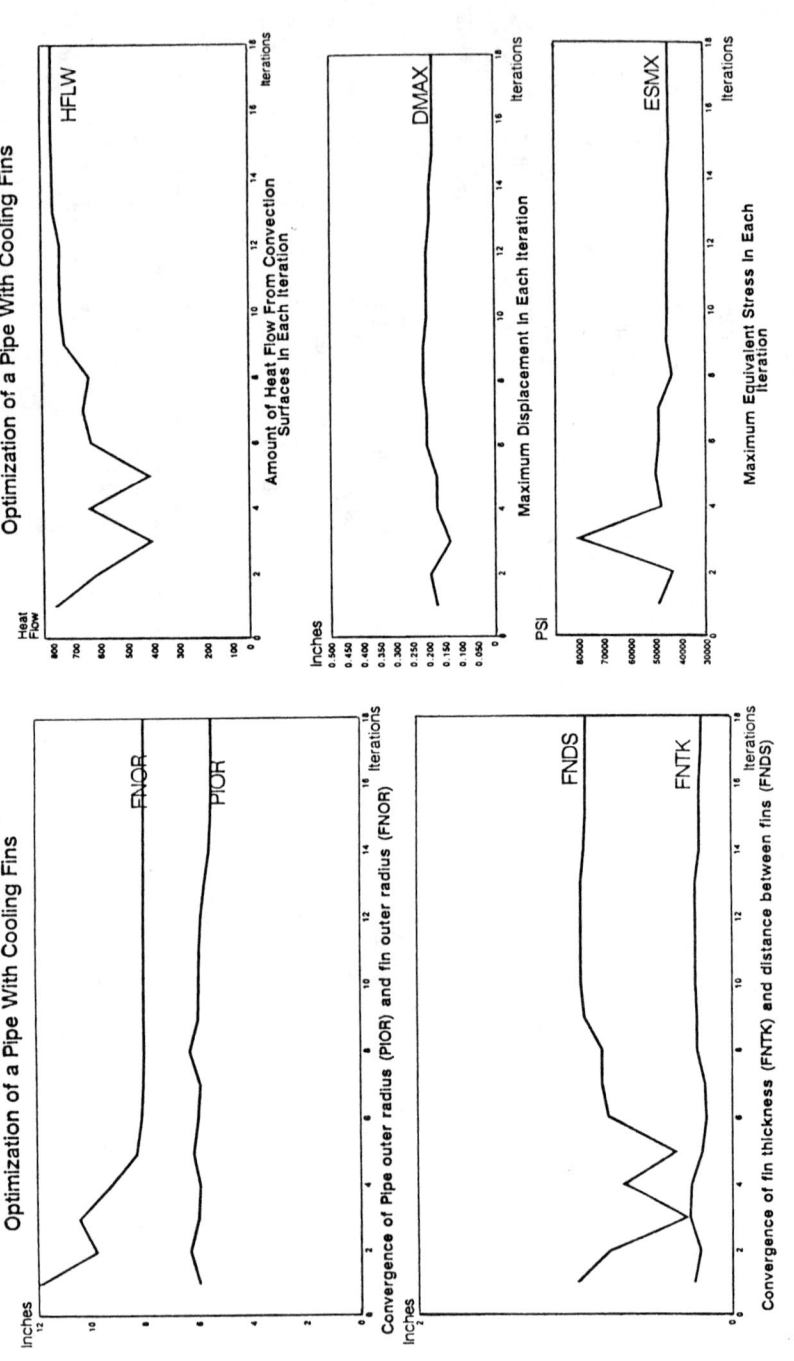

Fig. 5: Optimization of a Pipe with Cooling Fins - Results

Program 'BEAST' for the Analysis of Beam/Membrane Assemblies on a Desktop Computer
D. Kecman, I. Kecman, V. Bulat
Faculty of Mechanical Engineering, 27 Marta 80, Belgrade, Yugoslavia
SovaSoft, M. Tolbuhina 81, Belgrade, Yugoslavia

INTRODUCTION

The intention of this paper is to discuss the applicability of relatively small desktop or micro computers in a realistic design environment. Reasons for the development of program 'BEAST' (stands for BEA-m ST-ructures) will be given with an outline of the program features and examples of application in the analysis of vehicle structures.

EFFECTIVENESS OF MODERN METHODS OF STRUCTURAL ANALYSIS IN A REALISTIC DESIGN ENVIRONMENT

The effectiveness of modern methods of structural analysis in a realistic design environment depends to a great extent on the following points :

a) How important is the problem analysed in the light of the overall performance of the structure ?

For example, it may be far more effective to investigate alternative concepts of the design by computer analysis and then refine the best one, than adopt an inferior concept and spend far more time and money in optimising it.

b) Can the information obtained guide the design in the proper direction ?

The most important design features of a new structure are decided upon in the early stages of design when there may not be enough information or time for detailed modelling. Engineering experience in defining the essentials of the problem in terms of the simplified model, loads and interpretation of the results are of the greatest importance. Under such circumstances continuous access to a smaller, but dedicated, computer may provide a much shorter turn-round time than a bigger time-sharing system.

c) Is the information available in time for the implementation in the design ?

The intention of modern methods of analysis is to provide information on design alternatives that can be implemented within the tight product development schedules, otherwise the information becomes rather 'academic'.

d) What are the economic effects of the complete analysis ?

This is probably the main argument for or against the investment in the new design/analysis tools. The true return on investment has to be assessed allowing for many characteristics of the environment in which the equipment is supposed to operate. It does not appear reasonable to make large investments in high performance systems unless their capabilities are used and can be justified on hard economic grounds.

IS THERE ROOM FOR SMALL ANALYSIS SYSTEMS ?

In the light of the capabilities of many modern CAD and analysis hardware and software one wonders whether there is any room for a 'David among Goliaths'.

The arguments under the previous heading provide the initial ground for considering the potential role of the small systems.

Program 'BEAST', being one of the small packages, was developed for the following additional reasons :

e) There are still many 'Davids' among 'Goliaths' in the motor (and building) industry who may benefit from, but do not employ modern methods of structural analysis. The main reasons usually are:

- professional staff are too much involved in solving the current design and/or production problems so that they cannot devote time to considering, let alone adopting a new technology in their own job. It is often not easy to realise that lack of new technology contributes greatly to this very lack of time;

- hand in hand with human resistance to change, among smaller firms often goes further limitation of the investment funds and the need to employ new professional staff to operate a major analysis system;

- use of external consultants or computer centres is also much more an exception than a continuous practice among small producers, again due to time pressures (problems are rarely anticipated, but solved as they come) and the fact that the expenses are external;

- documentation accompanying most of the commercial software packages is written for professionals and not for the first time users. This is, of course, inevitable in very complex programs, but a first time user usually looks for a package that he may employ almost instantly;

- it is best if systems grow with increasing natural needs of the user, rather than try and force the needs to feed an 'overweight' system.

BASIC FEATURES OF THE PROGRAM 'BEAST'

Program 'BEAST' was developed with an intention to comply with the first needs of many first time users in small companies in the motor and building industry. Here are the basic features that contribute to this end :

A. Hardware
Program is written in modular form as a combination of BASIC, FORTRAN and C language routines running on micro and PC computers (APPLE, IBM compatibles, and also on Hewlett-Packard 9200 series). It can be transferred onto another small system without great difficulties, provided that suitable compilers and external hardware units are available.

Micro and PC computers with external memories, printers and plotters represent a small investment not only to companies but also to professional individuals.

B. Applicability of the program
Program 'BEAST', in its current state, is intended for the quasi-static analysis of 2 and 3-dimensional frameworks, trusses and grillages. The skeleton may be combined with membrane elements, so that sheet metal cladding (or walls and diaphragms) can be taken into account.

The loads include concentrated forces and moments in or between nodes, distributed loads and temperature effects.

C. Element library
The program includes the following elements:

- 2 dimensional beam with possible pins on either or both ends,
- 3 dimensional beam with possible pins on either or both ends,
- 2 dimensional compound beam for simulation of finite stiffness joints (important in vehicle structures)'
- 3 dimensional compound beam for simulation of finite stiffness joints,
- 2 dimensional triangular, constant strain membrane,
- 3 dimensional triangular, constant strain membrane.

D. Input module
Input module is very comfortable and particularly convenient to the first time user. Function keys are always displayed with clear indicators of the current options. Input module is organised in subsets of 'pages', with each subset corresponding to a particular segment of the input data. Subsets are selected by function keys, and further input or editing of previous data is done by simple cursor movements around each page. Various data generation options are also available.

Input data may be entered or edited in any order of subsets, and switching from one to another subset may be done simply and at any time.

The program incorporates an extensive data check with around 50 warning and error messages which are displayed before each calculation.

E. Graphical verification of the model
A model may be shown graphically at any stage of development, viewed from any angle.

ANALYSIS OF BEAM/MEMBRANE ASSEMBLIES

F. Program capacity and node/element numbering

Program incorporates a frontal solution routine, so that node numbering is arbitrary. This has great advantages when adding new, or deleting nodes and elements from the previous stage of model development. Both nodes and elements may be added or deleted anywhere in the input data list.

Program capacity can vary, but experience has shown that the arrangement with 450 nodes (2700 degrees of freedom), 900 elements and 50 'active' nodes in the 'front' cover the widest range of problems.

Program capacity can be extended to the capacity of the external disk space by using an out of core band solver. In order to keep the option of arbitrary node and element numbering, a special, very efficient renumbering subroutine has been developed.

However, PC computers may not be competitive with more powerful machines when solving very complex models. The capacity of the 'normal' version of program BEAST was therefore limited.

G. Post processing

Normal results of the calculation include nodal displacements, balance checks, reactions and internal loads in the elements. In order to reduce the time required to interpret the results some post-processing features are developed :

- Graphics presentation of the deformed shapes, viewed frm any angle,
- Combination of various factorised load cases,
- Special post-processing routines to aid the dimensioning of the structural elements. For example, a post processor for vehicle structures and steel skeletons provides and displays the following information on selected or all elements : length, weight, deformation energy, normal stress, shear stress, eqivalent stress and safety factor with reference to a material dependent stress level. A post-processor for reinforced concrete provides information on the selection of steel reinforcements.

H. Documentation

User documentation is extensive and intended for the first time user. It includes the engineering aspects of finite element modelling, program features, detailed information on the selection of the input data, computer operation and examples. In such a way the package can also be used for teaching.

EXAMPLES OF THE ANALYSIS OF VEHICLE STRUCTURES

The model used in the preliminary analysis of a heavy off road vehicle chassis frame is shown in Fig. 1. The frame was composed of closed section members, so that the effect of section warping was not significant. The vehicle is now in full production.

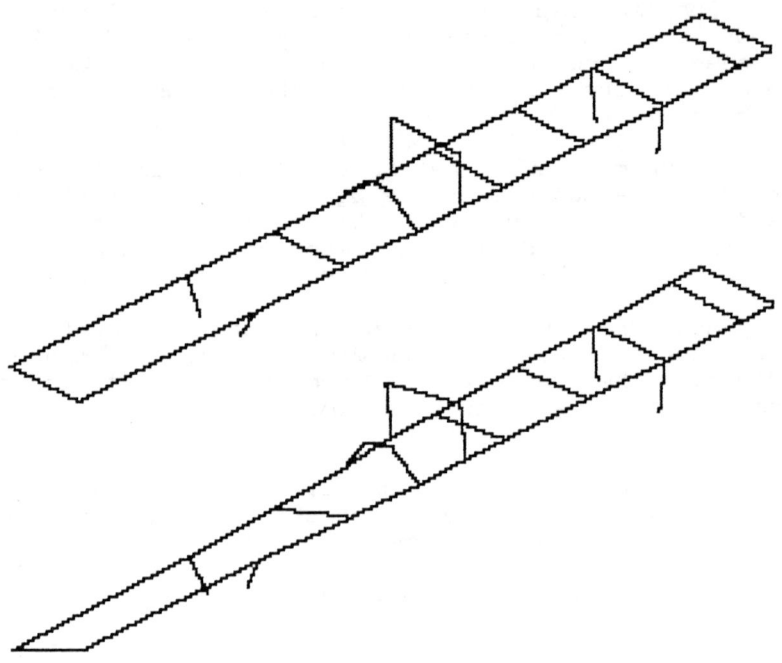

Fig. 1 The BEAST model and torsion of a chassis frame of a heavy off road vehicle

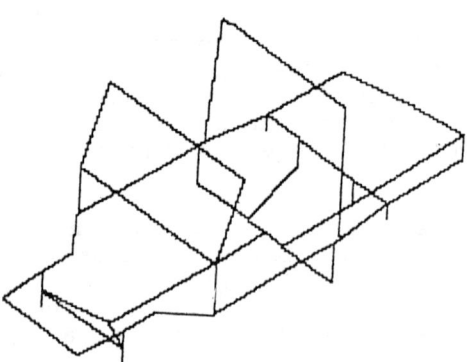

A model used in the selection of the main structural elements of a buggy car is shown in Fig. 2.

Fig.2 Model of a buggy car structure

ANALYSIS OF BEAM/MEMBRANE ASSEMBLIES 69

The application of program BEAST in the independent suspension design of a new light, 4 wheel drive off road vehicle is shown in Fig. 3. This example illustrates well the need to consider alternative concepts in the preliminary stages. After the kinematics of the suspension were determined, the design started with the concept whose model is shown in Fig. 3a. This design had very high moments in the lower arm, so an alternative concept was also considered. It had the lower link composed of two straight members, joined by a pin joint at the end of the rear beam. The BEAST model in Fig. 3b demonstrated the clear advantages and weight saving of this second concept, which was eventually incorporated into the new vehicle. More details can be found in the paper published at the XXI FISITA Congress in Belgrade, June 1986.

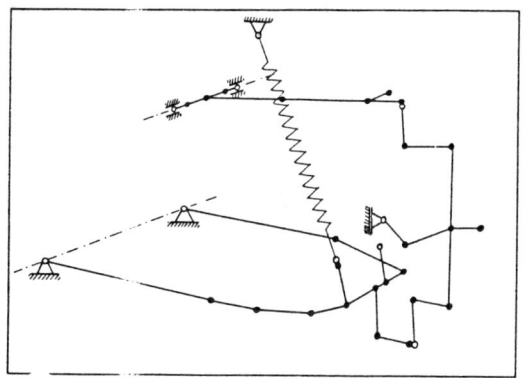

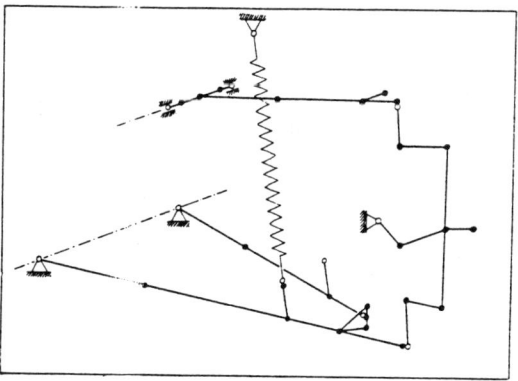

Fig. 3 BEAST models of the initial (a) and final design (b) of the independent suspension of a new light off road vehicle

70 ANALYSIS OF BEAM/MEMBRANE ASSEMBLIES

The last example shows the application of the program BEAST in the design and analysis of the chassis frame and body of the light off road vehicle presented at the XXI FISITA Congress. The model (Fig. 4) includes the suspension in order to simulate the load transfer as accurately as possible.

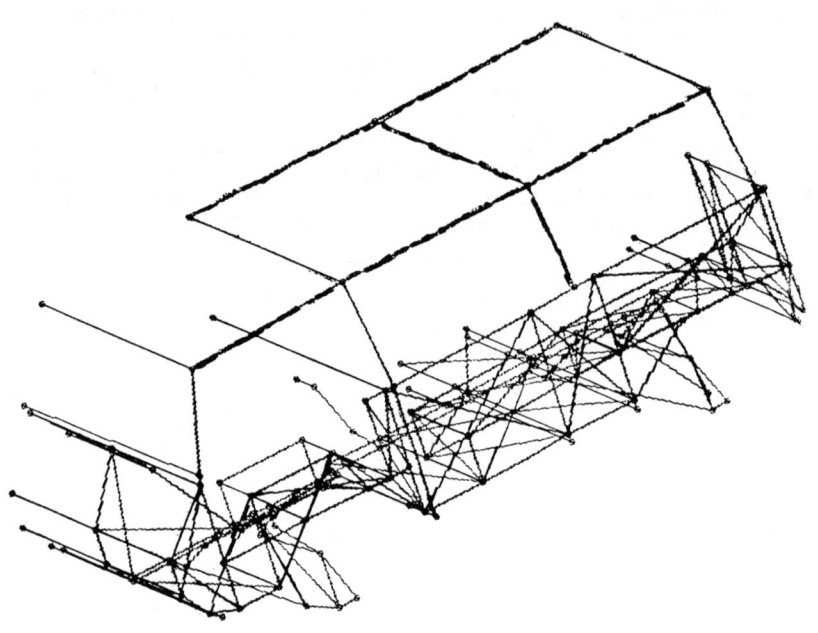

Fig. 4 BEAST model of the complete structure of a new off road vehicle (half of the structure is considered)

Program 'WEST-EX' for the Optimisation of the Rectangular Section Tubes Meeting Safety Requirements

D. Kecman

Faculty of Mechanical Engineering, University of Belgrade, 27 Marta 80, Belgrade, Yugoslavia
Consultant to the Cranfield Impact Centre Ltd., Cranfield, Beds. MK43 0AL, United Kingdom

INTRODUCTION

Rectangular and square section tubes are widely used in buses, coaches, special purpose vehicles, roll over and falling object protective structures (ROPS and FOPS). Some beams in car bodies can also be approximated by simplified rectangular sections. All these and some skeleton-type buildings may be subject to various safety requirements. The latest one, introduced in December 1986, in Britain and Hungary, is the ECE Regulation 66 on the roll over safety of buses and coaches. This Regulation was strongly supported by the research done in the Cranfield Impact Centre Ltd (summary given in reference 1). The provision that the type approval can also be done by calculation combined with some component testing was directly based on the results published in references 2 and 3.

A crashworthy vehicle structure must provide a satisfactory maximum strength, but should deform in a reasonably controllable manner and absorb sufficient impact energy without intruding into the survival space. It must also be weight and cost efficient and meet various further design constraints. It has been demonstrated widely that development of such structures can be aided efficiently by specially developed non-linear programs, such as CRASH-D, PLASH, EPSAP, KRASH, UMVCS-1, LAGS etc.

Program 'WEST-EX' was developed to enable an efficient weight and cost optimisation of safety structures composed of rectangular and square section tubes and great time saving in the preparation of input data for section collapse properties. It represents an extended version of the previously published (ref. 4) program 'WEST' (W-eight E-fficient S-afety T-ubes).

THEORETICAL AND EXPERIMENTAL BACKGROUND

Overloaded structural skeletons collapse due to development of localised bending failures in beams which act as hinges in mechanisms (hence the name 'plastic hinges'). Most of the impact energy is absorbed in hinges, so that good understanding of their behaviour is essential for both control of the collapse mechanism (i.e. distribution of hinges) and for the assessment of their energy absorbing capacity.

Hinges in thin walled vehicle components undergo large rotations (say 25 to 45 degrees) before the structure intrudes into the survival space. Instead of constant moment (curve A in Fig. 1), one can get a great variety of curves, depending on the location (beam or joint) and nature of local failures. Thin walled tubes usually buckle locally and display a moment drop-off (curve B), while curve C illustrates the effect of material separation at the hinge after the onset of collapse.

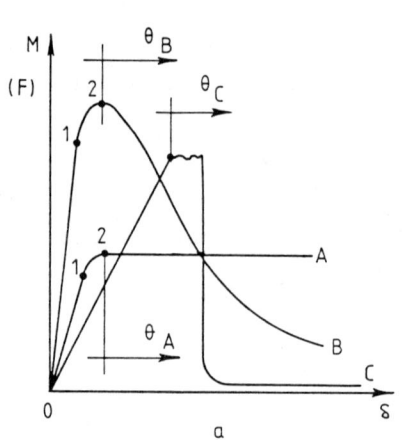

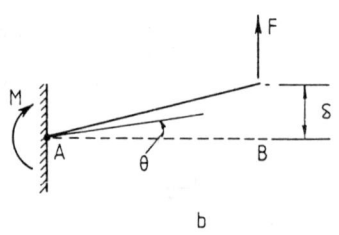

Fig. 1 Hinge moment-rotation curves of vehicle components

In further text the hinge angle (θ) will be assumed to start from the onset of collapse, while the elastic/plastic curvature will be allowed for by the stiffness properties of the appropriate finite element or rotary spring joint in the model.

Collapse mechanism in hinges which are directly exposed to impact may vary, but most of the hinges in a structure fail in a 'free', i.e. unrestrained mode. It has been observed, however, that the free bending collapse mode of rectangular section tubes is very repeatable and applies to sections with a wide range of aspect ratios and wall thicknesses (refs 3 to 8). The same mode was observed under both static and impact conditions, presumably due to the kinematics constraints of the collapse mechanism.

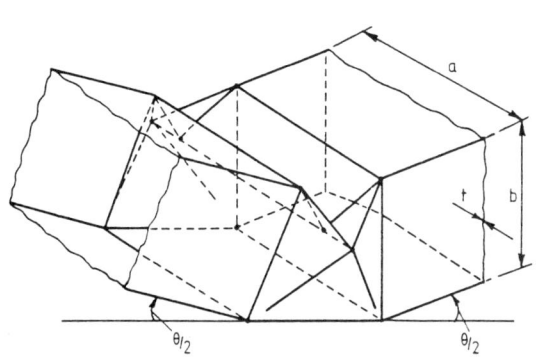

Fig. 2 Theoretical model of the hinge collapse mechanism

A typical hinge is symmetric in the cross and longitudinal planes. Theoretical study in ref. 3 established the theoretical model of the hinge collapse mechanism shown in Fig. 2. The plastic deformations are concentrated along the 'yield' lines of bending and 'rolling' deformation. Section walls are assumed non-extensible or compressible, although some in-plane deformation also took place in the real hinges, particularly in thicker walled tubes. Variation of the hinge kinematics during collapse was observed as well.

The maximum bending strength of the tube was determined allowing for the possibility of the elastic buckling in the compression flange, with boundary conditions depending on the aspect ratio of the section sides.

The theoretical model in Fig. 2 reflected the hinge kinematics between the angles of approximately 5 degrees and the angle of 'jamming', when the two opposite sides of the compressed flange in Fig. 2 come into contact.

The complete derivation of the theoretical hinge moment-rotation curves was presented in ref. 9, so only the basic principles will be given here. Bending and rolling deformations along the concentrated yield lines were related to the hinge angle (O). Work done by the hinge moment (M) over rotation (O) is absorbed by plastic deformation along the yield lines. The energy absorbed (E) can be expressed in terms of the material properties and yield line deformation. Due to the complexity of the formulae hinge moment at any angle O is then calculated as : $M(O) = (E(O + .O) - E(O))/ .O$, where .O represents a small, but finite increment.

The theory applies to angles of up to 30 to 50 degrees, but the angle O does not include the elastic curvature and starts from the onset of collapse as shown in Fig. 1.

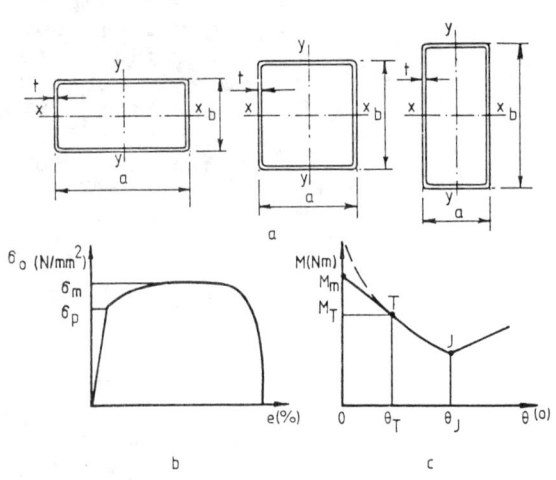

Fig. 3   Input parameters for calculation   of the M-O curve

If x-x indicates the bending axis (Fig. 3a), then the section data include width (a) depth (b), wall thickness (t), and material properties: Young's modulus (Y), nominal yield stress (p) and yield strength (m) shown in Fig. 3b. It is very important to note here that the material is assumed to be ductile enough not to fracture during hinge rotation. This is normally true for mild steel and some alluminium alloys.

By selecting a series of hinge rotation angles (O), one can produce a complete M-O curve in quasi-static bending (Fig. 3c). The initial theoretical 'overestimate' (dotted line) is corrected by a line through the point Mm which is also tangent to the basic M-O curve at the point (M., O.). The angle Oj corresponds to 'jamming' of the hinge mechanism. Another empirical formula is used beyond Oj.

OPTIMISATION OF RECTANGULAR SECTION TUBES 75

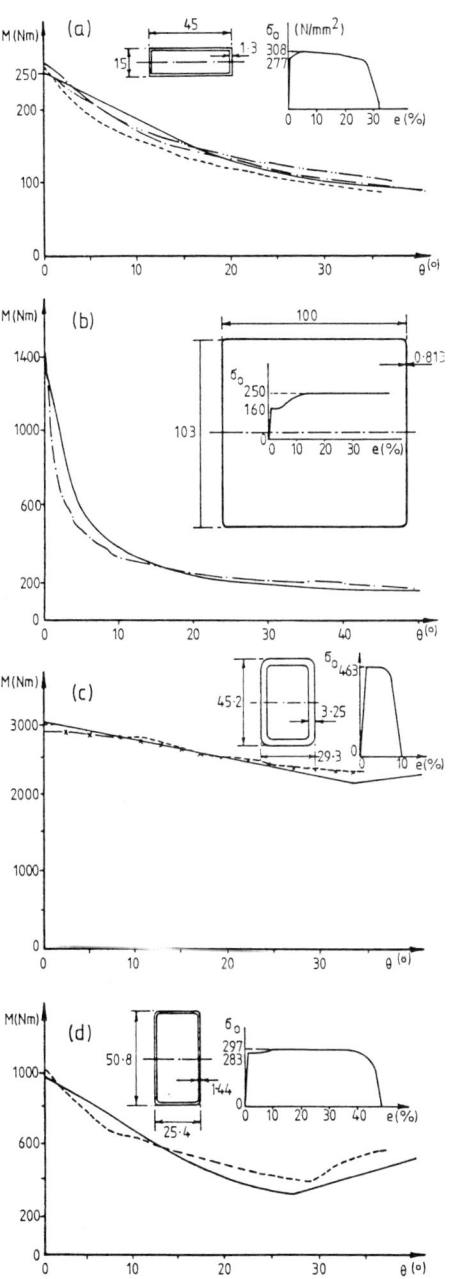

Fig. 4 Theoretical (solid) and experimental curves of a range of tube dimensions

Hence we have the following three sets of formulae :

1. for the maximum strength

$Mm = Mm(a,b,t, p)$

2. for the energy absorbed during hinge rotation (O)

$E = E(a,b,t, p, m, O)$

3. for the strength remaining after hinge rotation (O) :

$Mr = Mr(a,b,t, p, m, O)$

The theory was checked against 56 quasi-static cantilever bending tests on 27 different sections. Cantilevers were approximately 1m long and it was established by separate exercise (ref 3) that shear force did not have a noticeable effect on the hinge collapse behaviour (in short beams this may not apply).

Theoretical and experimental results in Fig. 4 illustrate the range of applicability of the method and versatility of the possible moment-rotation curves.

Energy absorbed is proportional to the area under the moment-rotation curve and can serve as a particularly useful

TABLE 2. THE EXPERIMENTAL AND THEORETICAL ENERGIES ABSORBED IN HINGES*

Section Number	a [mm]	b [mm]	t [mm]	σ_p [N/mm²]	σ_{pu} [N/mm²]	a/b	a/t	θ=10 Wexp [J]	θ=10 Wth [J]	θ=20 Wexp [J]	θ=20 Wth [J]	θ=30 Wexp [J]	θ=30 Wth [J]	θ=40 Wexp [J]	θ=40 Wth [J]
1	45	15	1.30	277	308	3.0	34.6	36	38	61	65	81	85	98	102
2	50.8	25.4	1.25	297	338	2.0	40.6	65	76	105	119	133	151	159	178
3	50.8	25.4	1.44	283	297	2.0	35.3	80	85	133	135	175	172	208	203
4	38	19	1.26	290	326	2.0	30.2	45	45	75	76	99	99	118	119
5	54	28.5	1.60	267	300	1.9	33.8	108	110	183	180	240	231	288	274
6	45.2	29.3	3.25	463	463	1.54	13.9	368	362	675	694	938	995	(1170)**	1263
7	38.1	25.4	1.62	352	363	1.5	23.5	101	101	178	174	236	229	284	275
8	50.8	38.1	1.26	253	284	1.33	40.3	93	107	145	162	187	202	214	236
9	50.8	38.4	1.6	380	430	1.33	31.8	198	213	318	340	398	433	457	511
10	104	87	0.813	161	250	1.2	128	93	102	135	146	166	178	201	205
11	103	99	0.813	161	250	1.04	127	83	116	127	166	163	202	-	232
12	44.4	44.4	1.6	313	348	1.0	27.8	186	196	298	313	379	398	(471)	470
13	38.4	38.4	1.6	374	390	1.0	24	170	178	288	291	378	374	(451)	443
14	45	45	1.94	340	416	1.0	23.2	286	282	482	487	616	638	716	765
15	45	45	2.15	324	360	1.0	20.9	307	296	510	512	677	674	(817)	809
16	25.4	25.4	1.48	329	353	1.0	17.5	73	67	130	121	177	163	214	198
17	25.4	25.4	2.0	418	418	1.0	12.7	117	114	218	216	315	305	-	381
18	100	103	0.813	161	250	0.97	123	100	121	147	173	188	210	223	241
19	45	40	0.86	160	245	0.96	52.3	52	50	75	76	97	94	(119)	109
20	38.4	50.8	1.6	380	430	0.756	24	260	264	423	428	537	546	611	643
21	38.1	50.8	1.26	253	284	0.75	30.2	120	126	186	194	230	242	(293)	282
22	38.1	50.8	1.67	308	351	0.75	22.8	219	226	368	372	-	476	-	562
23	29.3	45.2	3.25	463	463	0.66	9.14	508	498	980	953	1392	1364	-	1749
24	25.4	50.8	1.25	297	338	0.5	20.3	114	130	185	208	248	261	(325)	328
25	25.4	50.8	1.44	283	297	0.5	17.6	136	144	234	235	307	297	(397)	373
26	19	38	1.26	290	326	0.5	15.1	81	75	138	130	183	168	(225)	213
27	15	45	1.3	277	308	0.33	11.5	94	84	160	142	222	200	(300)	271

*Numbers are rounded to the nearest integer. **Numbers in parentheses indicate estimated values.

reference to the accuracy of the theory. A summary of the test data for all sections is therefore given in Table 1.

Past experience (refs. 2.3,6,7,8) has shown that if the impact speeds are below approximately 10 m/s, and if the collapsing mass is much smaller than the mass that is being retarded, then the overall and local collapse mechanisms in structural frameworks tend to be very similar. This implies that the quasi-static analysis is valid. Due to strain rate ($\dot{\epsilon}$), the dynamic yield stress (σ_{pd}) is higher than the static one (σ_p) and can be approximated by (ref. 10) :

$$\sigma_{pd} = \sigma_p K_p = \sigma_p \left[1 + \left(\frac{\dot{\epsilon}}{c}\right)^n\right]$$

where 'c' and 'n' are material dependent constants, e.g. for mild steel c = 40.4, n = 0.2.

The dynamic coefficient (K_m) for the dynamic yield strength (σ_{md}) is usually less than K_p in the equation above, although good results were obtained in some impact tests on bus rings using $K_m = K_p$.

It is important to note, however, that higher strain rates reduce material ductility and the possibility of material separation has to be considered.

OPTIMISATION APPROACH

Eight tube optimisation modes are possible (in contrast to five in the WEST program) in the current context :

(a) weight minimisation assuming that section dimensions represent continuous variables;
(b) weight minimisation by selection from a set of discrete data;
(c) price minimisation by selecting from a set of discrete data;
(d) minimisation of material properties for given section dimensions;
(e) minimisation of the wall thickness for given width, depth and material properties;
(f) minimisation of the section width for given depth, wall thickness and material properties;
(g) minimisation of the section depth for given width, wall thickness and material properties;
(h) minimisation of the time and cost of determining section collapse properties, either for design or analysis purposes.

A. Minimum weight theoretical sections

The objective function to be minimised is the section area $F = 2t(a + b - 2t)$, assuming for the practical purposes, that the wall thickness is constant. The objective function represents a hypersurface in the (a, b, t) coordinate system, with boundaries determined by the range of ratios a/b, a/t and b/t, within which the theory has been verified experimentally (Table 1).

Contraints imposed on the section collapse properties are typically defined as :

$$Mm - MX \quad 0,$$

$$E - EX \quad 0,$$

$$Mr - RX \quad 0,$$

where MX, EX and RX represent, respectively, the minimum required strength, energy absorbed and remaining strength after hinge rotation through a given angle O about the x-x axis of the section. Naturally, only some or all constraints may apply simultaneously.

In practice it is also necessary to specify additional constraints with reference to the other axis (y-y in Fig. 3), which is, indeed, essential in safety structures. A convenient way to do so is to specify the ratio 'R' between the corresponding properties about the y-y and x-x axes. Analysis of the experimental data established that the same ratio R applies well to all the three relevant characteristics.

It was established that the aspect ratio (a/b) of a section can be well approximated by

$$a/b \quad 0.2 R^2 + 0.9 R - 0.1.$$

The last conclusion greatly simplifies the optimisation process, because instead of a complex nonlinear optimisation problem, the task is reformulated in the following manner :

Optimisation constraints about one axis (say x-x) will apply exactly, while the collapse properties about the y-y axis will be very close, but possibly on either side of the values determined by the pre- selected ratio R (how close and on which side is, of course, always known after the results are produced).

Since the ratio a/b is now determined, the objective function can now be expressed in terms of two variables only (say 'a' and 't'). One can now choose a value of 'a' and solve one of the constraints as an equality in terms of 't'. The process can then be repeated with other values of 'a' and other constraints, until (with proper control of the process) the section with minimum area is found that meets all of the constraints.

Consider, for example, Fig. 5. Solid lines represent the constant area curves like contour lines on a complex surface originating from the 'a' and 't' axes. Assume now that the designer wants to find the lightest square section tube (R = a/b = 1), made of the same material as tube 13 in Table 1, and with the following constraints : MX = 1216 Nm, EX = 150 J and RX = 150 Nm after hinge rotation of O = 30 degrees.

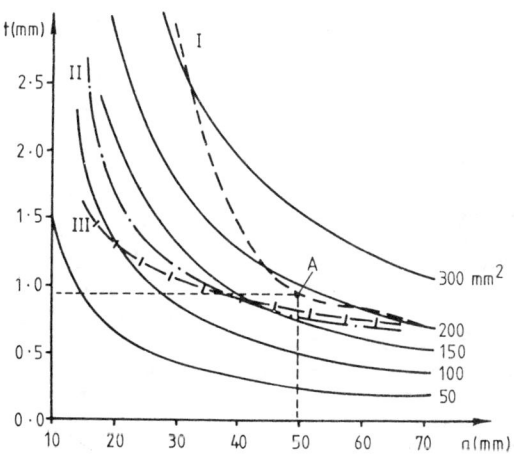

Fig. 5 Search for the minimum section when all three constraints apply

Curve I in Fig 5 corresponds to all sections with Mm =1216 Nm, curve II implies E = 150 J and III means that moment Mr = 150 Nm after O = 30 deg. The minimum section corresponds to the 'lowest' point (A) on the 'area' surface which does not fall below any of the three curves (I, II and III). This is because sections below a particular curve do not meet the appropriate safety constraint.

Constraints on energy and remaining strength produce only one minimum, while the competing effects of the fully plastic material deformation and elastic /plastic buckling on the maximum strength (Mm) may create two local minima in the curve I.

B. Lightest section from a data set
The objective function is still the same, but selection is now made from sets of discrete data. One set

may include 'standard' section dimensions (a,b,t), or preferable dimensions only, or sections available from a particular supplier e.t.c. Material properties (p) and (m) are also given for each section.

Since the section dimensions are known in advance, one can introduce new design constraints, say:

- collapse properties MX, EX, RX, MY, EY, RY about the x-x and y-y axes, with a given strain rate and the 'dynamic' coefficients 'c' and 'n';
- maximum section dimensions (a', b', c');
- minimum section dimensions (a", b", c");
- new material properties;

and others may be added very simply.

To find the lightest section meeting all of the criteria the program searches through the data set in an efficient manner and displays a chosen number of lightest sections meeting all of the constraints. The program automatically reverses the axes x-x and y-y if such 'rotation' helps to meet the constraints. Several sections may be useful because some may be more convenient than others even if slightly heavier.

It is interesting to note that the lightest 'standard' and 'non-standard' sections may not be the 'nearest' ones, because the slopes of the objective function need not be equal all around the minimum.

C. Cheapest section from a data set

The objective function is now the price index of the selected or all sections in the data set. Naturally, the number of price indexes usually corresponds to the number of materials in which a section may be purchased. In other respects the procedure is the same as in paragraph B.

D. Minimum material properties

Production, styling and assembly reasons may leave little freedom in choosing section dimensions. With dimensions and collapse properties specified, the objective function becomes the static yield stress (p) of the material. The user must also decide on the ratio m/ p (Fig. 3), strain rate, the dynamic parameters 'c' and 'n' and the ratio of the dynamic coefficients Km (for md) and Kp (for pd).

Optimisation is carried out by solving each of the constraints for the yield stress p (as an equality) and selecting the highest value.

E. Minimum wall thickness

It is sometimes convenient to keep the outer section dimensions, say when weight is to be taken off a structure without changes in the assembly tooling. The input data are the outer dimensions (a, b) and the static and dynamic material properties. The objective function is the section wall thickness (t) which is minimised as a continuous function and then the first equal or higher standard gauge can be taken for the element considered.

F. Minimum section width

Assembly or production reasons may sometimes fix the section depth and the choice of gauges and materials may also be quite limited. In such cases safety constraints are given and minimum section width is also found as a continuous function (which may be replaced by the first equal or higher standard value).

G. Minimum section depth

Argument is the same as for the width.

H. Time and cost savings for collapse properties

Prediction and modelling of the collapse properties of local failures (Fig. 1) is, arguably, the most difficult problem in the design and analysis of safety structures. A hybrid approach, combining component tests with the design and analysis of the complete structure often provides the best ground for a reliable prediction of the overall collapse performance. However, although preliminary component tests may prove to be very cost-effective in the long run, they still consume time, money and offer less flexibility for trial of design alterations than a reliable theoretical method.

Experimental verification of the theory behind the program WEST-EX on components (Table 1) and complete structures (refs. 3,11,12) demonstrates that these predictions do not introduce a greater level of uncertainty than do the variations in the material properties, component manufacture, and assembly of the complete structure. Since Table 1 was produced on the basis of measured material properties, the use of minimum guaranteed material specification can only increase the confidence in the theoretical prediction.

Time and costs of testing the collapse properties of tubes may vary from one place to another, but it is easy to imagine the benefits of getting a close estimate almost instantly from the computer. The advantages are even greater in an iterative, computer aided design/analysis process, involving trials of a variety of design alternatives.

EXAMPLES

A. Minimum weight - theoretical section

An example has already been shown in Fig. 5. Assume now that all the three safety constraints correspond to tube 13 in Table 1 : R = 1, p = 374 N/mm, .m=390N/mm, MX = 1216 Nm, EX = 374 J, RX = 430 Nm for O = 30 deg. The experimental and theoretical M - O curves for this section are shown in Fig. 6a. Boundary curves, as defined by WEST-EX (Fig. 6b) intersect at point A with a = b = 38.4 mm and t = 1.6 mm (as section 13, Table 1). How close to the exact dimensions one gets depends on the accuracy of definition of the collapse properties and the appropriate solution tolerance.

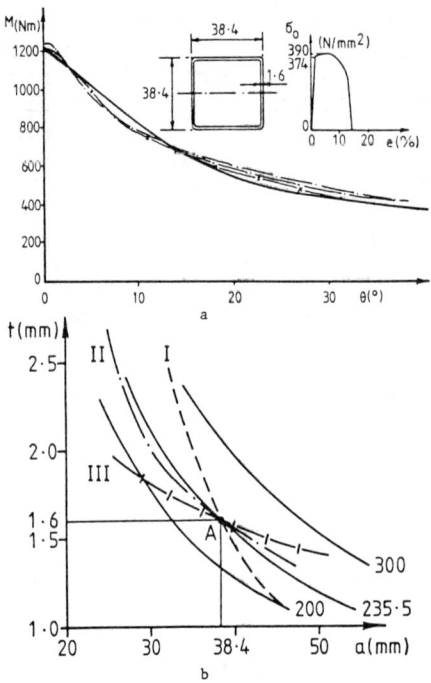

Consider also the constraints based on, say, section 25, Table 1: MX = 979 Nm, EX = 235 J, RX=411 Nm for O = 20 deg. The same tube, bent about the oter axis (Section 3 i Table 1) gives MY = 600 Nm, EY=135 J and RY = 239 Nm, again for O = 20 deg. The ratios of collapse properties 'R' are, respectively : R1 = 600/979 = 0.61, R2 = 135/235 = 0.57 and R3 = 239/411 = 0.58. With these values one gets the aspect ratios a/b of 0.52, 0.48 and 0.49 which are all very close to the actual aspect ratio 25.4/50.8 = 0.5.

Fig. 6 Collapse properties of section 13 (a) and the appropriate theoretical solution (b)

Weight minimisation allowing for the maximum strength only, tends to 'expand' the sections and reduce the wall thickness. For example, a minimum section of the same material as section 13 and with the same strength about both axes is (with tolerances on width 0.1 mm and 1 % on strength) : a = b =54.1 mm t = 0.9175 mm, area = 195.18 mm (weight reduction of 17 % in comparison with section 13).

It should be mentioned, however, that the very thin walled tubes are more sensitive to local damage or geometry error prior to bending collapse and may lose much of their original strength (Fig. 4b).

The estimated strain rate properties reduce further the section area. For example, assume that the material of section 13 is subject to a strain rate of 0.1 /sec. This gives K_p = 1.3 with the dynamic yield stress p_d = 1.3 374 = 486 N/mm, and let the same value correspond to m_d – hence K_m = 486/390 = 1.25. With this input and the same tolerances as above, the lightest section has : a = b = 27.6 mm, t=1.88 mm (weight reduction of 15 % with respect to the 'static' minimum.

One direction of bending is often regarded with preference. For example if we use again section 13, but reduce the y-y section properties by one third, so that R = 2/3 = 0.667, new minimum dimensions become : a = 22.6 mm, b = 38.38 mm, t = 1.79 mm, and the sec- tion is 13 % lighter than section 13.

B. Lightest standard sections

A choice has been made using the collapse properties of section 25 in Table 1, for O = 20 deg, from a set of standard sections as defined in DIN 2393 and/or 2394. If 5 lightest sections are asked for, the result is in Table 2.

Table 2

No	Area mm	a mm	b mm	t mm	MX Nm	EX J	RX Nm	MY Nm	EY J	RY Nm
1	264	30	40	2	1012	290	650	825	234	514
2	264	25	45	2	1084	312	701	710	202	446
3	280	34	40	2	1098	306	656	979	271	574
4	284	25	50	2	1278	357	770	776	214	453
5	300	25	40	2.5	1097	343	868	778	244	621
6	304	40	40	2	1227	328	664	1227	328	664
7	304	30	50	2	1414	387	803	984	262	529
8	304	20	60	2	1544	408	932	684	187	394

The program gave 8 (rather than 5) sections because tubes 1 and 2 have the same area, as well as tubes 6, 7 and 8 (i.e. there are 5 weight levels).

This also means that one can get a variety of collapse properties for the same and similar weight and a list like Table 2 may help to make the best choice. If one property, say EX, is preferential, one can get higher values from lighter sections, e.g. compare tubes 2 and 3 and also 4, 5 and 6, all passing the same basic requirements.

C. Cheapest standard sections
A table similar to Table 2 can also be produced, but with ranking according to the section price and not area.

D. Minimum material properties
Assume that all static properties of section 13, Table 1, should be increased by (at least) 30 % and that the new yield stress and strength are equal. The program gives p' = 513 N/mm. The ratio of the new and old maximum strengths is proportional to p'/p= 1.37, but the energies and remaining strengths are not (E'/E = 1.34 and RX'/RX = 1.3).

Before using a new material its dynamic ductility and tendency to fracture near welded joints should be examined.

E. Minimising one section dimension
Minimisation of one section dimension (a or b or t) with other data given was also successfully tested using data from Table 1.

F. Collapse properties of sections
Calculation of the collapse properties has already been demonstrated. These data can then be used independently, or as input information for the programs dealing with the non-linear behaviour of the complete structure.

Examples of the combined use of programs CRASH-D and WEST-EX are shown in Figs. 7 and 8, dealing with the prediction of the collapse behaviour of a bus ring. The input data to the program CRASH-D were generated by WEST-EX, and the comparison between the theoretical and experimental quasi-static load-deflection curves is shown in Fig. 7a, with the collapse mode in Fig. 7b. Results of a pendulum impact test on a similar ring are shown in Fig. 8. The strain rate was calculated from the pendulum impact speed and its effect on the material properties has been taken into account. The curve in Fig. 8a represents a 'quasi-dynamic' load-deflection curve. Maximum displacement of the impact point was calculated by looking for the point E on the curve

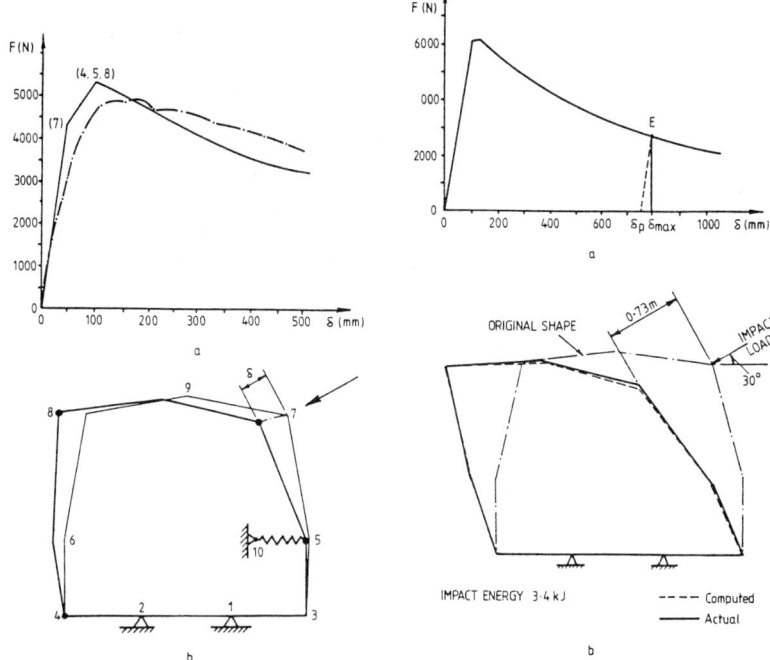

Fig. 7. - Experimental (dotted) and theoretical (solid), quasi-static load-deflection curves of a bus ring (a) and the overall collapse mode (b)

Fig. 8 - The theoretical 'quasi-dynamic' load-deflection curve of an impacted bus ring (a) and its final deflections (b).

corresponding to the area under the curve to the kinetic energy of the pendulum. Dotted line in Fig. 8a corresponds to the elastic spring-back. A very good prediction of the maximum deflection of the ring was produced (Fig. 8b).

PROCEDURE FOR OPTIMISATION OF A SAFETY STRUCTURE

The procedure for optimisation of a safety structure will be demonstrated using an example of a bus structure to meet the new ECE Regulation 66. The procedure involves the following steps :

(a) Choice of the general concept of the safety structure, or alternative ones to be examined.

(b) Assume starting section dimensions and perform an elastic analysis of the complete body (Fig.9a) to determine the main load paths and the effect of the non-collapsing members.

(c) Perform collapse analysis on a simpler model (Figs.9b and 9c), using collapse properties produced by program WEST-EX and allowing for the full range of

86 OPTIMISATION OF RECTANGULAR SECTION TUBES

Finite Element Model
for 'Stardyne' Elastic
Analysis of Complete Structure

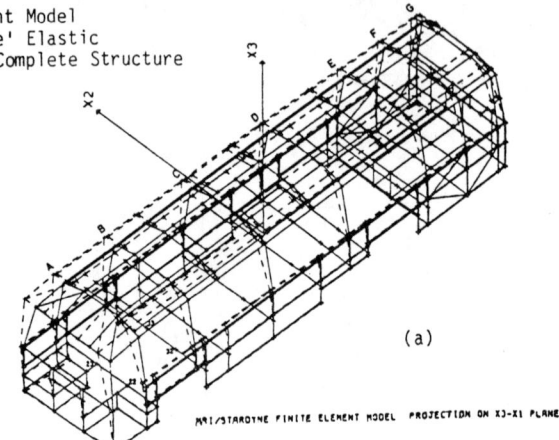

(a)

Simplified Framework Structure
for CRASH-D Analysis

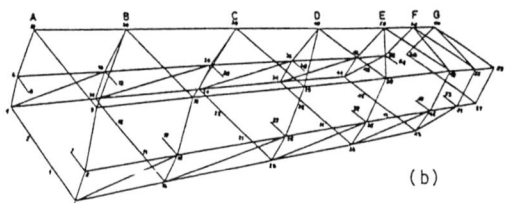

(b)

Output from CRASH-D Analysis
Showing Deformed Shape and
Sequence of Formation of
Plastic Hinges.

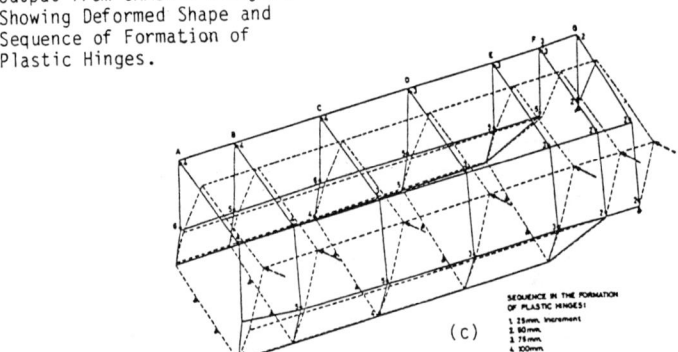

(c)

Figure 9. Computer Models of Bus Structure.

deformations required to absorb the energy specified.

(d) Analyse the results of step (c) and determine the hinge rotation angles and energies required. Use these as input data to the program WEST-EX to determine new section dimensions or material properties, depending on which of the program options is regarded as the most significant.

(e) Repeat steps (c) and (d) until the best solution is found.

(f) Repeat steps (b) to (d) to check that the alterations do not introduce important new effects on load redistribution, elastic stiffness, etc.

(g) Design and produce components (beams and joints) based on the theoretical analysis and test them to collapse statically and dynamically (by a small pendulum). This should prove that the assumptions concerning the beam and joint stiffness, strength and energy absorbing properties are correct.

(h) Accept the solution, or repeat the same procedure with appropriate corrections if results of step (g) so require.

CONCLUSIONS

Rectangular and square section tubes are widely used in vehicle and other structures which must meet various impact safety requirements. In order to make such structures cost efficient, one can employ modern non-linear finite element programs.

Based on an extensive theoretical and experimental support, program WEST-EX has been developed to enable optimisation of sections which provide sufficient maximum strength, energy absorbed and remaining strength when subject to quasi-static and impact conditions. Features include:

    a) weight minimisation (theoretical),
    b) weight minimisation of 'standard' sections.
    c) cost minimisation of 'standard' sections,
    d) minimisation of material material properties,
    e) minimisation of section wall thickness,
    f) minimisation of section width,
    g) minimisation of section depth,
    h) efiicient and reliable calculation of section collapse properties, which saves much time and cost for preparation of data to be used for design and/or analysis.

Examples of program use are presented, as well as instructions on the structure optimisation procedure with the aid of programs WEST-EX and another one for the collapse analysis of a complete structure.

REFERENCES

1. Kecman D. (1983), Analysis of Framework-Type Safety Structures in Road Vehicles. Chapter 13, Structural Crashworthiness, (Ed. Jones N, Wierzbicki T), pp. 371-396, Butterworths,London

2. Miles J. (1976), The Determination of Collapse Load and Energy Absorbing Properties of Thin Walled Beam Structures Using Matrix Methods of Analysis, Int. J. Mech. Sci., Vol.18.

3. Kecman D. (1978), Bending Collapse of Rectangular Section Tubes in Relation to the Bus Roll Over Problem, PhD Thesis, Cranfield Institute of Technology, U.K.

4. Kecman D. (1981), Program WEST for Optimisation of Rectangular and Square Section Tubes from the Safety Point of View, Int Conf. Vehicle. Struct Mech., Detroit, USA (SAE Paper 811312)

5. Cranfield Impact Centre (1980), Bending Collapse of Car Components, Report to FORD Motor Company

6. Cranfield Impact Centre (1977), Investigation of the Collapse Behaviour of Bus Rings, Report to the Dept. of Transport, London

7. Cranfield Impact Centre (1979), Investigation of the PSV Roll Over Accidents 1976-1979, Report to the Dept. of Transport, London

8. Kecman D., Hardy R. (1980), Analysis, Redesign and Testing of a Tractor Safety Cab, JUMV Masinstvo, Belgrade (in Serbocroatian)

9. Kecman D. (1983), Bending Collapse of Rectangular Section Tubes, Int. J. Struct. Mech.,Vol 25 No 9-10, pp.623-636

10. Manjoine M.J. (1944), Influence of Rate of Strain and Temperature on Yield Stress of Mild Steel, ASME Trans., Vol 66.

11. Wardill G.A., Kecman D. (1980), Theoretical Prediction of the Maximum Strength and the

Collapse mode of a Bus Structure when subject to a Standard Roll Over Test, Int. Congress FISITA, Hamburg, W. Germany

12. Kecman D., Tidbury G.H. (1982), Theoretical Prediction of the Complete Collapse Behaviour of a Coach Subject to the Proposed Standard Roll Over Test, Int Congrss FISITA, Melbourne, Australia

Torsional Rigidity of a Racing Car Frame

J.R. Banerjee
Department of Aeronautics, The City University, Northampton Square, London EC1V 0HB, U.K.

SUMMARY

Experiments have been conducted to determine the torsional stiffness of a racing car frame. Problems encountered in the experimental procedure and their possible remedies are mentioned. Use of software packages to analyse the frame is demonstrated in order to achieve a lighter frame. Theoretical and experimental results are discussed and commented on. Suggested guidelines for the proposed future work are highlighted.

INTRODUCTION

Torsional behaviour of a car frame is of great significance mainly because excitations arising out of sources such as rough road conditions, impact loading etc., often tend to produce a twist in the chassis. The amount by which the frame twists is governed by its ability to resist the twisting moment. This resistance is termed as torsional stiffness and is expressed as torque required to produce a unit twist. A representative figure for a space-frame chassis is 2.7 KNm/degree for a frame weighing about 50 kg. Figure 1 illustrates an example, where one wheel of a car is travelling over a bump in the road surface. As a result the spring attached to this wheel is compressed and the spring load is transmitted to the frame and the frame is then deflected under the application of an applied load i.e. a bump in the road surface. The angle of twist $\phi = \tan^{-1}(\frac{2D}{L})$ and the torque $T = FL$ (see Figure 1), then the torsional stiffness K is given by $K = T/\phi$. So for a given frame with appropriate support conditions if values of D are measured for a corresponding set of F values of applied loads, the torsional stiffness as given above can then be calculated.

PURPOSE OF A SPACE-FRAME CHASSIS

A motor car chassis connects all four wheels with a structure which should ideally have very small or negligible deformation in bending and torsion i.e. very small or negligible sag or twist. The structure must be capable of supporting all components and occupants and should absorb all loads fed into it without deflecting unduly. It should be designed to link up the mounting points for all the components that go into making up the car. A space-frame structure is regarded as a very efficient type of chassis which satisfies the above requirements. Furthermore, if a space frame has a very high torsional rigidity normally it automatically ensures an adequate bending rigidity which is also an important criterion of chassis design. A well designed space frame made from tubular construction is expected to be light, stiff and durable. However from the production point of view the space frame is probably the most expensive tubular chassis to make, because of the number of tubes used and the amount of welding involved. But it is undoubtedly the most efficient.

EXPERIMENTAL RESULTS

The frame under investigation has been taken from a racing car the details of which are not disclosed to abide by the manufacturer's company policy. The frame is schematically shown in Figure 2 with the left and right hand end representing the front and rear end of the car respectively. In order to recreate the road condition it was decided to take the load through the main suspension support so, the frame should be held horizontal and supported at the rear whereas the torque will be applied at the front. This resulted in supporting the frame at points P,Q,R and S and applying a pure torque in the vertical plane which contains points P',Q',R' and S' (see Figure 2). Deflections at various points on the frame are then measured using dial gauges. (It may also be noted that details of the testing apparatus are not reported here because of the classified nature of certain aspects of this work.) Every effort was made to minimize the errors such as due to gravitational effects etc. The loads were applied in a manner that would be as far as possible, similar to those encountered under normal road conditions.

Ideally the chassis is to be twisted about its torsional axis which is obtained by finding the flexural axis of each portion of the frame and joining them up with straight lines. The structure being very nearly symmetric, the flexural axis for the complete frame can be closely approximated to its axis of symmetry as shown by the solid lines in Figure 3. As seen in the figure a straight horizontal line is not obtained by joining the flexural axes of the front and rear portions of the frame. As an acceptable compromise it was decided to twist the chassis about an axis that persisted for the greatest length of the frame. The assumed flexural axis of the complete frame is shown by the chained line in Figure 3. Pure torque was applied both in the clockwise and anticlockwise directions as shown in Figure 4 and the dial gauges are placed under points A,B,C and D in Figure 2 to measure the required deflections. (The points A,B,C and D corresponds to nodes 2,1,19 and 20 of Figure 8 respectively.) A dial gauge is hereafter referenced by its location, e.g. gauge A refers to the dial gauge which has been placed under the point A. Representative results of a typical test are shown in Figures 5 and 6 where the load was applied in the clockwise direction and in the fashion shown in Figure 4. The points denoted by circles in the figure correspond to the readings taken during the loading of the frame whereas the ones shown by crosses correspond to the readings during unloading the frame. It may be noted that the deflections of gauge B has been reversed, i.e. had their signs reversed in order that they can be plotted on positive axes, and, therefore more easily compared with the graph obtained from gauge A.

Experimental results obtained from dial gauges indicate considerable errors and almost in all cases the left hand side dial gauge gave a reading which was approximately 1.5 times greater than that given by the right hand side dial gauge. It was soon realised that the way the experimental set up was designed and the manner in which the torque was applied were the two main sources of error. The supporting structure deflected quite appreciably under the applied loading which in turn introduced errors in the dial gauge readings. Thus it was noted that the dial gauges on either side of the chassis were giving repeatable but significantly different readings. This meant that when torsional rigidity figures were calculated the difference in values obtained could be as much as 150 Nm/degree. It was also realised that the 'torsion apparatus' used was not dividing the torque into two equally applied forces on either side of the chassis. This was soon rectified but no significant improvement in results was observed. It became clear that the frame deflected both laterally and in the vertical direction quite considerably. So a proper estimation of the twist of the frame from the dial gauge reading became almost impossible.

Against the above background, it was felt that the unpredictable vertical and horizontal 'errors' were most unsatisfactory and a solution was sought whereby they could be eliminated. A practical method of solution using 'a line of sight' that reduced the vertical errors to an insignificant level was deviced. The method is shown in Figure 7 which involves fixing a sight to the chassis that was aligned on a vertical scale placed at a distance 8.44m away from the chassis. The torque was then applied and the rotation of the chassis measured as a change in the reading on the scale. A value of the torsional rigidity could then be computed. The readings obtained using this method are almost identical irrespective of the direction of twist. The method proved very satisfactory because it gave the actual twist of the frame in a very straight-forward way. Representative results are shown in Table I.

THEORETICAL RESULTS

Two software packages namely BUNVIS[1] and LUSAS[2] were used to analyse the frame. The numbering of the nodes is shown in Figure 8. Accuracy of theoretical results was confirmed when both the packages gave similar displacements for the nodes. Figure 9 shows the displacements and rotations of the face 1,2, 3,4 (see Figure 8) of the frame. The load values are as shown in the figure. The horizontal load simulate the experimental condition.

PROPOSED WORK

The following work would enable a proper evaluation of the torsional stiffness of the chassis

(a) The frame should be analysed with and without the presence of some well selected members and the corresponding displacement pattern should be studied.

(b) The frame should be loaded in a manner that causes it to remain stationary and twist rather than displace in a horizontal direction.

(c) Displacements in a number of representative vertical plane should be treated when evaluating torsional rigidity figures.

(d) Theoretical figures obtained should be cross checked with experimental data to see that there is good correlation.

CONCLUSION

1. The torsional stiffness of a racing car frame is experimentally determined (see Table I).

2. The use of software packages for the structural analysis of of the frame is demonstrated but further work needs to be done to investigate the effects of individual members on the overall stiffness of the frame.

3. Problems encountered during the course of the experiment are highlighted.

ACKNOWLEDGEMENTS

The author is grateful to Dr. D.L.McDiarmid, Mr.G.Nearn and Mr. J.Coates for help, encouragement and many new ideas. He wishes to thank his student Mr.M.C.Nethercott who did all the ground work reported in this paper.

REFERENCES

1. Anderson, M.S., Williams, F.W., Banerjee, J.R., Durling, B.J., Herstrom, C.L., Kennedy, D. and Warnaar, D.B. User Manual for BUNVIS-RG, NASA. Technical Memorandum 87669, November, 1986.

2. LUSAS - Developed by Finite Element Analysis Ltd, London.

Table I Results obtained using the line of sight method

Applied Torque (Nm)	Scale Reading (m)	Deflection (m)	Torsional Stiffness (Nm/degree)
0.00	1.500	0.000	-
137.05	0.984	0.021	961.4
274.11	0.962	0.043	939.0
411.16	0.939	0.066	917.7
548.22	0.917	0.088	917.7
685.27	0.894	0.111	909.4

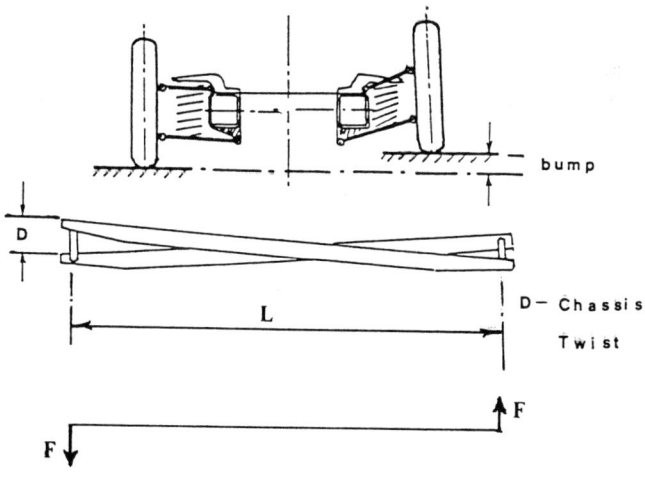

Figure 1. The twist of a car chassis when travelling over a bump.

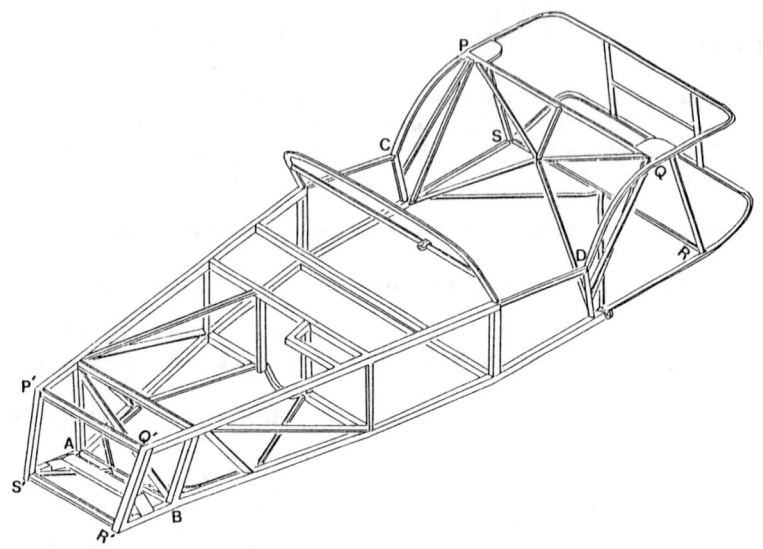

Figure 2. The racing car frame.

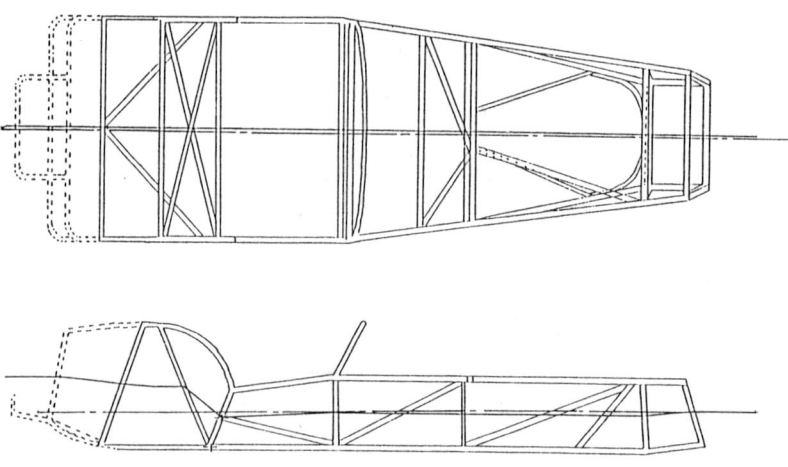

Figure 3. Flexural axis of the frame.

TORSIONAL RIGIDITY OF A RACING CAR FRAME 97

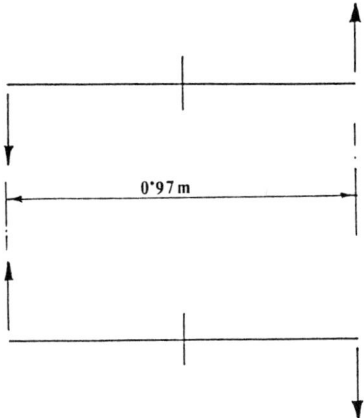

Figure 4. Direction of applied forces to produce a pure torque.

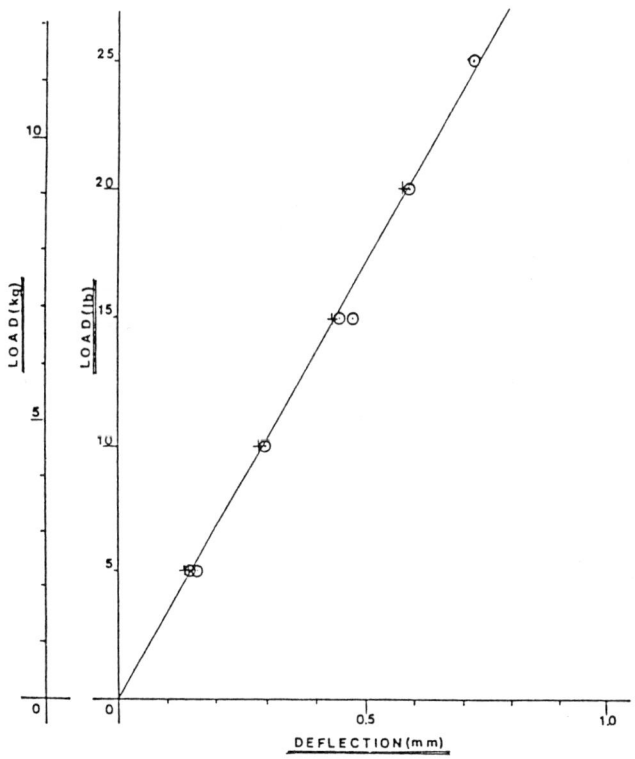

Figure 5. Load-Deflection characteristics obtained using dial gauge A.

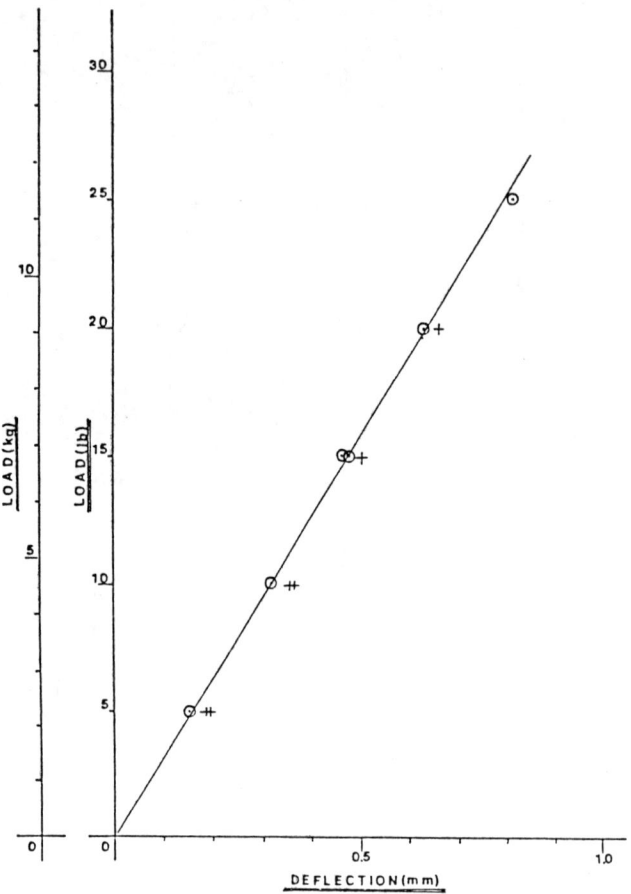

Figure 6. Load-Deflection characteristics obtained using dial gauge B.

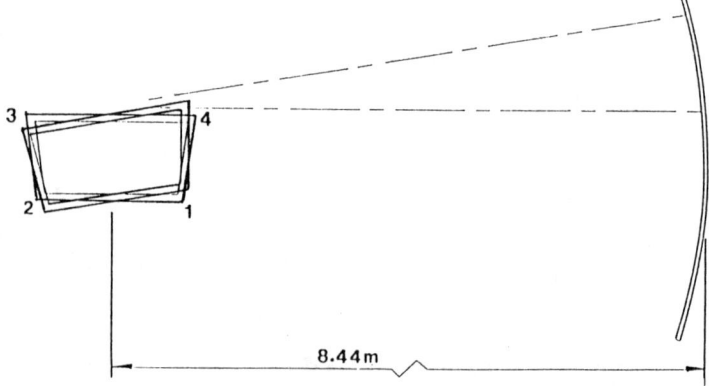

Figure 7. Line of sight method.

TORSIONAL RIGIDITY OF A RACING CAR FRAME 99

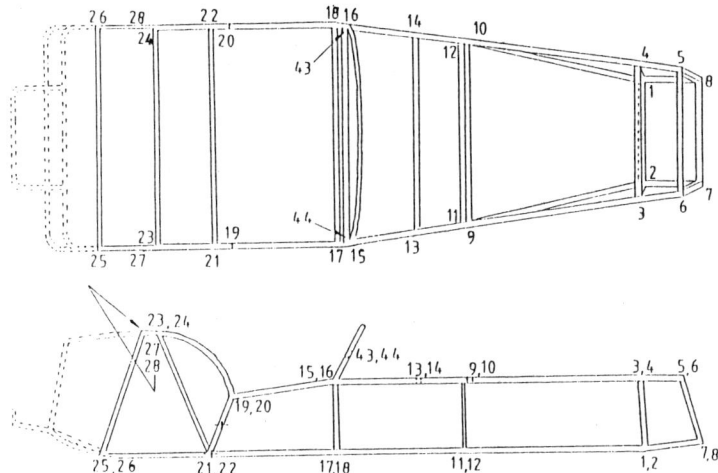

Figure 8. Node numbering for the BUNVIS and LUSAS run.

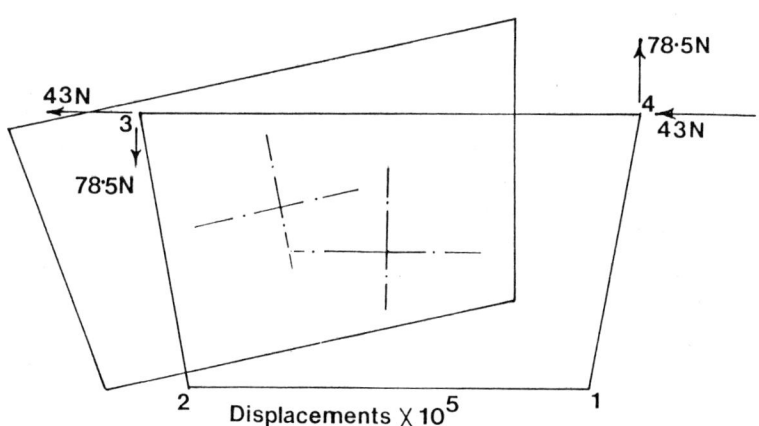

Figure 9. Theoretical results showing deformation of the frame front.

Thermal and Mechanical Analyses of Resistance Spot Welding: A Review of Existing Work
S.D. Sheppard
Department of Mechanical Engineering, Stanford University, Stanford, California, 94305, U.S.A.

INTRODUCTION

The purpose of this paper is to review analytical and experimental research concerned with the performance of resistance spot welds under fatigue loading. Furthermore, works focused on understanding residual stresses (as related to fatigue performance) in these weldments will be discussed.

Interest in spot weld performance under fatigue loading has increased in the last few years due to several changes in practices in the automobile industry. In search of lighter weight cars, for example, automakers have been gradually replacing many mild steel parts with parts made of high strength steel, thereby allowing for a reduction in gage. This change, along with a general industry design change from frame-body construction to unibody construction can make the fatigue behavior of spot welds a critical issue with respect to vehicle safety and reliability.

The effect of such changes on the fatigue performance of spot welds was reported by Fuji Heavy Industries (Subaru) [1]* when mild steel sheet metal in a particular automobile was almost entirely replaced by lighter gage, higher strength sheet. No other design modifications were made. Results of road tests showed fatigue damage at spot-weld connections that was attributable to a decrease in body stiffness caused by the reduction in sheet thickness, and the persistence of residual stresses in the stronger material. In light of such findings

---

* Numbers in brackets [] designate references listed at end of text.

it is not surprising that surveys conducted in 1982 by both
the Transportation Department of the AISI Committee of Sheet
Steel producers [2] and the Japanese Society of Automotive
Engineers (JSAE) [3] of companies using spot welding listed a
better understanding of fatigue behavior of spot welding as a
top research priority.

Fatigue performance of spot welds is influenced both by
the magnitude of the variable load applied to the structure
and by the overall quality of the weld. In today's welding
community the idea of spot weld quality indicates adequate
weld formation and static strength. Both of these parameters
can be measured directly with destructive tests [4] on random
samples of production weld joints, or by visual inspection,
which is inherently qualitative. There has also been research
done on relating real time signals such as acoustic emission
[5], dynamic resistance of the weld joint [6], hydraulic weld
force amplitudes [7], and electrode travel during welding [8]
to static strength. An understanding of the relationship
between such signals and strength opens up the possibility of
developing adaptive feedback control welders, a number of
approaches of which are summarized in [9].

Little is said by welding engineers or in the literature
of resistance weld quality in terms of fatigue strength. This
particular measure of strength may be markedly affected by,
for example, the presence of residual stresses (as is often
the case with arc welds). In fact, reviewing previous work
focused on gaining an understanding of the effect of residual
stresses on fatigue strength of fillet and butt weldments
provides insight into fatigue performance of resistance spot
welds.

FATIGUE LIFE IN SPOT WELDED JOINTS

As previously mentioned, fatigue performance of spot welded
joints has gained greater attention during the last few
years. There have been a number of efforts directed toward
increasing understanding of crack growth around spot welds,
and predicting the stress-life (S-N) or strain-life
(ε-N) behavior of spot welded structures. The influence of
joint geometry has been considered by several of these
researchers.

Lawrence et al. [10, 11] have developed a three stage
initiation-propagation model (TSIP) of fatigue failure in spot
welds loaded in tensile-shear. The three stages are fatigue
crack initiation (Stage 1), crack growth through the sheet
thickness to the surface (Stage 2), and finally, crack growth
across the specimen width (Stage 3). Stage 1 life (N_s)
predictions were made based upon the Basquin equation (plastic
strain)[12] and used Neuber's Rule [13] to predict weld strain
concentration. Stage 2 life (N_{pt}) and Stage 3 life (N_{pw}) used

linear elastic fracture mechanics principles to calculate the
number of cycles required for crack growth through the
thickness and across the width, respectively. Fatigue life,
as predicted by the model and observed experimentally,
increased both with sheet thickness and specimen width. This
is most likely due to increased joint stiffness. Ho [14] used
a similar approach to study fatigue life in tensile-shear spot
welds. He included the presence of residual stress as a
prestress of the spot weld.

Recently, Abe et al. [15] have also investigated crack
initiation and crack propagation in spot welds subjected to
fatigue. Their experiments were focused on identifying the
effects of thickness and specimen width on the number of
cycles spent in initiation and propagation.

A different approach to fatigue life prediction in spot
welds has been taken by Orts [16], and Barsom et al. [17].
Both of these research efforts focused on the role that weld
rotation plays in fatigue, and have attempted to relate this
parameter to life.

The Committee on Fatigue Strength and Structural
Reliability of the JSAE set up a special task force quantify
fatigue behavior of typical automotive weld joints. Results
from the three year study (1979-1983) were published in
[18]. In this work a series of fatigue tests of spot welded
samples were run by various Japanese automobile manufacturers
in order to establish alternating load or strain vs. life
characteristics. Test configurations included tensile-shear,
cross-tension, and plane bending. Various combinations of
sheet thicknesses (0.8mm, 1.2mm, 1.6mm) and sheet strengths
(high strength and low carbon) were considered. The Japanese
effort is continuing and is valuable in helping to establish a
knowledge base of fatigue behavior of spot welded
structures. A similar effort was carried out by Rivett and
Slater of The Welding Institute in Cambridge [19].

Investigations have also been made into factors that
might improve fatigue performance under constant amplitude and
variable load conditions. Lawrence et al. [20] have
undertaken an experimental study to establish the stress-life
characteristics of spot welded joints subjected to tensile-
shear loading when "modifications" are made to the "as welded"
condition. Mild and high strength sheet steels of nominal
thickness (1.25mm) were considered. "Modifications" included
mechanical treatments (e.g., prestressing prior to fatigue
testing, coining), and different welding conditions (e.g.,
stress relief subsequent to welding, cool-forging, weld-
forging, modified weld voltage/current). Broad conclusions
that can be drawn from this work are:

- Fatigue resistance of tensile-shear spot welds,

particularly in high strength sheet, could be greatly improved by treatments which either reduce tensile residual stresses resulting from welding (e.g., heat treatment), or induce residual compressive stresses (e.g., coining, weld-forging).

- The state of the sheet steel surface, that is galvanized or bare, has little, if any, influence on fatigue test results. (It may, however, greatly influence electrode tip wear).

- Increasing the base metal tensile strength does not greatly improve the fatigue resistance of as-welded tensile-shear spot welds. This has also been found to be true in arc welding [21-23], especially at long lives. Lawrence et al. conclude that this is due to greater (tensile) residual stresses in higher strength metals, but in arc welding it has been found that the size of the zone experiencing tensile residual stresses near yield strength is smaller in high strength steel compared with mild steel [24]. This is primarily because a smaller zone undergoes plastic deformation during welding in a higher strength steel. For example, the maximum mechanical strain observed one inch from the arc weld line during welding decreases as the yield strength of the steel increases. These findings indicate that the lack of improvement in fatigue strength with increased tensile strength may be due either to the general pattern of decreased fracture toughness in stronger metals, or to an overwhelming influence of the stress concentration that the weld represents.

- Improvements possible through modification of weld geometry (e.g., elliptical nugget) and the weld cycle seem to be smaller than those possible through control of residual stresses.

These basic trends are supported by the works of others, as summarized by Dickenson in his publication <u>Welding in the Automotive Industry,</u> [25], and by the investigation by Ewing et al. [26].

FATIGUE LIFE AND RESIDUAL STRESSES IN WELDMENTS

The heating and cooling cycle seen in most types of welding leads to the introduction of residual stresses in the structure or component. These residual or self-equilibrating stresses result from non-uniform yielding and have long been of concern to the welding engineer. Their effect on fatigue performance of butt and fillet welds is still a topic of some debate. For example, Newman and Gurney [27] found that minimizing residual stresses by thermal stress relief had no effect on fatigue strength at 2×10^6 cycles of fully reversed loading of transverse butt welds with or without the weld reinforcement machined flush. Navrotskii and Savelev [28] also found no effect with unmachined transverse butt welds or with transverse non-load-carrying fillet welds. Wiene [29] found an 18% improvement in fatigue strength due to stress relieving K-butt welds tested in unidirectional bending and Kudryavtsev [30] found a 150% increase in non-load carrying fillet welds. Ross [31] suggests that the effect is negligible in good welds, and Hebrant et al. [32] believe that stress concentration effects are much greater than those introduced by the presence of residual stress. A different opinion is held by Dugdale [33] who feels that there is significant evidence that fatigue performance is strongly influenced by the presence of residual stress. Furthermore, results presented by Nelson [34] indicate that life of load-carrying fillet welds is reduced when tensile residual stresses are present (e.g., when R=0, maximum stress at 4×10^6 cycles is reduced by approximately 30% when initial tensile residual stress of 240 MPa is present). In general more effect is present in higher strength materials.

Munse [35] summarizes these apparently conflicting opinions/results well when he states that "the effects of residual stresses (on fatigue performance) may differ from one instance to another, depending upon the materials and geometry of the members, the state of stress, the magnitude of applied stress, the type of stress cycle and perhaps other factors." Furthermore, there is little doubt that general features of these opinions and results are relevant to gaining an understanding of residual stresses and fatigue performance of resistance spot welds.

RESIDUAL STRESS PREDICTIONS IN WELDMENTS

Arc welding
There has been much research done in attempting to understand the residual stresses resulting from butt and fillet arc welding. Butt and fillet welding are commonly found in marine industries (e.g., ship building), as well as in nuclear and aerospace applications. Many of the experimental and theoretical techniques employed in studying residual stresses in these types of weldments are relevant to studying residual stresses in resistance spot welding and it is therefore appropriate to review some of these techniques.

Many of the early studies of fillet and butt welding were focused on gaining an understanding of the heating cycle. Appropriate physical and/or analytical models of the heating cycle experienced by the base metals being joined during arc welding have been developed, a large number of which are discussed in Masubuchi's recent book <u>Analysis of Welded Structures</u> [36]. For example, Rosenthal [37,38] in the late 1930's and early 1940's studied the pattern of heat conduction in a solid subjected to a moving heat source. His 2-D analysis assumed a line heat source, while his 3-D analysis assumed a point source. More recently finite element principles have been employed by researchers at M.I.T. to gain an understanding of the heat flow in weldments [39,40]. Experimental measurements of temperature and strain changes have been performed by Kihara [41] and Klein [42,43], among others, to support analytical studies.

The assumption that the heat conduction problem in welding can be uncoupled from the nonlinear thermal material behavior, an assumption that is generally made in arc welding studies, leads to the result that the solution of the heat flow problem (i.e., temperature vs. time) be input into the thermal-stress problem. This allows both the transient thermal stresses and the residual stresses to be found analytically. This is the approach that has been taken by such researchers as Muraki [44] in studying the thermal stresses caused by an arc traveling along the girth of a thin cylindrical shell, by Kihara [45-47] in doing an empirical and analytical study of residual stresses in restrained butt welds, and by Hwang [48], in studying both a butt weld and a weld located along the edge of a six inch thick plate.

Rybicki et al. [49,50] used the same basic procedure to study residual stresses and deflections in multi-pass girth butt welding of piping. Analytical results compared favorably with experimental data on deformation, and hoop and axial residual stresses. More recently, Dhalla [51] analyzed the effect of residual stresses introduced during arc welding on the creep rupture strength of a typical Liquid Metal Fast Breeder Reactor nozzle. This simulation correctly predicted weld shrinkage effects. Residual stress levels seemed reasonable, but no experimental results were available for comparison. Analytical work is also ongoing at Lawrence Livermore Laboratory [52] in the general area of material response during arc welding.

At this point, it is also worth mentioning the work of Toshioka [53,54] who included the effects of metallurgical transformation on transient thermal stresses in his simulation of arc welding. After analyzing heat flow, material properties were determined using a continuous cooling transformation (CCT) diagram. Dimensional changes due to metallurgical transformation were considered in addition to thermal strains. Hibbitt and Marcal [55] have also included metallurgical transformation in their analysis of the gas-metal arc welding process.

Resistance welding

Few attempts have been made at performing a similar analysis, first a heat flow study, then a temperature-driven stress study, on resistance welding, and in particular, spot welding. It should be emphasized, however, that it has been the recent advent of use of high strength steel in automobile construction which has prompted concern over spot weld fatigue performance.

Since the source of heat in resistance welding is not an external heat source as in arc welding, but rather internal heat generation resulting from resistance within and between the sheets being welded together, the works of Bowen and Williamson [56], and Greenwood and Williamson [57], concerning electric current flow in conducting solids are relevant. These researchers studied both the constrictive resistance between two contacting bodies which leads to asperity softening and an increased contact area, and the distribution of current density in the contact patch. More recently, Kaiser et al. [58] have investigated the influence of surface resistivity on heat flow during spot welding of mild and high strength steel sheet. They relate the resulting temperature profiles to nugget formation.

Over the last twenty-five years a few researchers have investigated, experimentally and analytically, portions of the thermal mechanical cycle of spot welding. This cycle involves stages of squeeze, welding, hold, and electrode release. During squeeze, a load of 800-2000 pounds is applied to the workpiece by the electrodes (see Figure 1). This load creates intimate contact between the two sheets of metal and a "controlled" pathway for current flow during the welding stage. It also serves to break up any surface oxides at the faying surface (see Figure 1). The hold stage involves

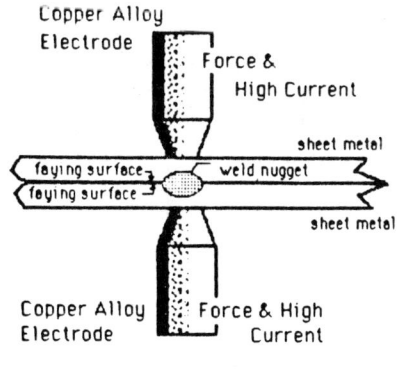

Figure 1. Resistance Spot Welding Process

Table 1: Thermal and Mechanical Studies of Spot Welding

D = Finite Difference
E = Finite Element
X = Experimental
V = Factor Considered

CONSIDERATION	Greenwood [59]	Bentley & Greenwood [60]	Rice & Fun [61]	Chakalley [62]	Houchens [63] 1-D model	2-D model	Nied [64] (Stainless Steel 1mm thickness)	Lindh & Tocher [65] (Ti alloy sheet 5mm thickness each)	Schroder & Macherauch [66]
1. 1-Dimensional Heat			V		V				
2. Axis-symmetric	V		V			V	V	V	V
3. Internal Heat generation	V	V					V		V
4a. Temperature dependent Thermal Prop.		V		V			V	V	V
4b. Temperature dependent Elec. Prop.	V		V			V			
5. Electrode Geometry Included							V	V	
6. Latent heat of fusion considered				V	V	V			
7. Residual stresses calculated (C), found by experim. (E)								(C) (E)	(C)
8. Nonlinear with temp. dependent material prop.								V	V
9. Effect of surface oxide, contact resistance incl.			V				V		
10. Solution technique	D	X	D	D	D	D	E,X	E	D,E
11. Thermal-mechanical response followed								V	
12. Electrode/workpiece & faying surface contact considered explicitly								V	

partial, if not complete cool down of the weld zone. The efforts of eight of these researchers are summarized in Table 1. It is worth pointing out that the early work of Bentley, Greenwood et al. [60] is particularly significant because it predicted the presence of a current singularity near the periphery of the contact patch at the faying surface. This singularity had been physically observed by Greenwood and Williamson [57].

While works [59-66] are all certainly significant in their contribution towards gaining a better understanding of thermal response during spot welding, the study by Nied [64] is unique in that it is the only one to consider the thermal-mechanical response during welding (i.e., expansion/contraction of contact surfaces during thermal cycling), and to explicitly consider faying surface contact during the squeeze stage of the welding cycle.

Nied's analysis, which used the finite element technique, consisted of a series of solution steps. The first step involved considering the squeeze stage of the weld cycle. Contact areas between the electrodes and the workpiece (two sheets of metal), and at the faying surface were determined by using the fact that only compressive tractions can be transferred during contact. Contact pressure peaks were near the periphery of each of the contact patches. Results for two 1mm thick sheets of Type 321 austenitic stainless steel squeezed together by truncated electrodes with a force of 1000 pounds showed a peak traction near the periphery of 38 ksi and 33 ksi between the electrode and workpiece, and faying surface, respectively.

The second step in Nied's study involved solving the nonlinear electrical-thermal problem. His procedure consisted of first solving for the voltage drop across the electrodes and workpiece at some specific time. This drop was then translated into a pattern of internal heat generation, using the fact that the heat q is equal to $(V^2/R)\ \Delta t$, where Δt is an increment of time, small, relative to the total weld time, and R is material resistance, which is itself temperature dependent. The internal heat generation was then used in the heat transfer equations to find the temperature pattern at the end of this particular Δt. Thermal expansion-contraction and transient elastic thermal stresses were also calculated at each specific time. However, the effect of expansion-contraction on the size of contact between the electrodes and workpiece, and at the faying surface was not included in any subsequent electrical-thermal calculations.

After solving the thermal problem, time was incremented slightly and the electrical problem was solved so as to reflect the new temperatures. In this incremental manner the analysis was carried out through the weld stage up to the point that the voltage was turned off. Response during the stages of cooldown and hold, and electrode removal were not considered. In fact, as the model did not consider material plasticity, it could not be directly extended through cooldown and hold, and electrode removal in order to predict final residual stresses.

Experimental and analytical results were presented describing nugget diameter and weld expansion as a function of welding time, and the author rightfully concluded that realistic analytic models of resistance welding could provide manufacturing engineers with additional information with which to determine welding schedules.

In 1967 Lindh and Tocher [65] considered the effects of material plasticity during the spot welding process. Internal heat generation was not included in their model, but the magnitude of equivalent heat flows at the electrode-sheet and faying interfaces were estimated from experimental data. Residual stresses determined by blind hole drilling of a spot welded workpiece made of two 5mm thick titanium alloy plates were consistent with those predicted by the finite element model.

More recently Schroder and Macherauch [66] developed a thermal-mechanical model of the resistance spot welding process. Temperature distributions during the process were calculated by using the finite difference method with heat input dictated by the planned welding time and the maximum temperature required. The generation of heat by electrical resistance and the presence of electrodes were not considered explicitly. The time dependent temperature distributions were then used to solve for the thermal and residual stresses using the finite element technique. Residual stress results were presented for X 4 CrNiMo 19 13 steel of sheet thickness equal to 10mm. This particular steel is well behaved as there are no solid phase transformations. The authors' findings confirm the importance of sheet thickness on the resulting residual stress pattern.

Works by Rybicki et al. [67-69] are also relevant to understanding welding. These researchers were interested in analytically predicting the effect of induction heating on the residual stresses seen in girth butt welded steel piping. Induction heating is seen as a prime candidate for imposing favorable residual stress profiles in piping susceptible to intergranular stress corrosion cracking, and involves introducing a current in the piping through magnetic field effects. The current results in resistive heating in the pipe, which in turn causes non-uniform yielding.

In [67] the electrical and thermal problems were solved in a serial fashion. Using the finite element technique, the

ANALYSES OF RESISTANCE SPOT WELDING   111

electrical problem was solved for current densities in the piping. Values of electrical resistivity throughout the piping were based upon measured steady state temperatures seen in testing. Relating current density to heat generation, as was discussed above, the thermal cycle was then simulated. Analytical and measured steady state temperature distributions compared favorable. The next step in this ongoing work will be to solve the electrical and thermal problems in parallel, thereby eliminating the need for experimental temperature input, and making the simulation more realistic.

In [68] these researchers predicted residual stresses at the end of induction heating of welded piping using experimentally determined temperatures in a nonlinear stress analysis. Predicted values of axial and hoop residual stress levels compared well with experimentally determined levels.

Related work has also been going on at Sandia Laboratory and at Cornell University in the area of upset weld simulation [70 - 72]. Upset welding is similar to spot welding in that the work piece is experiencing thermal, electrical, and mechanical cycles, but is further complicated by the fact that the work piece changes shape during welding. Viscoplastic effects are particulary important in this problem. The simulation developed by Dawson and Eggert employs the finite element technique. Experimental and numerical results presented in their work of time dependent variables such as voltage, surface temperatue, and axial displacement show good correlation.

SUMMARY

Analytical techniques (e.g., finite element and finite difference) have been applied by a number of researchers to study the thermal cycle and resulting residual stress pattern in fillet and butt arc welds. Analytical simplifications are demanded by the complex nature of this type of welding.

Researchers have also approached the problem of understanding the thermal, electrical, and mechanical cycles experienced during resistance spot welding. These works have been motivated primarily by concerns over nugget formation, and to a much lesser degree by concerns over residual stresses (as related to fatigue performance). Applying simulation techniques to this particular form of welding has several advantages; resistance spot welding is superior to all other welding processes with respect to reproducibility, the process does not involve filler metals and only relatively small volumes of material are affected for relatively short periods of time, and finally, the process is inherently 3 dimensional but can be accurately depicted in a 2 dimensional fashion. The underlying objective of the majority of these investigations has been to study temperatures in the workpiece during the welding process and the size of the resulting weld nugget. A few researchers have extended this objective to include predicting the resulting residual stresses.

To date no one has developed a comprehensive simulation, one which considers temperature dependent thermal and electrical properties of bulk and surface materials, the latent heat of fusion, as suggested in [73], as well as temperature dependent plastic material response. Such a simulation could be particularly valuable to welding engineers in determining weld schedules.

REFERENCES

[1] Yamamoto, T., Mem. Sci. Rev. Met., 77, 1980. Presented at IDDRG Congress, May 1980, Metz., France.

[2] Wood, J.T., Chairman AISI Committee of Sheet Steel Producers, Committee Correspondence of May 9, 1983, to D.S. Arnot, Chairman, Committee to Promote the Use of Steel.

[3] Nitto, H., Herai, T., Mizui, Mr., "The State and the Concept of Fatigue Evaluation of Steel Sheets for Automotive Use at Automakers and Steelmakers in Japan," Nippon Steel Corporation Report, 1982.

[4] Welding Handbook, 7th edition, 3, Chapter 3, W.H. Kearns, Editor, American Welding Society, Miami, Florida.

[5] Vahaviolos, S.J., "Method and Apparatus for the Real Time Evaluation of Weld Emitted Stress Waves," Patent No. 3,965,726.

[6] Schumacher, B.W., Dilay, W., "Adaptive Schedule Selective Weld Control," Patent No. 4,456,810 (Ford Motor Co.).

[7] Shearer Jr., T.W., "Method and Apparatus for Control of Resistance Welding," Patent No. 3,553,420 (General Motors Corp.).

[8] Stiebel, A., Ulmer, C., Kodrack, D., Holmes, B.B., "Monitoring and Control of Spot Weld Operations," presented at SAE International Congress, Detroit, MI, February 24-28, 1986, Paper 860579.

[9] Resistance Welding Control and Monitoring, The Welding Institute, Abington Hall, Abington, Cambridge CB1 6AL, 1977.

[10] Wang, P.C., Corten, H.T., Lawrence, F. V., "A Fatigue Life Prediction Method for Tensile-Shear Spot Welds," SAE paper no. 850279, presented at International Congress and Exposition, Detroit, Michigan, Feb. 25 - May 1, 1985.

[11] Lawrence, F.V., Wang, P.C., Corten, H.T., "An Empirical Method for Estimating the Fatigue Resitance of Tensile-Shear Spot Welds," SAE paper no. 830035, presented at International Congress and Exposition, Detroit, Michigan, Feb 28 - Mar 4, 1983.

[12] Basquin, O.H., "The Exponential Law of Endurance Tests."

Proceeding of ASTM, 10, 1910, 625.

[13] Fuchs, H.O., Stephens, R.I., Metal Fatigue in Engineering, John Wiley and Sons, New York, 1980, 136.

[14] Ho, H.L., "Fatigue-Life Prediction for Spotweld Using Neuber's Rule," Design of Fatigue and Fracture Resistant Structures, ASTM STP 761, P.R. Abelkis and C. M. Hudson, Eds., American Society for Testing and Materials, 1982, 296-309.

[15] Abe, H., Kataoka, S., Satoh, T., "Empirical Formula for Fatigue Strength of Single-Spot-Welded Joint Specimens under Tensile-Shear Repeated Load," SAE paper no. 860606, presented at International Congress and Exposition, Detroit, Michigan, Feb. 24-28, 1986.

[16] Orts, D.H., "Fatigue Strength of Spot Welded Joints in a HSLA Steel," SAE paper no. 810355, presented at International Congress and Exposition, Detroit, Michigan, Feb. 23 - 27, 1981.

[17] Barson, J.M., Davidson, J.A., Imholf, Jr., E.J., "Fatigue Behavior of Spot Welds under Variable Amplitude Loading," SAE paper no. 850369, presented at the International Congress and Expository, Detroit, Michigan, February 25 - March 1, 1985. .

[18] Kitagawa, H., Satoh, T., Fujimoto, M., "Fatigue Strength of Single Spot-Welded Joints of Rephosphorized High-Strength and Low-Carbon Steel Sheets," SAE paper no. 850371, presented at International Congress and Exposition, Detroit, Michigan, Feb. 24-28, 1986.

[19] Rivett, R.M., Slater, G., "Assessment of Single Resistance Spot Welds in Low Carbon and High Strength Steel Sheet-Part 2. Fatigue and Impact Properties," Research Report 212/1983, The Welding Institute, Abington, Cambridge, 1983.

[20] Lawrence, F.V. Jr., Corten, H.T., McMahon, J.C., Final Report to the American Iron and Steel Institute on the Improvement of Steel Spot Weld Fatigue Resistance, April, 1985.

[21] Gurney, T.R., Fatigue of Welded Structures, Cambridge University Press, 1979, Chapt. 5.

[22] Gurney, T.R., "Fatigue Tests on Butt and Fillet Welded Joints in Mild and High Tensile Structural Steel," Br. Weld, J., 9(11), 1962, 614-620.

[23] Gurney, T.R., "Some Fatigue Tests on Fillet Welded Mild

and High Tensile Steel Specimens in the As-Welded and Normalized Conditions," Br. Weld. J., 13(11), 1966, 648-651.

[24] Andrews, J.B., Arita, M., Masubuchi, K., Analysis of Thermal Stress and Metal Movement During Welding, NASA contractor Report NASA CR-61351, prepared for the G.C. Marshall Space Flight Center, Dec. 1970.

[25] Dickinson, D.W., Welding in the Automotive Industry, supported by Committee of Sheet Steel Producers, American Iron and Steel Institute, Washington, D.C., August 1981.

[26] Ewing, K.M.W., Wilson, M.L., Heimbruch, R.A., Watney, D.K., Houchers, A.F., "Fatigue of Welded High Strength Low Alloy Steels," SAE paper no. 800374, presented at International Congress and Exposition, Februay 25 - 29, 1980.

[27] Newman, R.P., Gurney, T.R., "Fatigue Tests on Plain Plate Specimens and Transverse Butt Welds," Br. Weld. J., 6, no. 12, 1959, 569-594.

[28] Navrotskii, D.I., Savelev, V.N., "The Effects of Residual Stresses on the Fatigue Strength of Specimens with Transverse Welds," Svar. Proiz, no 5., 1960, 15-17.

[29] Wiene, P.E., "Effect of Annealing on Bending Fatigue of Large Welded Test Pieces," Weld. Res. Suppl., 21, no. 5, 1956, 261s-264s.

[30] Kudryavtsev, I.V., "The Influence of Internal Stresses on the Fatigue Endurance of Steel," Inc. Conf. on Fatigue I. Mech. E., 1956, 317.

[31] Ross, M., "Experiments for the Determination of the Influence of Residual Stresses on the Fatigue Strength of Structures," Welding Research BWRA, 4(5), 1950, 83r-93r.

[32] Hebrant, F., Louis, J., Soete, W., Vinckier, A., "The Relaxation of Residual Welding Stresses of Static and Fatigue Loading," Welding Research Abroad, 1957, 58-63.

[33] Dugdale, D.S., "Effect of Residual Stress on Fatigue Strength," Welding Journal, 33(1), 1959, 45s-48s.

[34] Nelson, "Fatigue Consideration in Welds," 1982 SAE Transactions.(*)

[35] Munse, W.H., Fatigue of Welded Steel Structures, Welding Research Council, New York, 1964.

[36] Masubuchi, K., Analysis of Welded Structures, Pergamon Press, New York, 1980.

[37] Rosenthal, D., "Mathematical Theory of Heat Distribution During Welding and Cutting," Welding Journal, 20(5), 1941, 220s-234s.

[38] Rosenthal, D., Schmerber, R., "Thermal Study of Arc Welding," Welding Journal, 17(4), 1938, 208s.

[39] Muraki, T., Masubuchi, K., Thermal Analysis of M551 Experiment for Materials Processing in Space, Final Report under Contract NAS8-28732 for the G. C. Marshall Space Flight Center, NASA, from M.I.T., Dec. 1973.

[40] Muraki, T., Masubuchi, K., Thermal Analysis of M552 Experiment for Materials Processing in Space, Final Report under Contract NAS8-28732 for the G.D. Marshall Space Flight Center, NASA, from M.I.T., Dec. 1973.

[41] Kihara, H., Suzuki, H., and Tamura, H., Researches of Weldable High-Strength Steels, 60th Anniversary Series, 1, The Society of Naval Architects of Japan, Tokyo, 1957.

[42] Klein, K.M., "Investigation of Welding Thermal Strains in Marine Steels," M.S. Thesis, M.I.T., May 1971.

[43] Klein, K.M., Masubuchi, K., "Investigation of Welding Thermal Strains in High-Strength Steels for Marine Application," paper presented at the Second International Ocean Development Conference, Tokyo, Oct. 5-7, 1972.

[44] Muraki, T., Masubuchi, K., "Finite Element Analysis Based Upon the Generalized Variational Principle of Plastic and Elastic Distortion of Plates and Shells," paper presented at the International Conference on Computer Applications in the Automation of Shipyard Operation and Ship Design, Tokyo, Aug. 28-30, 1973.

[45] Kihara, H., Masubuchi, L., "Studies on the Shrinkage and Residual Welding Stress of Constrained Fundamental Joint," Reports of Transportation Technical Research Institute, No. 7, 1954, No. 20, 1956.

[46] Kihara, H., Masubuchi, K., Matsuyama, Y., "Effect of Welding Sequence on Transverse Shrinkage and Residual Stresses," Report No. 24 of Transportation Technical Research Institute, Tokyo, 1957.

[47] Kihara, H., Masubuchi, K., Ogura, Y., "Radial Contraction and Residual Stresses in Circular Patch

Weld," Parts I and II, J. Society of Naval Architects of Japan. 99, 111-112, 100, 163-180, 1956.

[48] Hwang, J.S., "Residual Stresses in Weldments in High Strength Steels," Thesis for M.S. degree, M.I.T., May 1975.

[49] Rybicki, E.F., Schmueser, D.W., Stonesifer, R. W., Groom, J.J., Mishler, H.W., "A Finite-Element Model for Residual Stresses and Deflections in girth-butt welded pipes". J. Pressure Vessel Technology, 100, Aug. 1978, 256-262.

[50] Rybicki, E.F., Stonesifer, R.B., Computation of Residual Stresses due to Multipass Welds in Piping Systems, J. Pressure Vessel Technology, 101, May 1979, 149-154.

[51] Dhalla, A.K., "Analytical Simulation of Weld Effects in Creep Range," Nonlinear Constitutive Relations for high Temperature Application-1984, NASA Conference Publication 2369, June 15-17, 1984, Cleveland, Ohio, 329-339.

[52] A workshop on weld modelling, held at Lawrence Livermore Laboratory, Feb., 26, 1986, chaired by K. Mahin.

[53] Toshioka, Y., "Deformation of Quenched Steel Bar," M.I.T., March 1974, unpublished.

[54] Toshioka, Y., "Effects of Material Properties on Residual Stresses and deformation of Welded Parts," M.I.T., June 1974, unpublished.

[55] Hibbitt, H., Marcal, P., "A numerical Thermo-mechanical Model for the welding and Subsequent Loading of a Fabricated Structure," Contract No. N00014-67-A-D191-0006, Brown University, 1972.

[56] Bowden, R.P., Williamson, J.B.P., "Electrical conduction in Solids I. Influence of the Passage of Current on the Contact between Solids," Proceedings from the Royal Society of London, Series A, 246, July 1958, 1-12.

[57] Greenwood, J.A., Williamson, J.B.P., "Electrical Conduction in Solids II. Theory of Temperature-Dependent Conductors," Proceedings from the Royal Society of London, Series A, 246, July 1958, 13-31.

[58] Kaiser, J.G., Dunn, G.J., Eager, T.W., "The Effect of Electrical Resistance on Nugget Formation During Spot Welding," Welding Journal, June, 1982, 167S-174S.

[59] Greenwood, J.A., "Temperatures in Spot Welding," British

Welding Journal, 8(6), 316-322.

[60] Bentley, K.P., Greenwood, J.A., Knowlson, P., Baker, R.G., "Temperature Distributions in Spot Welds," BWRA report, 1963, 613-619.

[61] Rice, W., Fun, E.J., "An Analytical Investigation of the Temperature Distributions during Resistance Welding," Welding Journal, 46(4), 175s-186s.

[62] Chakalley, A.A., "Evaluation of the Thermal State of the Metal in Spot Welding with the Help of a Computer, Svar. Proiz., 10, 1973, 5-7.

[63] Houchens, A.F., Page, R.E., Yang W.H., "Numerical Modeling of Resistance Spot Welding," Numerical Modeling of Manufacturing Processes, eds. R.F. Jones, H. Armen and J.T. Fong, presented at ASME WAM, Atlanta, Georgia, Nov 27-Dec 2, 1977, 117-129.

[64] Nied, H.A., "The Finite Element Modeling of the Resistance Spot Welding Process," Welding Journal, April 1984, 123s-132s.

[65] Lindh, D.V., Tocher, J.R., "Heat Generation and Residual Stress Development in Resistance Spot Welding," Welding Journal, Aug 1967, 351s-360s.

[66] Schroder, R., Macherauch, E., "Calculating thermal and residual stresses in resistance spot-welded joints using different thermal-mechanical characteristics for the material," Schweisser und Schneider, V35(6), June 1983, 270-276.

[67] Koch, R.L., Rybicki, E.F., Strattan, R.D., "A Computational Temperature Analysis for Induction Heating of Welded Pipes," Engineering Materials and Technology, 107, April, 1985, 148-153.

[68] Rybicki, E.F., McGuire, P.A., "A Computational Model for Improving Weld Residual Stresses in Small Diameter Pipes by Induction Heating," J. Pressure Vessel Technology, 103, Aug 1981, 294-299.

[69] Rybicki, E.F., McGuire, P.A., Merrick, E., Wert, J., "The Effect of Pipe Thickness on Residual Stresses due to Girth Welds," J Pressure Vessel Technology, 104, Aug. 1982, 204-209.

[70] Springarn, J.R., Mason, W.E., Swearengen, J.C., Computer Simulation of Upset Welding, Sandia Report, SAND82-8663, April 1982.

[71] Eggert, G.M., Dawson, P.R., "A Comparison of a Theromomechanical Model of Upset Welding with Experiment," Cornell University, Masters Thesis, August 1985.

[72] Dawson, P.R., "Viscoplastic Modeling of Upset Welding Using the Finite Element Method," Process Modeling Tools, Proceedings of ASM 1980 Process Modeling Sessions, Materials Congress, 151-172, 1980.

[73] Erickson, W.D., "Computer Simulation of Solidification," Los Alamos Scientific Laboratory NTIS LA-UR-78-1852, 1978.

Applications of the 'BEASY' Boundary Element Code for Thermal and Stress Analysis within the Automotive Industry
J. Trevelyan, C.A. Brebbia and A. Mercy
Computational Mechanics Institute, Southampton, England

1. INTRODUCTION

The Boundary Element Method has now become a well established tool for the analysis of automotive components. The technique was formalized around 1978[1,2] as an alternative to the finite element method (FEM) and in order to resolve some of the shortcomings of FEM. It gained rapid acceptance during the beginning of this decade and several important advanced books have now been published[3,7] including the Proceedings of the International Conferences regularly held since 1978[8] to [15] and the more recent Boundary Element Technology meetings started in 1985 [16, 17].

Forerunners of the boundary element method are the so-called panel techniques which were mainly due to Hess[18] who has contributed to research in this field for many years. Panel methods have been extensively applied for aerodynamic simulation of flows around aircraft and also automotive structures. As will be shown in this paper, the boundary element technique can also be used to solve the same type of problem.

The advantages of boundary elements over finite elements are that

i) The method requires only the discretization of the body surface into elements making the boundary elements very well suited for engine design;

ii) The techniques usually give more accurate results than finite elements, as the influence functions used - fundamental solutions - are more complete than the polynomials used in finite elements, and in addition the unknowns of the problems are mixed (i.e. temperature and fluxes, displacements and tractions or streamfunctions and velocities are in each case both problem unknowns);

iii) The type of influence functions used is such that in many cases problems extending to infinity can be analysed without requiring any special boundaries, and therefore very economically.

The main advantage of boundary elements in automotive engineering is the simplicity of the input required to run a program. This renders the method ideally suited to Computer Aided Design applications, as it is a comparatively simple task to discretize the surface only of a body, by contrast with the domain discretization needed for finite elements. In addition, boundary element models are interfaced readily with Computer Integrated Manufacturing (CIM) systems, for which only boundary information is required.

In this paper some representative applications of boundary elements are presented and discussed. All results were obtained using the BEASY Boundary Element code developed at the Computational Mechanics Institute, Southampton, England.

2. GOVERNING EQUATIONS

Consider first the case of a problem governed by the Laplace equation, i.e.

$$k \nabla^2 u = 0 \quad \text{in } \Omega \qquad (1)$$

with boundary conditions of the form,

$$u = \bar{u} \quad \text{on } \Gamma_1$$
$$q = k \frac{\partial u}{\partial n} = \bar{q} \quad \text{on } \Gamma_1 \qquad (2)$$

where Ω is the domain, and $\Gamma = \Gamma_1 + \Gamma_2$ the boundary and n its normal. k is a coefficient of conductivity, which for the moment can be considered to be constant. For thermal problems u is the temperature and q the fluxes. In the case of perfect fluids, u can be interpreted as a potential or stream function and the normal derivatives q are the normal or tangential velocities. The objective is to solve equation (1) with the boundary conditions (2) and to reduce the problem to a boundary only formulation. In order to do so one uses another function u* which is the fundamental solution to the Laplace equation, i.e.

$$k \nabla^2 u^* = -\Delta_i \qquad (3)$$

where Δ_i indicates a Dirac delta function equal to zero everywhere except at the point i (or source point).

Applying Green's second identity one can relate the two fields through the following integral expression,

$$\int_\Omega (u^* k \nabla^2 u - u k \nabla^2 u^*) d\Omega = \int_\Gamma (u^* q - u q^*) d\Gamma \qquad (4)$$

where $q^* = k \frac{\partial u^*}{\partial n}$.

Substituting (3) into (4) one obtains

$$u_i + \int_\Omega u^* k \nabla^2 u \, d\Omega = \int_\Gamma u^* q \, d\Gamma - \int_\Gamma u q^* \, d\Gamma \qquad (5)$$

where u_i denotes the value of u at the source point.

Notice that $k \nabla^2 u \equiv 0$ and hence (5) reduces to

$$u_i = \int_\Gamma u^* q \, d\Gamma - \int_\Gamma u q^* \, d\Gamma \tag{6}$$

Equation (6) gives the value of the potential at any internal point i in function of the boundary values. If the source point is taken to the boundary one will have a jump for the integral in q* and obtain instead (Figure 1)

$$c_i u_i = \int_\Gamma u^* q \, d\Gamma - \int_\Gamma u q^* \, d\Gamma \tag{7}$$

Discretizing the Γ boundary into elements and carrying out the necessary integrations one obtains a system of equations for each source point 'i' on the boundary. This system can be written in matrix form as

$$\underset{\sim}{H}\, \underset{\sim}{U} = \underset{\sim}{G}\, \underset{\sim}{Q} \tag{8}$$

where the $\underset{\sim}{U}$ and $\underset{\sim}{Q}$ represent the potentials and fluxes at the boundary nodes. One can then apply boundary conditions on Γ_1 and Γ_2 and rearrange the above equations to obtain,

$$\underset{\sim}{A}\, \underset{\sim}{X} = \underset{\sim}{F} \tag{9}$$

where $\underset{\sim}{X}$ is now the vector of unknowns u and q, $\underset{\sim}{A}$ is obtained by rearranging columns of $\underset{\sim}{H}$ and $\underset{\sim}{G}$, and $\underset{\sim}{F}$ is a vector obtained as a result of taking to the right-hand-side all known values and their respective columns.

The same type of considerations apply for elasticity problems, which are governed by the following equilibrium equations, which can be written in function of the stress components σ_{jk} derivatives, i.e.

$$\sigma_{jk,j} = 0 \qquad \text{in } \Omega \tag{10}$$

with boundary conditions in terms of displacements or tractions, i.e.

$$\left. \begin{array}{ll} u_j = \bar{u}_j & \text{on } \Gamma_1 \\ \\ p_j = \bar{p}_j & \text{on } \Gamma_2 \end{array} \right\} \quad \Gamma = \Gamma_1 + \Gamma_2 \tag{11}$$

A fundamental solution can now be proposed (the Kelvin solution) which satisfies the following equation.

$$\sigma^*_{jk,j} = -\Delta^{i\ell} \tag{12}$$

where the $\Delta^{i\ell}$ is the Dirac delta function representing a unit load at i in the ℓ direction.

The equivalent to equation (4) in this case can be written as

$$\int_\Omega (u^*_k \sigma_{jk,j} - u_k \sigma^*_{jk,j}) d\Omega = \int_\Gamma (u^*_k p_k - u_k p^*_k) d\Gamma \tag{13}$$

Substituting equation (10) and (12) in the above, one obtains the following boundary integral expression,

$$u^{i\ell} + \int_\Gamma u_k p^*_k d\Gamma = \int_\Gamma p_k u^*_k d\Gamma \tag{14}$$

where $u^{i\ell}$ represents the displacement at 'i' in the direction 'ℓ'.

Note that p^*_k and u^*_k are components of the fundamental solution, i.e. tractions and displacements due to a unit concentrated load at the point 'i' in the 'ℓ' direction. If we consider unit forces acting in the three directions the equation can be written,

$$u^{i\ell} + \int_\Gamma u_k p^*_{\ell k} d\Gamma = \int_\Gamma p_k u^*_{\ell k} d\Gamma \tag{15}$$

where $p^*_{\ell k}$ and $u^*_{\ell k}$ represent the tractions and displacements in the k direction due to unit forces acting in the ℓ direction.

When the point i is taken to the boundary the singularity in the integral on $p^*_{\ell k}$ produces a 'jump' term, which originates a series of c coefficients.

$$c^{i\ell} u^{i\ell}_k + \int_\Gamma u_k p^*_{\ell k} d\Gamma = \int_\Gamma p_k u^*_{\ell k} d\Gamma \tag{16}$$

The upper indices i and ℓ refer to the source being applied at i and in the direction ℓ. Notice that the u_k components can contribute to the equation corresponding to any 'ℓ' direction.

After discretization the equations corresponding to applying equations (16) to all boundary nodes can be written

$$\underset{\sim}{H}\,\underset{\sim}{U} = \underset{\sim}{G}\,\underset{\sim}{P} \tag{17}$$

After applying boundary conditions this reduces to a form similar to (9) i.e.

$$\underset{\sim}{A}\,\underset{\sim}{X} = \underset{\sim}{F} \tag{18}$$

where X represents now all the unknown values of displacements and tractions on the boundary. Once the tractions are known one can obtain the boundary stresses and if required any stresses or displacements inside the body by applying (15) and its form in terms of derivatives.

A large variety of body force type effects (gravity, thermal stresses, centrifugal forces) can be introduced into (16) by considering an extra boundary integral such as

$$\int_\Omega b_k\, u_k^*\, d\Omega \tag{19}$$

This integral can then be taken to the boundary using different approaches. Analytical integrations such as those proposed in Reference [2] are the most elegant way of doing this, although they are not always feasible. Sometimes it is necessary to integrate over the Ω domain by dividing it into a series of cells. These cells, although they may appear similar to finite elements are different as they do not introduce any extra unknowns and are not required to satisfy any continuity requirements being rather arbitrary in shape and the way their boundaries match with those of the continuous cells or boundary element

More recently however, a new technique to reduce the domain integral has been proposed by Brebbia and Nardini[19,20] and used extensively in engineering practice (the technique is now implemented in some of the BEASY modules). To illustrate the technique consider the case of a diffusion rather than Laplace equation, i.e.

$$\nabla^2 u = \frac{1}{\kappa}\frac{\partial u}{\partial t} \tag{20}$$

which solves boundary conditions as (2). κ is the diffusivit coefficient which will be assumed constant in time and space in what follows.

Replacing equation (20) into (5) one obtains the following equation,

$$c_i u_i + \frac{k}{\kappa} \int_\Omega u^* \dot{u} \, d\Omega = \int_\Gamma u^* q \, d\Gamma - \int_\Gamma q^* u \, d\Gamma \qquad (21)$$

Brebbia and Nardini[19] proposed to approximate the function $\dot{u}$ at any point inside the domain by a set of N coordinate functions multiplied by unknown functions of time, i.e.

$$\dot{u}(x,t) = \sum_{j=1}^{N} f^j(x) \, \dot{\alpha}^j(t) \qquad (22)$$

The domain integral then takes the form

$$\int_\Omega u^* \dot{u} \, d\Omega = \sum_{j=1}^{N} \dot{\alpha}^j \int_\Omega f^j u^* \, d\Omega \qquad (23)$$

Let us assume that for each function $f^j(x)$ there exists a function $\hat{u}^j(x)$ such that

$$k \nabla^2 \hat{u}^j = f^j \qquad (24)$$

Using this substitution the domain integral becomes

$$\int_\Omega u^* \dot{u} \, d\Omega = \sum_{j=1}^{N} \dot{\alpha}^j \int_\Omega (k \nabla^2 \hat{u}^j) u^* \, d\Omega \qquad (25)$$

Notice that the term under the integral in equation (25) has the same Laplacian form as $\nabla^2 u$ and hence one can apply the transformation given by (5) to obtain instead of (21) the following expression

$$c_i u_i + \int_\Gamma q^* u \, d\Gamma - \int_\Gamma q u^* \, d\Gamma = \sum_{j=1}^{N} \frac{1}{\kappa} \left(c_i \hat{u}_i^j + \int_\Gamma q^* \hat{u}^j \, d\Gamma \right.$$

$$\left. - \int_\Gamma u^* \hat{q}^j \, d\Gamma \right) \dot{\alpha}^j \qquad (26)$$

Notice that the above equation involves only boundary integrals. The reduction has been accomplished by a double application of reciprocity principles. Because of this the resulting technique is called the Dual Reciprocity Boundary Element Method.

One can now approximate the u, q and $\hat{u}$, $\hat{q}$ fields using the same type of boundary integration function and obtain,

$$H\underset{\sim}{U} - G\underset{\sim}{Q} = \frac{1}{\kappa}[H\underset{\sim}{\hat{U}} - G\underset{\sim}{\hat{Q}}]\underset{\sim}{\dot{\alpha}} \qquad (27)$$

where $\hat{\underset{\sim}{U}}$ and $\hat{\underset{\sim}{Q}}$ represent square matrices given by the analytical solution equation (29) which can be easily obtained for the type of f^j functions used in practice. $\underset{\sim}{\dot{\alpha}}$ are unknown parameters which can be related to the boundary nodes of $\dot{u}$ by evaluating (22) at all boundary nodes, i.e.

$$\underset{\sim}{\dot{U}} = F\underset{\sim}{\dot{\alpha}} \qquad (28)$$

which upon inversion, produces the relation

$$\underset{\sim}{\dot{\alpha}} = F^{-1}\underset{\sim}{\dot{U}} \qquad (29)$$

Substituting the above into equation (27) results in

$$C\underset{\sim}{\dot{U}} + H\underset{\sim}{U} = G\underset{\sim}{Q} \qquad (30)$$

where

$$\underset{\sim}{C} = -\frac{1}{\kappa}[H\underset{\sim}{\hat{U}} - G\underset{\sim}{\hat{Q}}]F^{-1} \qquad (31)$$

Notice that equation (30) can now be integrated in time using some standard scheme as usual but the dimensions of all vectors and matrices in (30) are equal to the degrees of freedom of the boundary nodes.

The technique can be easily extended to transient elasticity and has also been used to solve wave propagation [21] and elastodynamics problems [19]. Furthermore it can be combined with the use of the Kirchhoff transform to analyse the case of thermal dependent material properties [22].

3. THE BEASY SYSTEM

This section describes the overall layout and capabilities of the Boundary Element Analysis System BEASY. Since BEASY has become established as an engineering analysis tool, the description in this paper is concentrated on the new developments and enhancements which have been made.

The BEASY suite[23,24] may be used to solve 2D, 3D and axisymmetric problems in the following fields:

* linear stress analysis (see Section 2).
* linear "field" problems - e.g. heat transfer, electrostatics simple fluid flow, as described in the first part of Section 2.
* transient diffusion (using the dual reciprocity principle of Section 2)
* non-linear diffusion (in which material properties are temperature dependent).

In addition to the boundary element analysis program itself, a new pre and post processor has recently been developed. This allows flexible and fully interactive model generation, and simple interpretation of the results. The new pre and post processor is described more fully below. As an alternative to this type of processing, interfaces to popular CAD-packages (such as SUPERTAB, PATRAN, etc.) are also available.

The layout of the BEASY system is shown in Fig. 2.

BEASY allows a wide range of boundary condition types[25] to be specified, and body forces can also be considered. This enables a wide variety of loading to be applied, including rotational and gravitational loads.

New developments to BEASY

i) Pre and post processor

Boundary element models are very easily built with the new pre and post processor. The program may be run in either of two modes - alphanumeric and cursor mode - according to the graphics facilities available and to the users preference. Simple commands are arranged in a series of "menus", in which points, lines, surfaces, loads, etc. are defined.

Once the geometry of the problem has been defined, an automatic mesh generator may be used to place elements on all or part of the model. Alternatively, by placing elements on each geometry line (for 2D problems) or surface (3D) more control in areas of mesh refinement can be achieved.

In this new program, full advantage is taken of the major attraction of the boundary element method, the fact that the data preparation time is reduced by an order of magnitude compared with other popular analysis techniques.

Post processing of BEASY results has also been improved, as a wide range of new types of plot have been introduced. These include

- hidden line displays of geometry
- shaded image of geometry
- shaded colour-fill contours of results
- solid-band colour-fill contours of results

and complement the existing range of contour, x-y graph and deformed geometry plots.

ii) <u>Transient diffusion analysis</u>

The diffusion equation[20] may now be solved by BEASY. An innovative time-stepping technique is used to make the BEM an efficient tool for the solution of problems governed by the diffusion equation. Constant or variable duration time steps may be considered for appropriate types of problem. For example, for problems in which there is an initial thermal shock, most of the diffusion is likely to occur very soon after the start of the analysis. In this case, the variable time-stepping scheme should be adopted to enable short time steps at the important initial stage, but longer time steps later in the analysis as the new steady state is approached.

Many problems of thermal conduction involve temperature dependent material properties. These can now be considered using a new iterative scheme in BEASY.

iii) <u>Improved elements and run times</u>

Two approaches have been made with a view to improving the c.p.u. performance of BEASY. Firstly, BEASY now uses a combination of "continuous" and "discontinuous" elements. Continuous elements (Fig. 3) are those in which nodes are shared between adjacent boundary elements, forcing continuity of variables. With discontinuous elements (Fig. 4) there are no shared nodes. Discontinuous elements generally give better results (particularly in areas of stress concentration), but in many cases continuous elements are satisfactory.

Since continuous elements share common nodes with neighbouring elements, the total number of degrees of freedom is reduced, so the run time is improved. The BEASY preprocessor automatically decides where to use continuous and discontinuous elements, although this may be overridden.

The second area in which run times are improved is in integration. Because of the complicated integrals which are required to be evaluated, the integration scheme (or schemes) used are the heart of a boundary element analysis program. A new integration scheme is used in the latest version, ensuring that BEASY remains a state-of-the-art analysis tool.

In addition to the introduction of continuous elements, a new family of triangular elements has been developed. Constant, linear and quadratic elements are available, as shown in Figure 5, which facilitate modelling of 3D problems.

These complement the existing families of line, quadrilateral, tube and source elements.

4. AUTOMOTIVE APPLICATIONS OF BEASY

As a general purpose program for the analysis of engineering problems, BEASY may be applied in a wide variety of fields commonly encountered by automotive engineers, and is commonly used in thermal problems and stress analysis. This section presents three different examples, which illustrate various possible applications of boundary element analysis to engineers, including one on vehicle aerodynamics.

Axisymmetric Case: Thermal Stress Analysis of Valve

This problem shows the use of BEASY for the analysis of stresses and displacements arising from a thermal "loading". The geometry of the valve, and its boundary element model are shown in Figure 6. The elements are lines which form the surface of the valve, since the assumption that the valve and its boundary conditions are axisymmetric can be made. No elements are placed on the axis of symmetry, since this is not a boundary (or surface) of the problem. Internal points are shown '+' in the figure. These are points at which the solution is found (i.e. potential, displacement, stress, etc.) after the boundary solution has been performed. These internal points are used as individual points, or lines of points, at which it is desired that the results be known.

A constant temperature is applied to the bottom face of the valve, and a temperature steadily decreasing to ambient around the side of the valve.

The results of the thermal stress analysis are shown in Figures 7 and 8, which give the deformed shape and stress contours respectively. These give a convenient overall picture of the behaviour of the valve under a thermal load.

2D Case: Potential Flow around Car Body

The Laplace equation solution in BEASY, the theory of which

is discussed in Section 2 of this paper, may also be used to analyse linear potential flow. While it is recognised that this is a fairly crude approach to the problem of the flow of air past a moving vehicle, this method can be used to give an economical first approximation.

The problem considered in this example is illustrated in Figures 9 and 10. Figure 9 shows the whole boundary element model of a 2D section through a car body. The flow around the car is found when a set of boundary conditions is applied to a large "box" around the model. A zoomed view of the region around the car is shown in Figure 10.

The potential flow streamlines are illustrated in Figure 11. Once flow separation has taken place, the boundary element formulation as described in Section 2 is no longer capable of solving the new set of equations. However, a wake position may be postulated, and an appropriate set of boundary conditions applied to obtain the next approximation to the solution. This type of analysis provides a cheap and quick method for studying vehicle aerodynamics.

3D Case: Connecting Rod

The third example selected is a fully three-dimensional analysis of a connecting rod. For 3D applications, the boundary is modelled using "patch" type elements, in this case the elements are all quadrilateral (Figure 12). In the figure, the elements have been shrunk for clarity. Symmetry has been applied about one coordinate plane.

The boundary element stress analysis of this connecting rod was performed, subject to boundary conditions consistent with a compression loading of the component between the two bearings.

Figure 13 shows the undeformed (a) and deformed (b) shape of the connecting rod, with the deformation being shown exaggerated.

5. CONCLUSIONS

The boundary element method provides a powerful analysis technique for the study of automotive components. The advantages of the method are that

i) It requires only the discretization of the body surface into elements.

ii) It usually gives more accurate results than domain type techniques.

iii) It can model more accurately domains tending to infinity.

The need to discretize only the surface of the body is the main attraction of the technique and it allows boundary element codes to be easily integrated in Computer Aided Engineering Systems.

Boundary elements can now be used for a wide variety of problems in automotive engineering and the range of applications is constantly increasing. In addition to the time dependent problems discussed in this paper and already implemented in the BEASY Code[23] the method is used for shape optimization and nonlinear material problems.

REFERENCES

1. BREBBIA, C.A. (1978) "The Boundary Element Method for Engineers" Pentech Press, London, 1st Edition.

2. BREBBIA, C.A., TELLES, J. & WROBEL, L. (1984) "Boundary Elements - Theory and Applications in Engineering" Springer-Verlag Berlin & NY.

3. BREBBIA, D.A. (Ed.) (1981) "Progress in Boundary Element Methods" Vol.1, Pentech Press, London.

4. BREBBIA, C.A. (Ed.) (1983) "Progress in Boundary Element Methods" Vol.2, Springer-Verlag, Berlin & NY.

5. BREBBIA, C.A. (Ed.) (1984) "Topics in Boundary Element Research" Springer-Verlag, Berlin & NY.

6. BREBBIA, C.A. (Ed.) (1985) "Topics in Boundary Element Research" Springer-Verlag, Berlin & NY.

7. BREBBIA, C.A. (Ed.) (1987) "Topics in Boundary Element Research" Springer-Verlag, Berlin & NY.

8. BREBBIA, C.A. (Ed.) (1978) "Recent Advances in BEM" Proc. Conference, Southampton, Pentech Press.

9. BREBBIA, C.A. (Ed.) (1980) "New Developments in Boundary Element Methods" Proc. Conference, Southampton, CML Publications.

10. BREBBIA, C.A. (Ed.) (1981) "Boundary Element Methods" Proc. Conference, California, CML Publications and Springer-Verlag, Berlin & NY.

11. BREBBIA, C.A. (Ed.) (1982) "Boundary Elements in Engineering" Proc. Conference, Southampton, CML Publications and Springer-Verlag, Berlin & NY.

12. BREBBIA, C.A. et al (Eds) (1983) "Boundary Elements V" Proc. Conference, Hiroshima, CML Publications and Springer-Verlag, Berlin & NY.

13. BREBBIA, C.A. (Ed.) (1984) "Boundary Elements VI" Proc. Conference Queen Elizabeth 2, CML Publications, Southampton Springer-Verlag, Berlin & NY.

14. BREBBIA, C.A. et al. (Eds) (1985) "Boundary Elements VII" Lake Como, ITALY. CML Publications, Southampton, Springer-Verlag, Berlin & NY.

15. BREBBIA, C.A. et al. (Eds) (1986) "Boundary Elements VIII" Proc. Conference Tokyo, CML Publications Southampton, Springer—Verlag, Berlin & NY.

16. BREBBIA, C.A. et al. (Eds) (1985) "BETECH/85" Proc. Conference Adelaide, Australia, CML Publications Southampton, Springer—Verlag, Berlin & NY.

17. BREBBIA, C.A. et al. (Eds) (1986) "BETECH/86" Proc. Conference MIT, USA, CML Publications, Southampton.

18. HESS, J. & SMITH, A.M.O. (1967) "Calculation of Potential Flow about Arbitrary Bodies". Progress in Aeronautical Sciences, Vol.8 (D. Kirchemann, Ed.) Pergamon, London.

19. BREBBIA, C.A. & NARDINI, D. (1983) "Dynamic Analysis in Solid Mechanics by an Alternative Boundary Element Approach" Int. J. Soil Dynamics and Earthquake Engng., Vol.2, 228-233.

20. WROBEL, L., BREBBIA, C.A. & NARDINI, D. (1986) "Analysis of Transient Thermal Problems in the BEASY System". BETECH/86 Proc. Conf. Computational Mechanics Publications, Southampton.

21. NARDINI, D. & BREBBIA, C.A. (1986) "Transient Boundary Element Elastodynamics using the Dual Reciprocity Method and Modal Superposition" Boundary Elements VIII, CML Publications Southampton and Springer—Verlag, Berlin & NY.

22. SKERGET, P. and BREBBIA, C.A. (1985) "Time Dependent Non-Linear Potential Problems" Chapter in Topics in Boundary Element Research, Vol.2, Springer—Verlag, Berlin & NY.

23. BREBBIA, C.A., DANSON, D. & BAYNHAM, J. (1985) "The BEASY Boundary Element Analysis System" in Finite Element Systems, A Handbook. (C.A. Brebbia, Ed.) Springer—Verlag and Computational Mechanics Publications, Berlin and Southampton.

24. TREVELYAN, J. (1986) "New Developments in the BEASY Boundary Element Program for Thermal and Stress Analysis" in Supercomputer Applications in Automotive Research and Engineering Development. Computational Mechanics Publications, Southampton.

25. MERCY, A.C., NAGESWARAN, S. & TREVELYAN, J. (1986) "New Developments in the BEASY Boundary Element Analysis System" Boundary Elements VIII, Computational Mechanics Publications, Southampton & Springer—Verlag, Berlin & NY.

136 'BEASY' CODE FOR THERMAL AND STRESS ANALYSIS

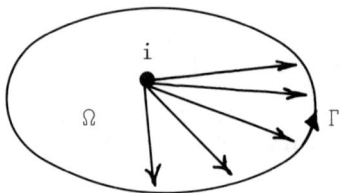

Initial point 'i'

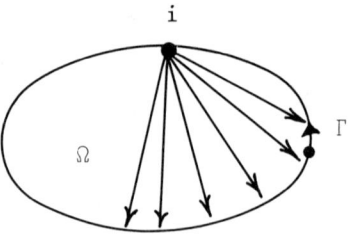

Point 'i' on the body

Figure 1 Different positions of the same point

'BEASY' CODE FOR THERMAL AND STRESS ANALYSIS   137

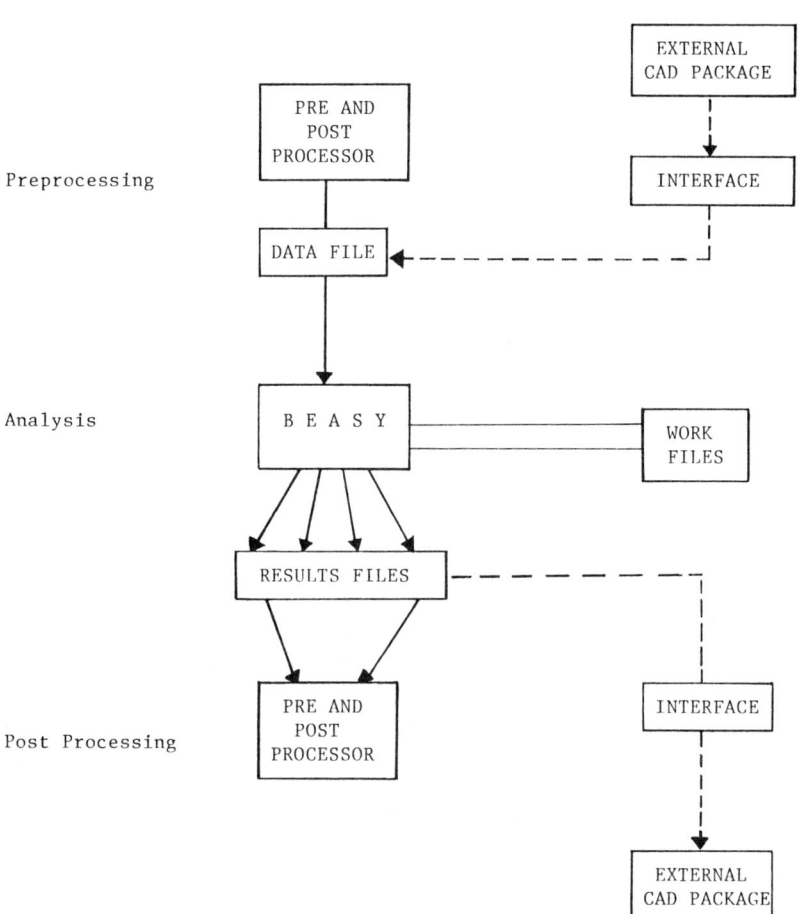

Fig. 2   Layout of programs in BEASY system

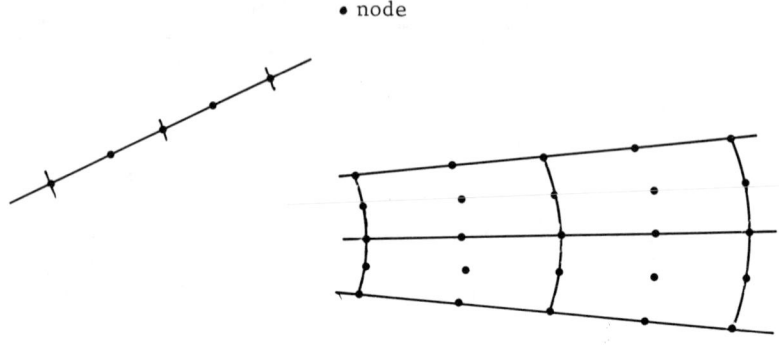

Figure 3 Fully continuous elements for 2D and 3D problems (quadratic elements shown only)

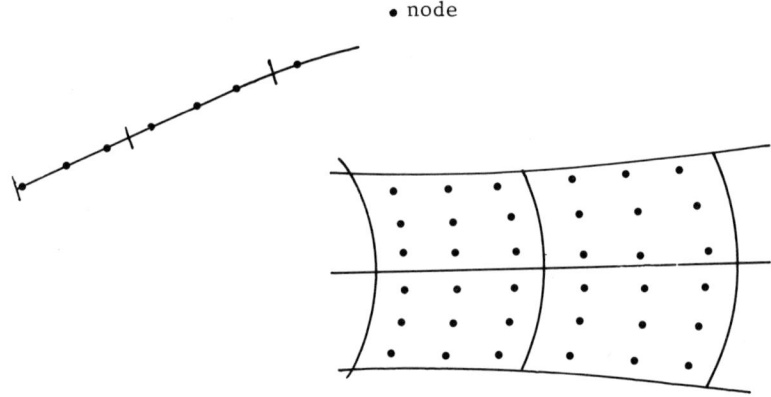

Figure 4 Fully discontinuous elements for 2D and 3D problems (quadratic elements shown only)

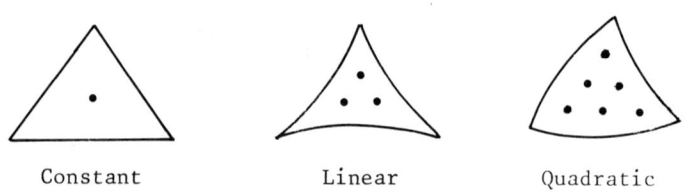

Figure 5 Family of triangular elements for 3D problems (only discontinuous elements shown)

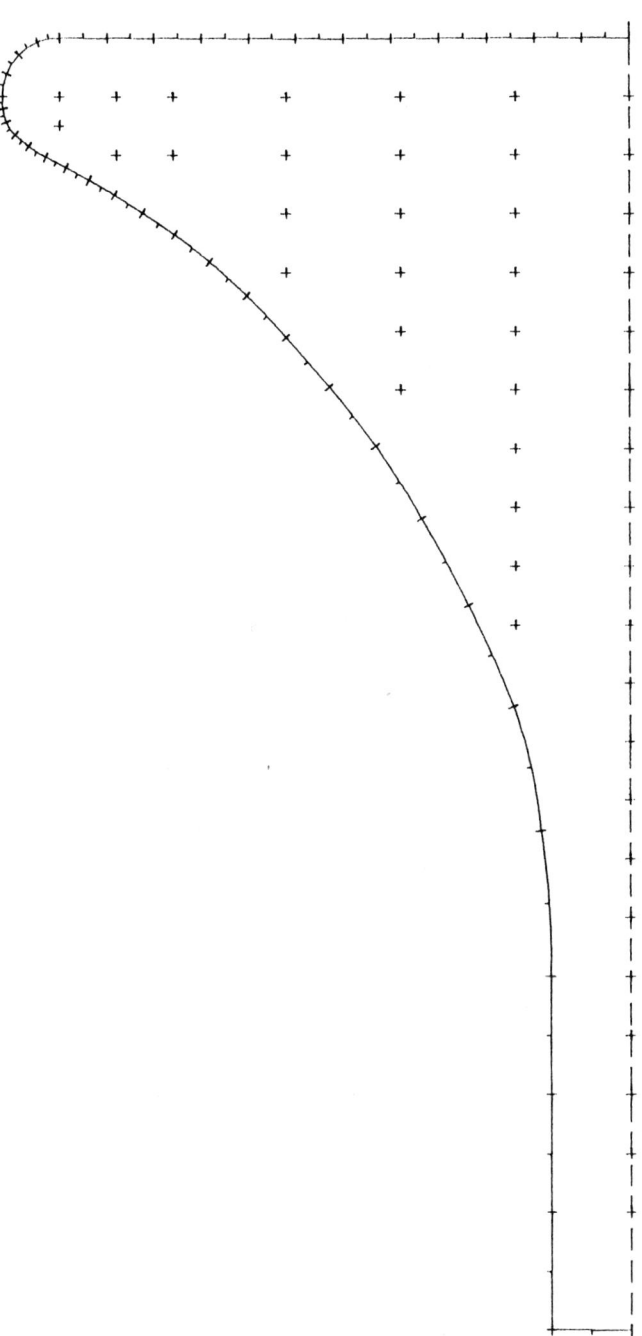

Fig.6 Valve boundary element model

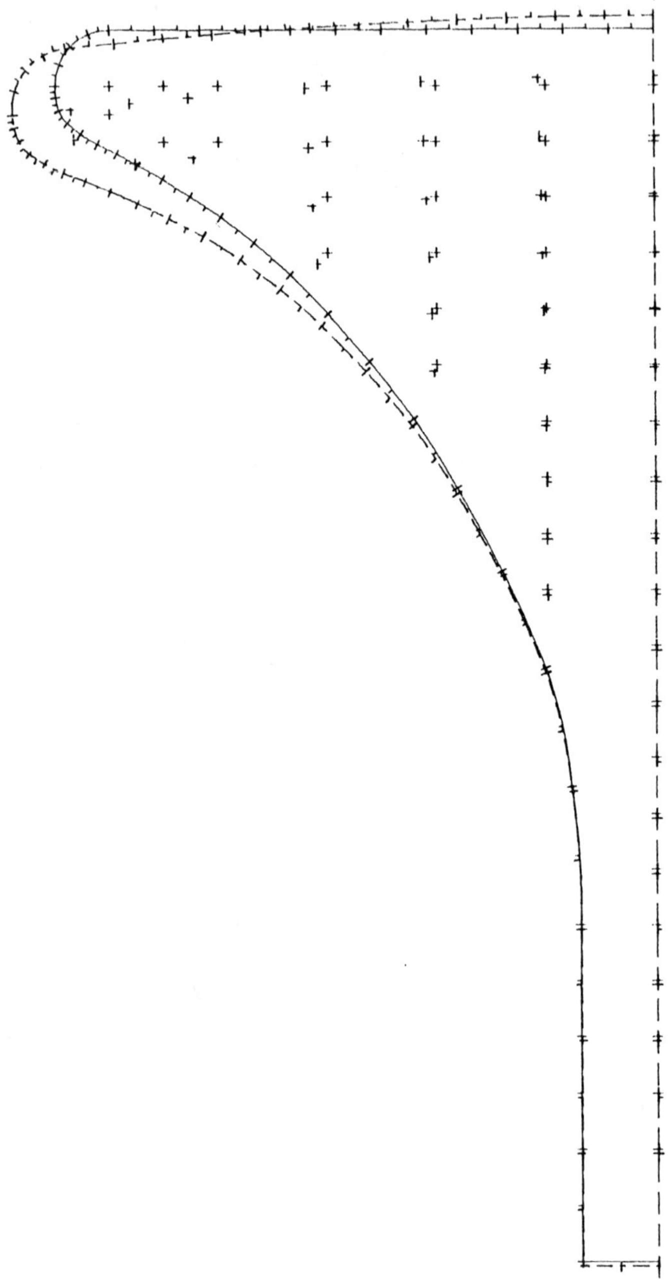

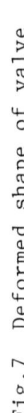

Fig.7 Deformed shape of valve

'BEASY' CODE FOR THERMAL AND STRESS ANALYSIS 141

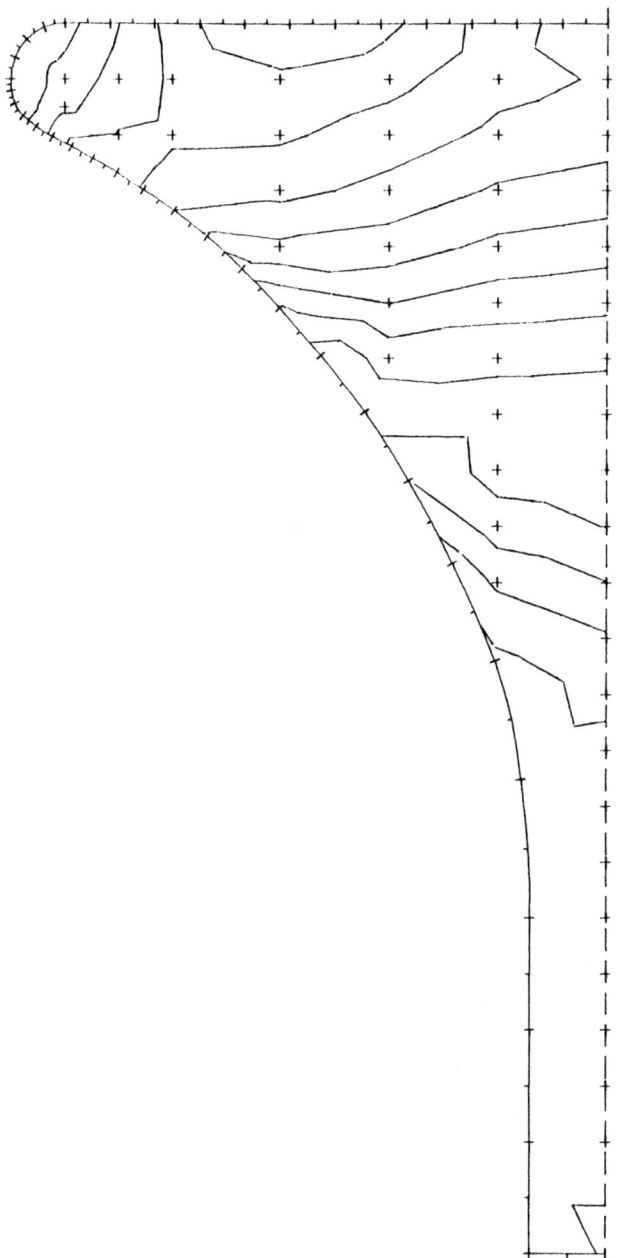

Fig. 8 Contours of thermal stresses in valve

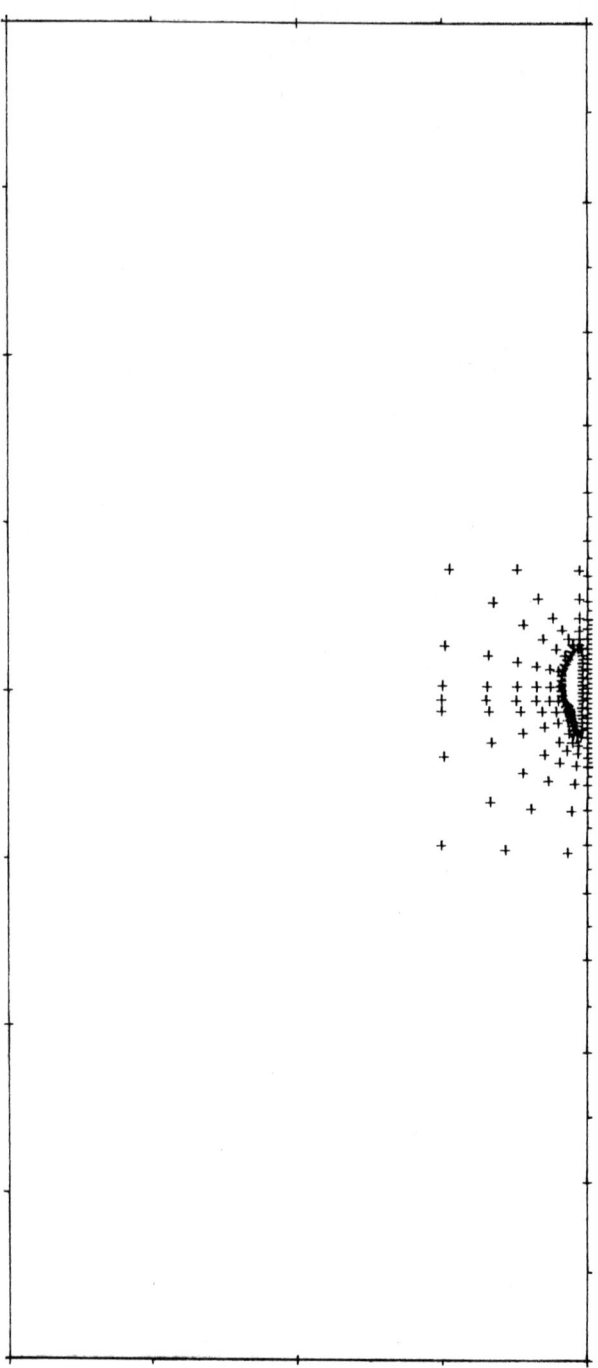

Fig. 9 2D model for potential flow around car

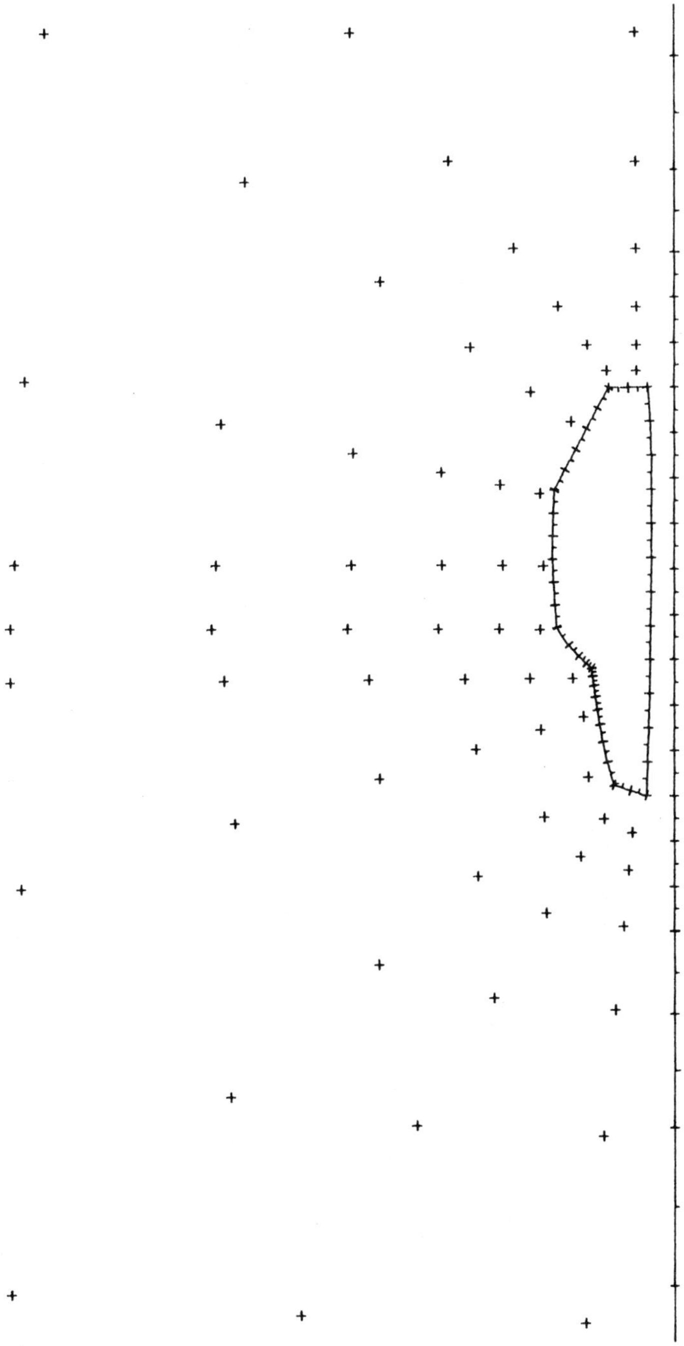

'BEASY' CODE FOR THERMAL AND STRESS ANALYSIS   143

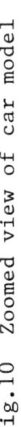

Fig.10 Zoomed view of car model

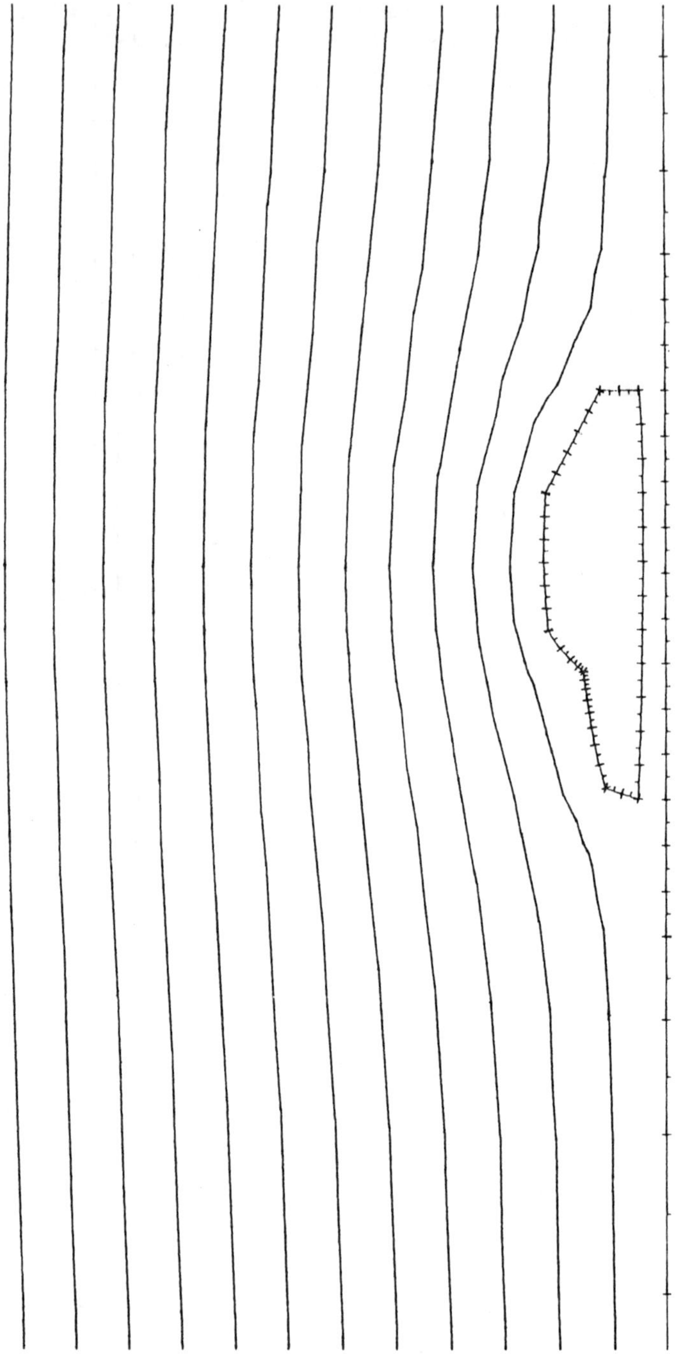

Fig.11 Streamlines calculated for air flow around car

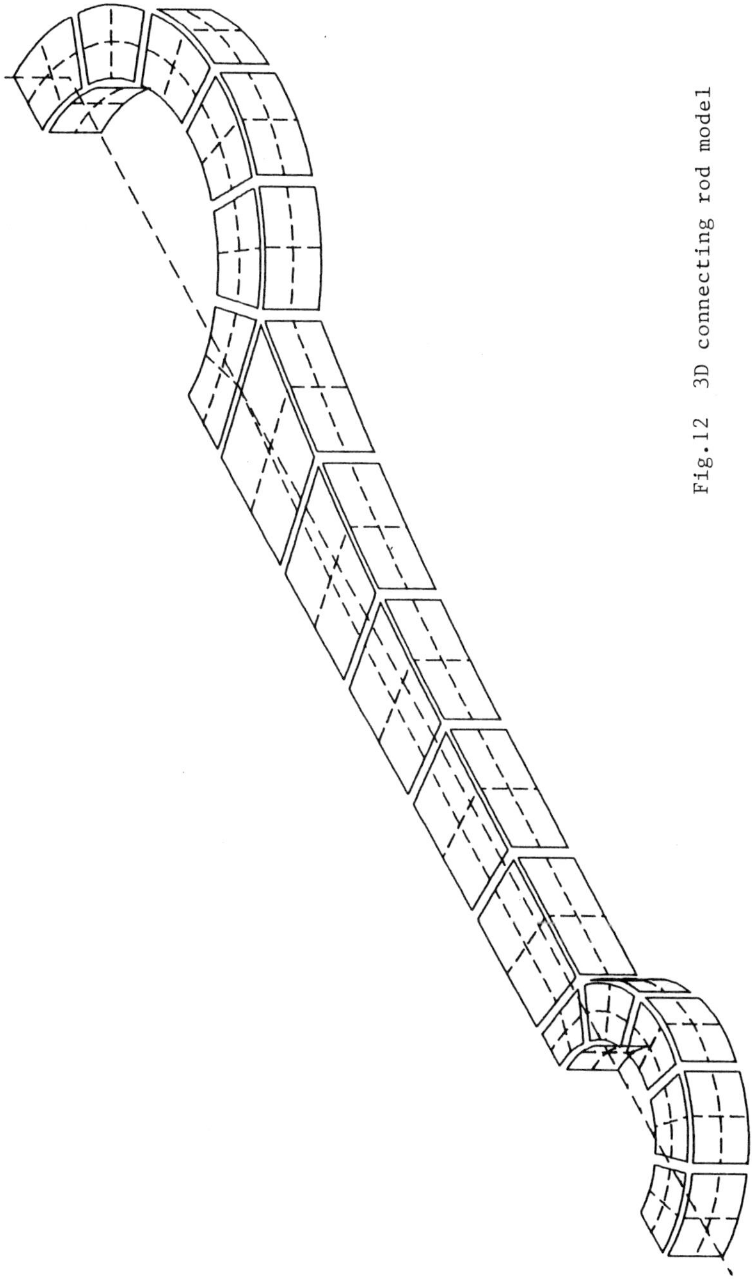

Fig.12 3D connecting rod model

146 'BEASY' CODE FOR THERMAL AND STRESS ANALYSIS

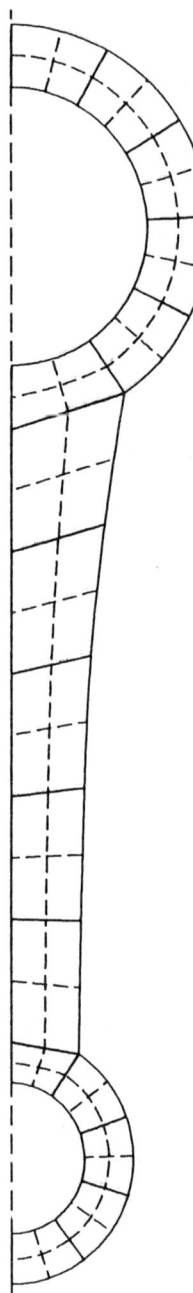

Fig.13a Undeformed shape of connecting rod

'BEASY' CODE FOR THERMAL AND STRESS ANALYSIS 147

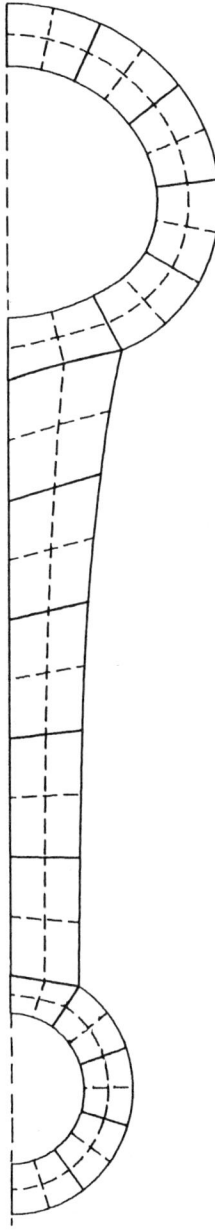

Fig. 13b Deformed shape of connecting rod

Hot Spot Stress Concept for Spot-Welded Joints
D. Radaj
Daimler-Benz AG Stuttgart and Technical University Braunschweig, Germany

SUMMARY

Finite element calculation for thin sheet metal structures in automotive engineering is employed to determine the shear, peel and cross tension forces transmitted at the individual weld spot. Sustainable weld spot forces are determined in Woehler fatigue tests using single spot and multiple spot specimens (e.g. tensile-shear specimen, cross tension specimen, peel tension specimen, torsion bar specimen). The maximum structure stress at the edge of the weld spot, the so-called hot spot stress, is a suitable means of transferring the sustainable forces determined in the specimen to the structure itself. The hot spot stresses which are calculated using the technical plate theory suppress the stress singularity at the edge of the weld spot, although they do provide a measure of its intensity and are thus of relevance for the strength. The weld spot itself is modelled elastic or rigid. The hot spot stress concept is demonstrated on the rectangular plate with a weld spot subjected to transverse shear, on the tensile-shear specimen and on the torsion bar specimen. There is surprisingly little difference in the hot spot stress concentration factors of the tensile shear specimen and the torsion bar specimen.

INTRODUCTION

Spot-welded joints in the load-bearing (thin sheet metal) structure (sheeting up to 3 mm thick) of vehicles (cars, light vans, truck cabs, minibuses, traincars and railway coaches) are subject to cyclic stresses and are thus at risk from fatigue. The layout of such welded joints (location, spacing and diameter of the weld spots and width of the flange) was hitherto the responsibility of the production engineer without consulting the designer. He verified his decisions by conducting Woehler fatigue tests with the (unrestrained) tensile-shear specimen

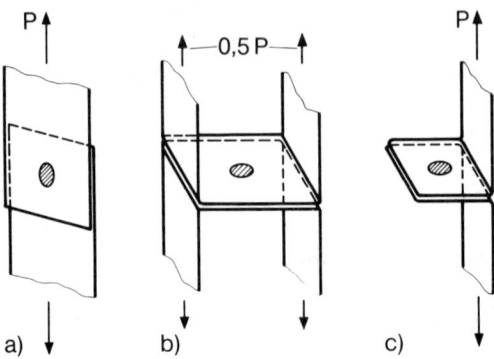

Figure 1: Single-spot specimens for testing fatigue strength: Tensile-shear specimen (for static loading standardized by DIN 50124 [1] (a), cross tension specimen (for static loading standardized by DIN 50164 [2]) (b), peel tension specimen (see [3]) (c); schematic presentation according to [4].

conforming to DIN 50124 [1]. In addition to the tensile-shear specimen, use was also made from time to time of the cross tension specimen conforming to DIN 50164 [2] and the peel tension specimen [3], Fig. 1.

More design-oriented engineers in the automotive industry are today also making use of Woehler fatigue tests performed on the torsion bar specimen which is similar to the actual structural components, Fig. 2. In both cases, the tests provide only relative statements. It has not been possible to reach an absolute statement regarding the strength or durability of the weld spot in the structure especially as the more precise stress conditions existing in the specimen and the actual component remained unknown.

There is a fundamentally new situation developing as a result of the work done by design and stress analysis engineers. Finite element analysis for the types of thin sheet metal structures mentioned, which has been performed for some 15 years now to predict static stiffness and behaviour under dynamic loading, has now reached such a level of sophistication as to make it possible to determine the resultant shear, peel and cross tension forces acting on the individual weld spot in the structure. It is therefore an obvious next step, and is also urgently desirable in view of new structural designs for which there is no empirical background, to estimate strength and durability of the weld spots in the structure on the basis of the weld spot forces mentioned, to provide recommendations regarding the structural design and to optimize this. This calls for a procedure enabling us to draw conclusions in quantative terms from

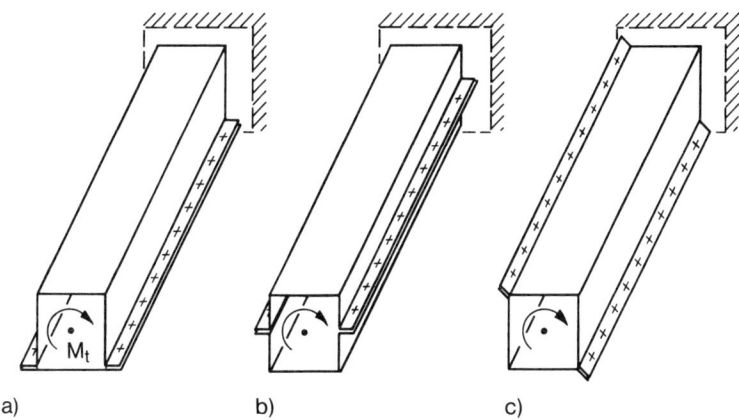

Figure 2: Multiple-spot torsion bar specimens subject to tensile-shear at the individual spot, various versions according to [5].

the strength of the weld spot in the specimen regarding the strength of the weld spots in the actual structure.

This is not a task which can be solved by elementary means, by, for instance, transferring to the weld spot in the structure the sustainable weld spot forces determined from the specimen. This can be concluded from a simple experiment in reasoning. The weld spot resultant forces Q_x, Q_y, Q_z, M_x, M_y, M_z which are presented in Fig. 3 at a flange element can be supported in an infinite variety of ways at the outer edges. Equally numerous are the local stress states at the edge of the weld spot and thus the likely strengths. Consequently, there can also not be any simple, generally applicable method of approximation which transfers the sustainable forces from the specimen to the structural component. Approaches and solutions based on plate theory are essential. As will be shown this largely avoids complex three-dimensional modelling.

The following contribution presents some results of the detailed work [6, 7] which the author has performed into the hot spot stress concept relating to spot-welded joints (refer to [8] for a general assessment of the hot-spot stress concept). This contribution is restricted to the transverse shear loading of the weld spot which is particularly significant in practice. This in the general systematics of basic design loading cases at the weld spot, Fig. 4, is mode II.1, supplemented by mode II.4 in the tensile-shear specimen and mode II.5 and III.1 in the torsion bar specimen.

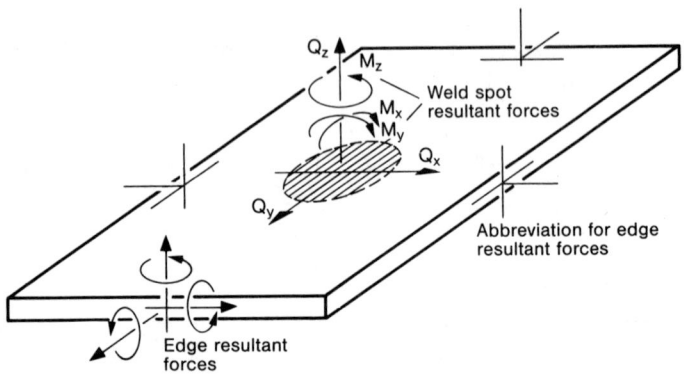

Figure 3: Flange element with edge and weld spot resultant forces.

HOT SPOT STRESS CONCEPT

A procedure which has been successfully employed on seam-welded joints on slightly thicker sheets is to use the maximum local structure stress at the seam weld toe (without the notch stress concentration and without the corner and crack effects) as the strength characteristic, [8]. A Woehler S-N curve of sustainable maximum structure stresses can identify the risk of crack initiation at the weld seam toe when the same material and the same type of weld seam (notch severity) is used. The term "hot spot" refers to the point of the weld toe at which the maximum structure stress exists because crack initiation here is preceded by a marked local heating-up (due to the cyclic alternating strain), this being particularly so with low-cycle fatigue.

Neglecting the notch, corner and crack effects in the stress field is synonymous with the assumptions of the technical theories which apply to load-bearing structures (rod, beam and plate theories) and the finite element calculation methods which are based on these. These theories linearize the pattern of the stress over the thickness of the component and thus eliminate the effects mentioned.

The hot spot stress concept can be applied to thin sheet metal structures with weld spots. The most practical method for the stress analysis engineer is to represent the sheet metal outside the weld spot by finite plate elements (with membrane and bending stresses) and to use this model to calculate the hot spot stress. Due to the flow of forces being concentrated on the weld spots, the hot spot stress generally occurs at the

HOT SPOT STRESS CONCEPT FOR SPOT-WELDED JOINTS 153

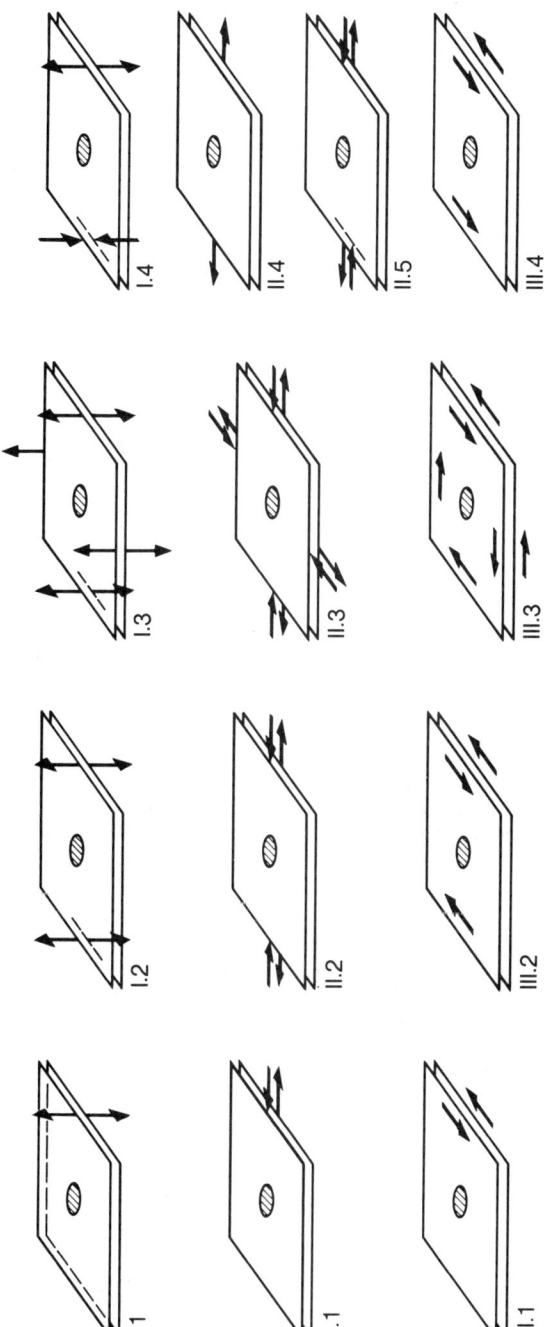

Figure 4: Systematics of basic loading cases at the flange element with weld spot, arrows for edge displacement.

edge of the weld spot. The crucial area is the inside of the sheet at which the notch effect of the slot end superposes on the hot spot stress initiating the crack here. By contrast, there is a reduction of the calculated structure stresses on the outside of the sheet due to the geometrically smooth transition to the inside of the weld spot which is only slightly stressed. Irrespective of what has been said above on a more theoretical basis, practical experience with the calculation procedure reveals that the maximum structure stresses occur nearly always on the inside of the sheet.

The structure stresses in plate models are, as is known, biaxial. They are generally variable along the edge of the weld spot. The maximum value on the inside of the sheet is not normally opposite the maximum value on the outside of the sheet. In what follows, the von Mises equivalent stress is regarded as being the parameter determining the initiation of the crack.

The hot spot stress concept with its linearisation of the stresses over the thickness of the sheet suppresses the stress singularity actually occurring at the edge of the weld spot, although it does provide an indication of the intensity of this singularity, which is the essential parameter determining crack initiation. That is why the hot spot stress is a suitable measure of the strength of weld spots. First of all, the hot spot stress enables various design versions to be compared and evaluated under the assumption that the material and the fabrication process is identical. Comparing the hot spot stress with the sustainable values of a Woehler S-N curve or a life characteristic is a second and more sophisticated step. The correlation between the concepts of hot spot stress, notch stress and fracture mechanics at the weld spot are discussed in greater detail in [6]. Of the concepts just mentioned, the hot spot stress concept appears to be the one most suitable for general practical application.

Although this contribution does deal only with the calculation of hot spot stresses, mention should be made of the possibility of determining hot spot stresses by measurement too. The hot spot stress concept relating to seam-welded joints was in fact developed on the basis of a stress measurement regulation [8]. It was only at a later date that finite element calculations were introduced as an alternative. In the case of spot-welded joints, considerable difficulties are encountered in measuring the hot spot stress at the edge of the weld spot on the inside of the sheet. In many cases the location of this hot spot stress is not initially known and in any case a miniaturised (if possible multi-axial) strain gauge has to be applied through a hole drilled into the overlapping sheet. Such investigations do exist. The weld spot cant angle, on the other hand, is not a measure of the hot spot stress or of the strength (contrary to a number of claims to this correlation).

STRESS MECHANICS OF THE LAP JOINT

The mechanical feature of the lap joint is that the jointed sheets are offset in the direction of the thickness, which produces bending moments in the sheets if the joint is subject to tensile loading. This results in considerable bending stresses being superposed on the membrane stresses and in deflections which attain the magnitude of the thickness of the sheet in the case of thin sheets even under low stresses (primarily outside the area of the joint) or which cause mutual supporting of sheet areas contacting each other (primarily in the area of the joint). The latter, non-linear effects of large deflection or variable support are ignored at first. Only the linear initial state is considered.

The plane contour model of the lap joint in the form of the tensile-shear specimen, Fig. 5a, has been reduced to a further simplified beam model, Figs. 5b to 5e. The beam model is point-symmetrical relative to the centre point M if the thickness, the length and the loading to the left and right of M are the same. The effect of the point-symmetry is that there is no bending moment transmitted in M, for bending deformation with a moment in M would break the point-symmetry. The moment vanishing in M is illustrated by a hinge in M. This hinge is the key to understanding the additional bending stresses in the lap joint subject to tensile loading.

The deformation due to bending as shown in Fig. 5 is greatly enlarged. No account is taken of the influence of deflection and end face rotation on the equilibrium conditions, however, a fact to be considered in visualizing the processes involved. Fig. 5 does not include the deformation due to tension in order to graphically emphasise the deformation due to bending.

Fig. 5b shows the deflection in the case of tension applied centrically to the middle of the weld spot and thus eccentrically to the middle of the beam. This is achieved in the standardized tensile-shear test by using a packing plate at one side of the sheet in the clamping jaws (suitable for sheets of larger thickness). In addition to the shear tension force S, the offset-bending moment also acts in the sheet (not at the weld spot as often claimed):

$$M_b = \frac{S\,s}{2}\,. \tag{1}$$

The following tensile and bending stresses are acting in the sheet of depth 1:

$$\sigma_z = \frac{S}{s}\,, \tag{2}$$

$$\sigma_b = \pm\frac{S\,s\,6}{2\,s^2}\,. \tag{3}$$

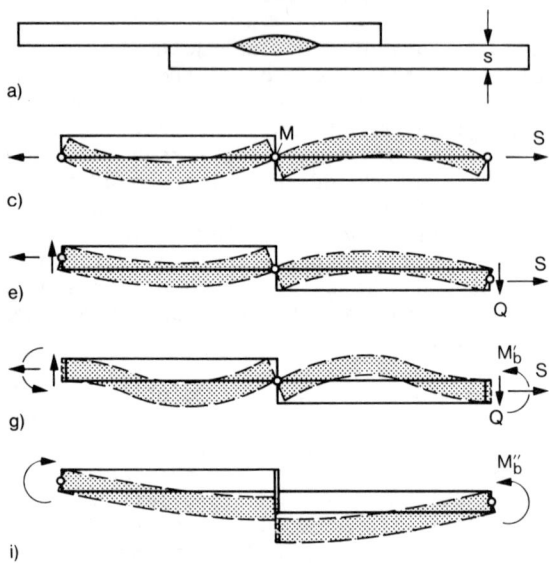

Figure 5: Mechanism of deformation due to bending in the tensile shear specimen subject to different loading cases; point M on edge of weld spot.

The stresses σ_i and σ_a on the inside and outside of the sheet in the beam model under small displacements are thus:

$$\sigma_i = \frac{4\,S}{s}, \tag{4}$$

$$\sigma_a = -\frac{2\,S}{s}. \tag{5}$$

In Fig. 5c the shear tension force is introduced free of moment in the middle plane of the sheet. In the standardized tensile-shear test this is achieved by not using a packing plate at one side of the sheet in the clamping jaws (suitable for sheets of smaller thickness). The equilibrium of the external forces is achieved in this loading case by self-positioning of the specimen at a slight angle causing (relatively small) transverse forces Q at the ends of the specimen. The direction of the resultants of S and Q is specified by the line connecting the three hinges shown. This corresponds to the slightly inclined position of the specimen. The stresses in the area of M are unchanged. These stresses drop linearly toward the ends of the specimen to the level of the tensile stress without the bending stress. In addition to S, Q is also transmitted in M. So, there is a slight cross tension in the weld spot.

Fig. 5d shows the case of horizontal parallel displacement of the end faces of the specimen. The external forces shown are the reaction forces to the specified displacement. This loading case, starting from Fig. 5c, can be presented by the additional equiaxed bending moments M_b' producing the horizontal end tangents. The entire moment has to be equalized by increased transverse forces Q. The shear tension force S in this conversion remains in the centre of the sheet, but without the hinge. If M_b' has been represented by displacing S, S would then be positioned further out. As a result, this loading case is the consequent continuation of the preceding one. There is a linear drop to zero and a rise with opposite sign to the ends of the specimen. Q is increasingly transmitted in M.

A common feature of the loading cases of Figs. 5b to 5d is the same tensile and bending stress state at the point of symmetry M with an increasing (relatively small) transverse force.

Fig. 5e presents the behaviour of the welded joint subject to a moment load. It is not point-symmetric. The hinge in M has to be eliminated in order to be able to transmit the moment. There is also a moment in M to be transmitted even in the case of tensile-shear if the two sheets are of different thickness, of different length or subject to different loading or clamping.

HOT SPOT STRESS CONCENTRATION FACTORS

The hot spot (structure) stress σ_{smax} is best stated in the form of a hot spot stress concentration factor, there being three different definitions depending on the reference stress (see [6]).

The stress concentration factor α_s relates to the basic (or nominal) stress σ_n in the plate:

$$\alpha_s = \frac{\sigma_{smax}}{\sigma_n} . \qquad (6)$$

The stress concentration factor α_s^* relates to the mean stress σ_n^* in the perimeter face of the weld spot which is obtained from the resultant of the internal forces at the weld spot:

$$\alpha_s^* = \frac{\sigma_{smax}}{\sigma_n^*} . \qquad (7)$$

The stress concentration factor α_{ns} relates to the nominal structure stress σ_{ns}, which is calculated using the elementary formulae derived from plate theory:

$$\alpha_{ns} = \frac{\sigma_{smax}}{\sigma_{ns}} . \qquad (8)$$

The stress concentration factor which most closely reflects reality is α_{ns}. The most important influencing parameters are contained in σ_{ns} and so α_{ns} represents a correction factor which is not too far off 1.0. A particular drawback of α_s^* is that the bending effects of the external forces in cross and peel tension are incorporated in the stress concentration factor, resulting in extremely high values of the factor.

The reference stresses (with specimen width b, sheet thickness s, weld spot diameter d, shear tension force S) which apply to the tensile shear specimen dealt with below are:

$$\sigma_n = \frac{S}{bs}, \qquad (9)$$

$$\sigma_n^* = \frac{S}{\pi d s}, \qquad (10)$$

$$\sigma_{ns} = 1.273 \frac{S}{ds}. \qquad (11)$$

The contents of σ_n and σ_n^* are clear to see. The nominal structure stress σ_{ns} is obtained from the shear tension force per perimeter face area of the weld spot times the factor 4 according to equation (4).

Equations (10) and (11) apply identically to the torsion bar specimen which is dealt with below, whereas equation (9) has the following form (with flange width e and support of S half at the front and half at the rear of the weld spot):

$$\sigma_n = \frac{S}{2es}. \qquad (12)$$

WELD SPOT MODELLING

Finite element modelling of the spot-welded joint by means of plate elements with membrane and bending effect comes up against its natural limit at the edge of the weld spot. It is not such a simple matter to present the inside of the weld spot. Fig. 6 takes the tensile-shear specimen as an example to show the different modelling possibilities which exist. The graphical representation shows the plane contour model in which beams have replaced the plates. Shown is the centre line of the beam. The shear tension force is applied centrically to the weld spot and thus eccentrically to the plate or beam.

In the simplest case, a rigid connecting pin takes the place of the weld spot, Fig. 6b, providing a correct simulation of the offset of the overlapping sheets. However, the (singular) concentration of forces at the pin and the altered bending lengths of the sheets falsify the hot spot stresses. In the next step, the rigid pin is replaced by a rigid cylinder, Fig. 6c, which eliminates this falsification. The model can be easily handled although it may represent too severe a restraint on the defor-

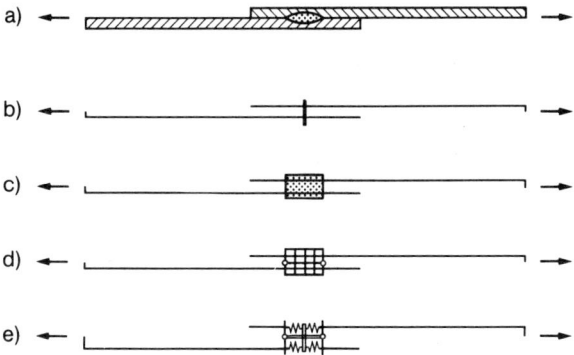

Figure 6: Modelling of weld spot in tensile shear specimen (a): rigid pin (b), rigid cylinder (c), elastic cylinder (d), spoked star with membrane elements visualized as springs (e).

mation (for instance with tension loading of only one of the two sheets). A further improvement of the model is therefore achieved if volume elements are provided in the inside of the weld spot, Fig. 3d. The pins with centre hinges at the edge of the weld spot convert the translational degrees of freedom of the volume elements into the translational and rotational degrees of freedom of the plate elements. Finally, the model can be simplified by replacing the volume elements with membrane elements, which does, however, necessitate introducing a nondeformable weld spot shear face for mounting the hinges, Fig. 3e. The rigid face is achieved by using a star of tensile- and bending-rigid spokes, their torsion elasticity being matched to the torsion elasticity of the weld spot (further details are given in [6]). The "spoked star model" has been mainly used in the investigation which is described in the sections which follow.

RECTANGULAR PLATE SUBJECTED TO TRANSVERSE SHEAR

The results of the calculations relating to the rectangular plate subjected to transverse shear as per mode II.1 are presented in Fig. 7. With the edges unrestrained, the plate with transverse-free weld spot moves out of its plane (bending primarily in the direction of the transverse shear). Whereas the edge which has been displaced transversely is held in the plate plane, maximum deflection takes place at the transverse edge which is not under load. With the edges restrained, the sheet forms cups in opposite direction (down-bending and up-bending) in front of and behind the weld spot while the weld spot cants (in the direction of the transverse shear). The hot spot stresses occuring at the front face of the weld spot, inside tension almost twice as great as outside compression, are significantly greater if the edges are unrestrained than with restrained edges. They are approximately as great with the rigid cylinder as with the elastic spoked star model, Table 1. The restrained outer edge produces a more balanced transmission of the forces at the edge of the weld spot, in particular a greater involvement of the rear (relative to the loading) weld spot edge. The ratio of the tensile stresses on the inside and the compressive stresses on the outside (approximately 2:1) corresponds to the predictable ratio with a weld spot subjected to a shear load applied centrically. Radial tensile force and radial bending moment dominate at the weld spot edge.

The effect of a parameter variation to α_s and α_{ns} is shown in Fig. 8 (α_s^* is not shown separately because $a_s^* = 4\,\alpha_{ns}$). In the case of an elastic weld spot in the plate with unrestrained edges α_s increases with b and s, or decreases with l (very little) and d. α_{ns} on the other hand decreases with b and l, or increases with d and s. The different behaviour of α_s and α_{ns} is attributable to the different parameter content of σ_n and σ_{ns}. The stress concentration factors for the rigid weld spot are smaller than the stress concentration factors for the elastic weld spot. Restrained sheet edges (edge deflection suppressed) produce an even greater reduction in α_s and α_{ns}, in the case of α_{ns} to values close to 1.0.

Table 1: Hot spot stress concentration factors, plate subjected to transverse shear, dimensions of plate 25x25x1 mm, diameter of weld spot 5 mm (unrstr. = unrestrained, rstr. = restrained).

Weld spot model	Plate face	Plate edge unrstr. α_s	rstr. α_s	unrstr. α_s^*	rstr. α_s^*	unrstr. α_{ns}	rstr. α_{ns}
elastic	outside	5.74	3.38	3.61	2.12	0.90	0.53
	inside	11.68	7.55	7.34	4.74	1.84	1.19
rigid	outside	5.61		3.52		0.88	
	inside	10.37		6.52		1.63	

Figure 7 (on next page): Results of calculation for rectangular plate subjected to transverse shear, mode II.1; unrestrained (a...f) and restrained (g...l) edge, deflection (a, b, g, h), principal stress crosses (c, d, i, j) and von Mises equivalent stresses (e, f, k, l), outside (c, e, i, k) and inside (d, f, j, l) of plate; crosses 0.62 mm for 1.0, graduation of contour lines 0.5, MAX = 11.68 for f and 7.55 for l; reference stress σ_n.

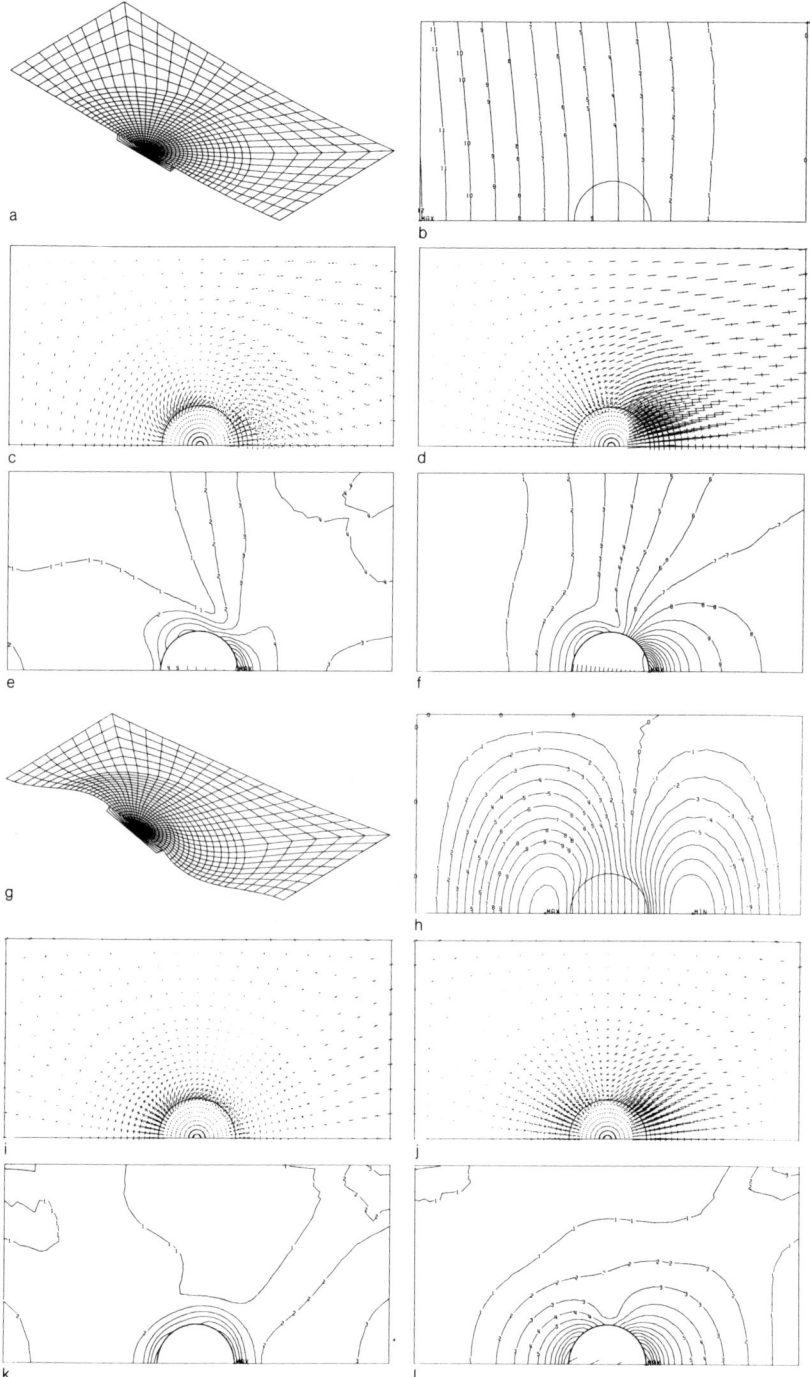

Figure 7

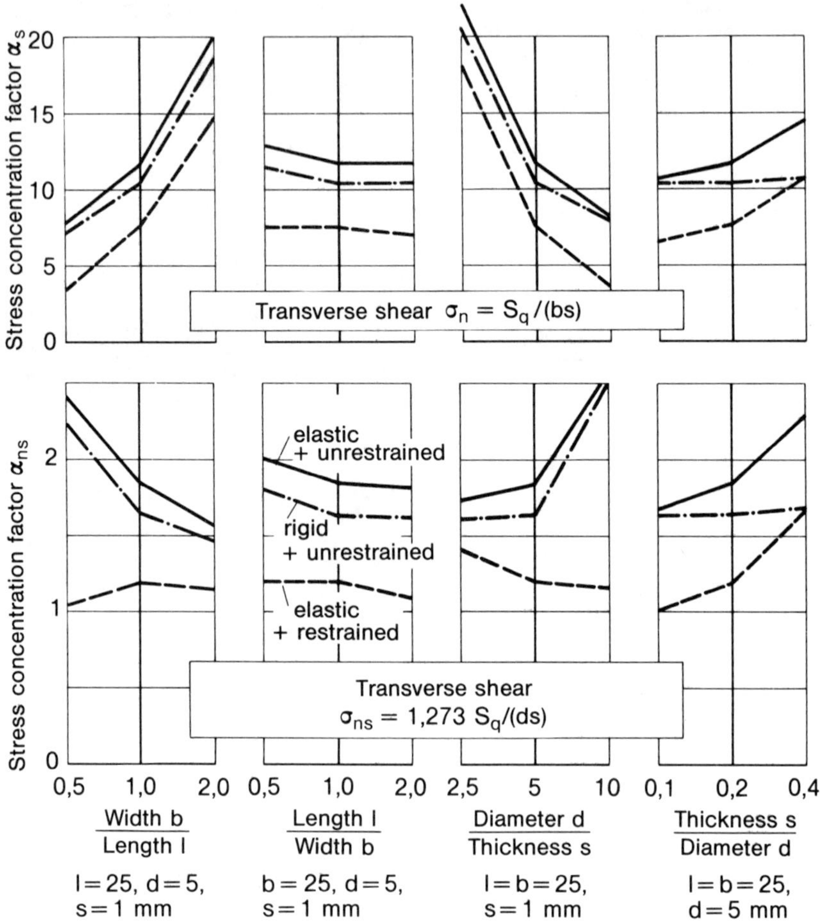

Figure 8: Hot spot stress concentration factors α_s and α_{ns} on inside of plate with transverse shear and variation of dimension parameters, elastic and rigid modelling of weld spot, plate edge unrestrained and restrained.

TENSILE-SHEAR SPECIMEN

The results of the calculation relating to the tensile shear specimen, Figs. 9 and 10, show similarity with the results relating to the transverse shear model. The tension sheet bends in front of and behind the weld spot to form cups in opposite direction while the weld spot itself cants. The hot spot stress occurs at the front face ahead of the weld spot on the inside of the sheet. Table 2 shows the hot spot stress concentration factors and it can be seen from this that the three different models investigated produce approximately identical stress concentration factors. The cross tension force is 1.6 % of the shear tension force. As regards the question of the influence of the model assumption of the shear face remaining plane (bending rigid spokes) the boundary element calculation performed on the contour model (surprisingly) revealed complete validity of the assumption with a relatively high degree of accuracy in the calculation.

Table 2: Hot spot stress concentration factors for tensile shear specimen 40x32x1 mm conforming to DIN 50124 different weld spot models, diameter of weld spot 5 mm.

Loading case	Weld spot model	Sheet face	Stress concentration factors		
			α_s	α_s^*	α_{ns}
Tensile shear specimen	Tensile soft spokes	outside inside	7.71 13.80	3.03 5.42	0.76 1.36
	Tensile rigid spokes	outside inside	7.28 14.23	2.86 5.59	0.72 1.40
	Rigid cylinder	outside inside	6.36 12.90	2.50 5.07	0.63 1.27

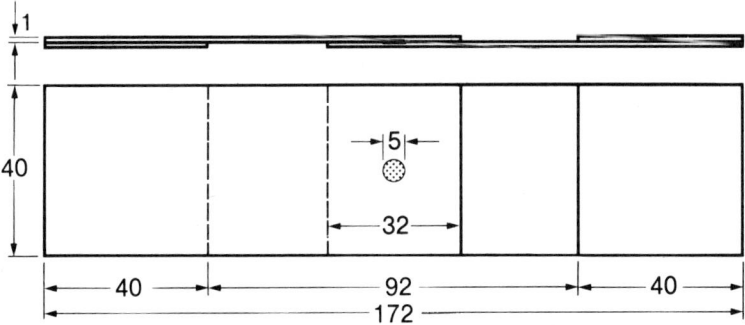

Figure 9: Tensile shear specimen conforming to DIN 50124 for sheet 1 mm thick, packing plates for clamping in jaws centrically relative to weld spot shear face.

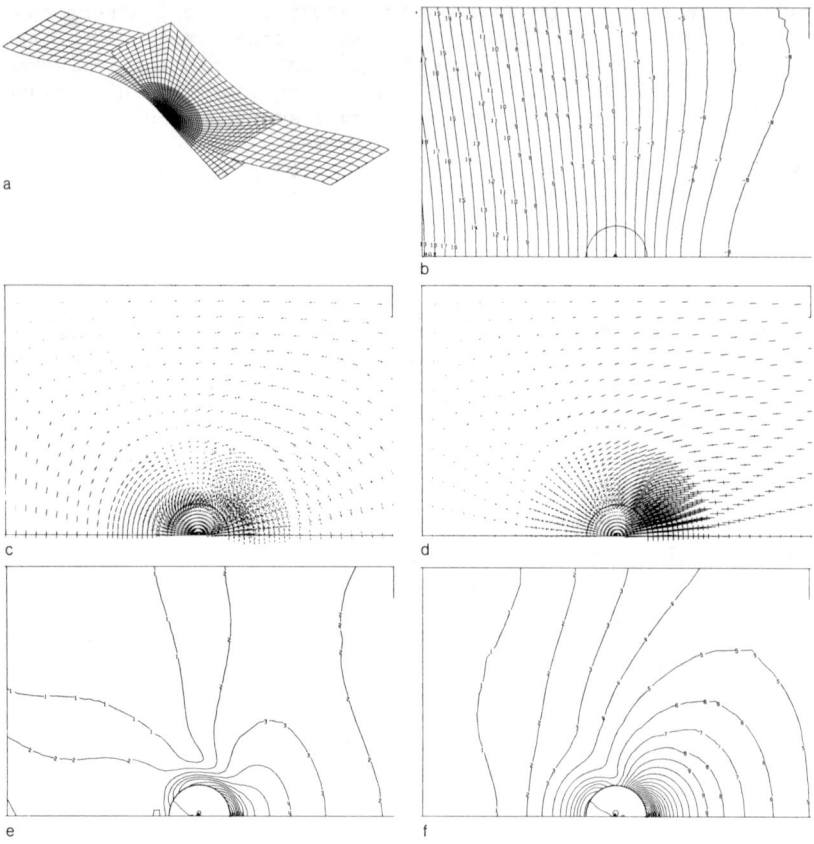

Figure 10: Unrestrained tensile-shear test conforming to DIN 50124; deflection (a, b), principal stress crosses (c, d) and equivalent stresses (e, f), outside (c, e) and inside (d,f) of sheet; crosses 0.9 mm for 1.0 with c and 0.5 mm for 1.0 with d, graduation of contour lines 0.5, MAX = 13.80 with f; reference stress σ_n.

TORSION BAR SPECIMEN

In the torsion bar specimen, Fig. 11, the weld spots are subjected primarily to shear forces in the direction of the bar similar to the tensile shear specimen. In contrast to the latter specimen, the shear force at the weld spot acts anti-symmetrically on both sides in the direction of the shear force and non-symmetrically on both sides transverse to the direction of the shear force. Moreover, the shear face is prevented from canting due to the proximity of the folded web.

The magnitude of the shear force S at the weld spot can be approximately determined using the Bredt formula for thin-walled closed sections. The constant shear flow in the cross section contour can be equated with the shear flow in the longitudinal direction of the bar. Hence it follows for the bar segment of length l between two weld spots (torsional moment M_t, width b and height h of the bar box):

$$S = M_t \frac{l}{2bh} . \qquad (13)$$

The reference stress used in the stress concentration factor α_s is the mean normal stress in the flange cross section (flange width e, thickness of sheet s), equation (12).

The mean shear stress in the longitudinal or cross section is also suitable for use as the reference stress:

$$\tau_s = \frac{M_t}{2bhs} . \qquad (14)$$

Hence, either from equations (12) to (14) or also direct from the equilibrium condition at the bar segment:

$$\sigma_s = \frac{l}{2e} \tau_s . \qquad (15)$$

In the calculation example selected, $l/e = 4$ and thus $\sigma_s = 2\tau_s$, in other words there is approximately equal straining in the

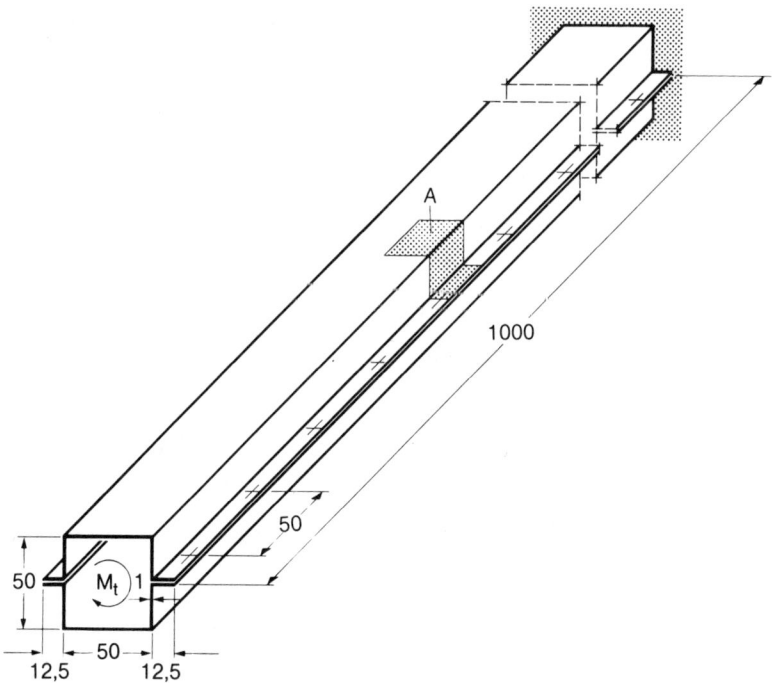

Figure 11: Torsion bar specimen; segment A for fe modelling.

flange and in the box on the basis of the strength hypothesis of principal shear stress.

The angle of twist is not correctly approximated by the (second) Bredt formula because the bar reacts torsionally stiff as a closed section only in the cross sections with the weld spots but torsionally flexible as an open section between them. The (second) Bredt formula applies only to the closed section.

Finite element calculation was used to determine the precise distribution of the structure stresses in the middle part of the torsion bar specimen. It is sufficient to model the segment which has been emphasised in Fig. 11 by the grey shading, see Fig. 12. This is due to the periodic anti-symmetry of the stress state, or rather deformation state in the specimen. The deflection pattern has been drawn as part of the deformation state. The suppressed or prescribed (in parenthesis) degrees of freedom are stated at the edges of the segment. The cross section contour is inherently rigid at the two end faces of the segment. This well-known assumption of the technical bar theories (specifically of the torsion-bending theory) is exactly satisfied due to the conditions of anti-symmetry in the end cross sections, it is in other words not an approximation. The cross section contours are mounted so as to be movable in the longitudinal direction of the bar. This movement is suppressed only at the top longitudinal edge and at the weld spots. The spoked star of the weld spot model is held fixed in the longitudinal direction of the bar and transverse to this too. The

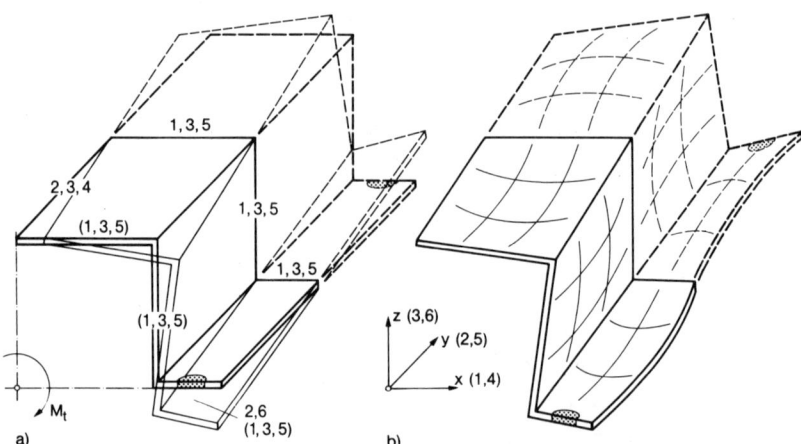

Figure 12: Model of segment of torsion bar specimen; suppressed degrees of freedom at edges from anti-symmetry condition at rear edge, at side edge and at front of spoked star (figures not in parenthesis), prescribed degrees of freedom at front edge (figures in parenthesis) (a), deflection pattern on deformed structure (b).

HOT SPOT STRESS CONCEPT FOR SPOT-WELDED JOINTS

translation normal to the flange is given due to the rotation of the end cross section. The spoked star is free to cant only in the longitudinal direction of the bar.

The conclusion to be drawn from the periodically anti-symmetrical deformation normal to the flange and in the flange plane as shown in Fig. 13 is that no resultant forces occur in the weld spot transverse or normal to the flange, in other words there is neither (flange) transverse shear nor cross tension. However, the weld spot transmits not only the (flange) longitudinal force but also a torsional moment. The resultant forces which nevertheless occur at the quarter weld spot of the segment model transverse and normal to the flange thus balance each other within the upper or lower half of the weld spot without appearing in the shear face of the weld spot.

The result of the finite element calculation is summarised in Fig. 14 and Table 3. Only the longitudinal shear force of the finite element model is used in the reference stresses for the hot spot stress concentration factors. The torsional moment M_t^* at the weld spot of the finite element model is so small compared with the rectangular plate model in 6, longitudinal shear as to mode III.1, $(M_t^*/(Se/2) = 0.09)$ that it can be ignored in the reference stresses. The longitudinal shear forces calculated using the Bredt formula, equation (13), and determined from the finite element model are identical with a high degree of accuracy if the inside area of the bar cross section (width b times height h) in Bredt's formula is enlarged by the slot area on both sides (width e times thickness s) (factor 1.005).

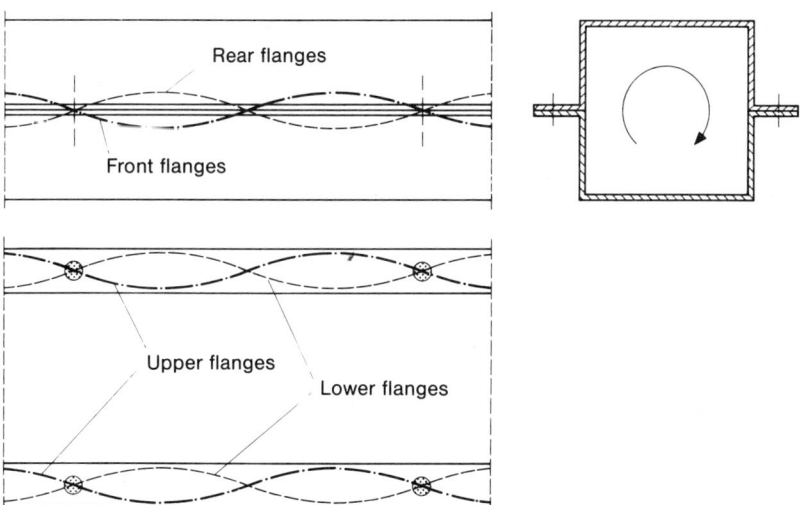

Figure 13: Deflection curves normal and transverse to flanges of torsion bar specimen.

Table 3: Hot spot stress concentration factors for torsion bar specimen 50x50x1 mm, different weld spot models, diameter of weld spot 5 mm.

Weld spot model	Weld spot spacing	Sheet face	Stress concentration factor		
			α_s	α_s^*	α_{ns}
elastic	50 mm	outside	3.92	2.46	0.62
		inside	7.26	4.56	1.14
rigid	50 mm	outside	3.83	2.41	0.60
		inside	6.61	4.15	1.04
elastic	100 mm	outside	4.26	2.91	0.73
		inside	7.58	5.17	1.29

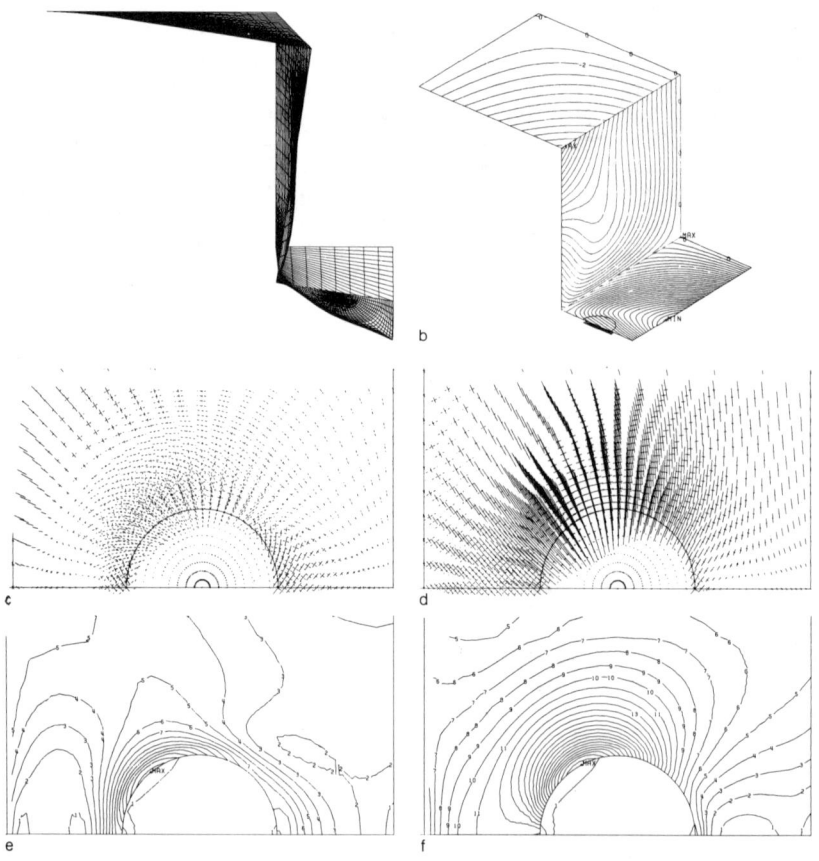

Figure 14: Segment model for torsion bar specimen; deflection normal to sheet faces (a,b), principal stress crosses (c,d) and equivalent stresses (e,f); crosses 0.9 mm for 0.47, graduation of contour lines 0.25, MAX = 7.26 for f; reference stress σ_n.

It is possible to only make a very rough comparison of the stress concentration factors α_s of the torsion bar specimen and the tensile-shear specimen because the reference stresses are not the same. The stress concentration factors α_s^* and α_{ns} agree well with the values for the rectangular plate subjected to longitudinal shear (l/b = 2.0 for l = 50 mm), restrained sheet edge, refer to Table 5 in [6], Part III. Compared to the tensile-shear specimen (refer to Table 2, stress concentration factors on inside, tensile rigid spokes), the stress concentration factors determined are 18 % less for l = 50 mm and 8 % less for l = 100 mm. The relatively high degree of agreement of the stress concentration factors of the tensile-shear specimen and the torsion bar specimen was unexpected.

CONCLUSIONS

Judging from the calculated stress concentration factors or hot spot stresses, it is possible to transfer the fatigue strength of the weld spot from the tensile-shear specimen to the torsion bar specimen, at least for relatively low cyclic stress close to the fatigue limit. In the case of higher cyclic stress in the direction of low-cycle fatigue strength, it is necessary to make a correction for large deflections which particularly occur in the tensile-shear test and increase the superposed cross tension to an over-proportional extent. The "transfer problem" which was hitherto unsolved for spot-welded test specimens and structures can be regarded as having been basically solved on the basis of what has been stated in this paper. Further investigations are required for practical introduction and verification of the method, in particular a comparison with results form fatigue strength tests as are currently being performed as part of an industrial research project.

REFERENCES

1 DIN 50124: Scherzugversuch an Widerstandspunkt-, Widerstandsbuckel und Schmelzpunktschweißverbindungen. Beuth Verlag, Berlin 1977.

2 DIN 50164: Kopfzugversuch an Widerstandspunkt-, Widerstandsbuckel und Schmelzpunktschweißverbindungen. Beuth Verlag, Berlin 1982.

3 Radaj, D., A. Schlüter and A. Baur: Schälzugschwingfestigkeitsversuch für Punktschweißnähte und Bruchflächenanalyse. Schweißen und Schneiden 38 (1986), No. 3, pp. 113/18.

4 Krause, H.J., and G. Simon: Über das Verhalten widerstandpunktgeschweißter Proben aus unlegiertem Stahl bei unterschiedlichen statischen Beanspruchungen. Schweißen und Schneiden 29 (1977), No. 1, pp. 22/25.

5   Eichhorn, F., and B.H. Schmitz: Vergleichende Prüfung standardisierter punktgeschweißter Hohlprofile aus Stahlblech mit und ohne zusätzliche Verklebung der Fügespalte. Schweißen und Schneiden 36 (1984), No. 3, pp. 113/16.

6   Radaj, D.: Strukturspannungserhöhung an Punktschweißverbindungen. Teil I: Grundbeanspruchungsfälle. Teil II: Beanspruchungskonzepte, Kreis- und Konturmodelle. Teil III: FE-Berechungen für Rechteckmodelle. Konstruktion 38 (1986) No. 2, pp. 41/47 (Teil I), 38 (1986) No. 10, pp. 397/404 (Teil II) and 39 (1987) No. 2 (Teil III).

7   Radaj, D.: Hot-Spot-Strukturspannungsberechnung für die punktgeschweißte Scherzug- und Hutprofilprobe. Schweißen und Schneiden 39 (1987) No. 1.

8   Radaj, D.: Gestaltung und Berechnung von Schweißkonstruktionen, Ermüdungsfestigkeit. Deutscher Verlag für Schweißtechnik, Düsseldorf 1985.

Efficient Computer Optimisation of Vehicle Structures within the Constraints of a Limited Time and Budget Allowance

S.L.M. Hall
Structural Engineering Group, I.A.D. (U.K.) Ltd., I.A.D. House, Dominion Way, Worthing, West Sussex, England

PRIMARY ACTIVITIES OF I.A.D. (U.K.) Ltd.

International Automotive Design (I.A.D) provides a consultancy service to the automotive world encompassing a complete spectrum of styling, engineering design, prototype build and validation. To provide this service on a complete basis requires the expertise of I.A.D.'s Structural Engineering Group. It is the activities of this group within the particular field of automotive structural engineering and their use of a variety of Computer Aided Engineering techniques which are the concern of this paper.

Styling projects progressing from clay modelling to structural design require constant guidance and structural input to ensure a well engineered final product, completely acceptable to both client and contractor. Support of these projects represents the bulk of the work undertaken by the Structural Engineering Group. In terms of conventional automotive design today this very often involves spot-welded sheet metal Body-in-White design. More and more, this dictates a high degree of interfacing with Computer Aided Design activities. The importance of C.A.D. to automotive applications is paramount to I.A.D. with four major systems running on site: CATIA; CADAM; PDGS and Computer Vision.

As well as Body-in-White design, more specific tasks such as detailed component design are addressed, ensuring a wide range of design activities within the group as a whole.

Design from a clean sheet, current design update or modification and troubleshooting tasks are all undertaken. Whereas the majority of full vehicle projects are undertaken in conjunction with I.A.D. Styling and Design Departments, the Structural Engineering Group has the potential to function in it's own right and does indeed undertake work of an unrelated nature.

With such a broad range of activities, the use of Computer Aided Engineering techniques must be varied and the approach to problems flexible in order to succeed.

Factors governing the approach to analyses
The automotive consultancy business is extremely competitive and survival necessitates assuring the client of first rate service at competitive rates. For continued success and growth, the quality of the product must maintain a high standard. Achieving this balance on a continued basis is a constant challenge and often requires careful use of analysis techniques less common within larger automotive companies, although the basic tool of the trade, Finite Element Modelling, is the same in each case.

To elaborate, a high degree of 'first sight' design is required in order to meet stringent timing and budget restrictions. This may well lead to development of coarse finite element models to assist in determination of structural performance levels where, in a perfect world, a more detailed model might be preferable for determination of performance in absolute terms. However, such coarse models have proved invaluable in establishing reliable results rapidly in projects tackled to date. The success of this approach relies heavily on a development/correlation process whereby simple models constructed rapidly are validated with reference to current test results and established yard-sticks for both analytical and physical investigations previously conducted. To be able to approach problems arising in this manner, it is imperative that comprehensive data is available. Information currently available at I.A.D. represents the collective experience of the Structural Engineering Group and the results of extensive literature searches. By way of the approximations that must be made to keep models simple, typically beam element representation of thin walled sections, the utmost care and consideration must be taken in construction of the model. The different effects of particular approximations can only be gauged by experience.

The favoured approach, wherever possible, is model development in relation to physical test programmes. Finite Element Analysis is a very powerful tool for comparative analysis but, within the particular applications of the motor industry, is not normally as reliable in absolute terms. The performance of a given model can be quantified absolutely by means of correlation with relevant physical test results. In this manner, by ensuring that the significant attributes of a given model are faithfully represented, the required complexity of that model can be reduced significantly with a minimal reduction in confidence in the subsequent results.

Where budget and/or timing constraints do not allow execution of a full development test programme, relevant information from previous test procedures can be used in a similar manner to optimize the model in terms of cost and effectiveness.

In amassing sufficient information to consider this as a general approach, physical testing plays a vital role. Consequently, the Structural Engineering Group is responsible for the majority of structural test and validation procedures undertaken. Increasingly, test work will be undertaken in-house as the existing test facility within I.A.D. is developed to incorporate a wider range of test activities.

Test activities to date, both in-house and external, have made this coarse approach wholly successful.

A general approach to Computer Aided Engineering in terms of specific applications to the automotive field.

Most of the work of the Structures Group is related to automotive activities and centres around preparation of vehicle structures to meet both market regulations and in-house standards. General structural integrity is also considered, particularly where market regulations are lenient.

The general approach to solution methods outlined above makes extensive use of finite element techniques. Excluding internal software developments, the finite element packages available on I.A.D.'s computer system are MSC/Nastran and

Abaqus. The majority of analysis tasks can be tackled with a good degree of confidence with this combination. Additional commercial software of direct relevance includes A.C.S.L. (Advanced Continuous Simulations Language), mounted on a desk-top micro computer. Pre- and post-processing of analytical results is undertaken with CAEDS.

The different techniques used to investigate the majority of automotive body engineering applications with limited resources using these packages are addressed on an individual basis in the following sections.

LINEAR STATIC ANALYSIS

A large part of the analysis required falls into this category. With minimal restriction placed on time and cost, the majority of situations can be modelled with a high degree of confidence in the outcome in absolute terms. This type of analysis typically covers body stiffness requirements. Target values and limits for these criteria are more often dictated by client standards than market regulations. For full body analyses of this nature within tight constraints on time and budget, a composite beam and shell element model may well be used. Nastran provides a very flexible approach to this type of modelling in view of it's general beam section handling routines and it's proven track record. For this type of model the correlated development approach discussed earlier is vital to successful validation of the model and consequently to instilling a high level of confidence in the results.

Detailed approach

Beam elements are used in order to minimize model size and, in most cases, preparation time. To represent specific regions of a classic automobile structure with beam elements, for example pillars and rails, certain approximations have to be made about the behaviour of the structure represented and it's interaction with adjacent body panels. Based on pure beam theory, these assumptions are invariably optimistic in terms of stiffness in the instance of this particular analysis and collapse in general. Behaviour of thin walled sections is difficult to predict with a good degree of accuracy in specific terms and unqualified generalizations can be very dangerous.

To make allowances for the inherent optimism of this approach, section cut-offs must be carefully controlled. Local discontinuities and joint performance are also catered for with use of spring elements. Ideally, joint stiffness and section performance figures are provided by test procedures.

Shear and significant bending contributions of body panels are represented with shells or shear panels. Attachment of the panel structures to the beam framework again is critical to the final performance of the model. Care is taken to ensure that only significant modes of load transfer are considered in connection of the shells. Beam locations in relation to body panel representation may be adjusted with offsets if required to achieve true neutral axis and shear centre location or attached by means of relevant multi-point constraint conditions. A typical full body model generated in this manner is shown in fig 1. Alternatively, framework designs with exact beam dimensions and no structural body panels can be modelled even more precisely (fig 2).

Through this approach, stiffness results can be achieved quickly as an aid to design development with a reasonable degree of confidence.

Component and sub-assembly analysis is better investigated with more detailed models, for example complete shell element models in the case of sheet steel construction (fig 3). Results from this sort of analysis can very often contribute to the coarse beam and shell full body approach at a later stage in the programme. For example, joint stiffness figures obtained from a detailed joint analysis with a complete shell element model.

DYNAMIC ANALYSIS

A similar approach to full body modelling can be adopted for this category of analysis with good results within tight time and budget restrictions.

Detailed approach
The beam and shell model construction again affords a relatively quick means of establishing performance levels in terms of normal modes of a complete body for example, provided that care has been exercised in constructing the model to make adequate allowance for all approximations.

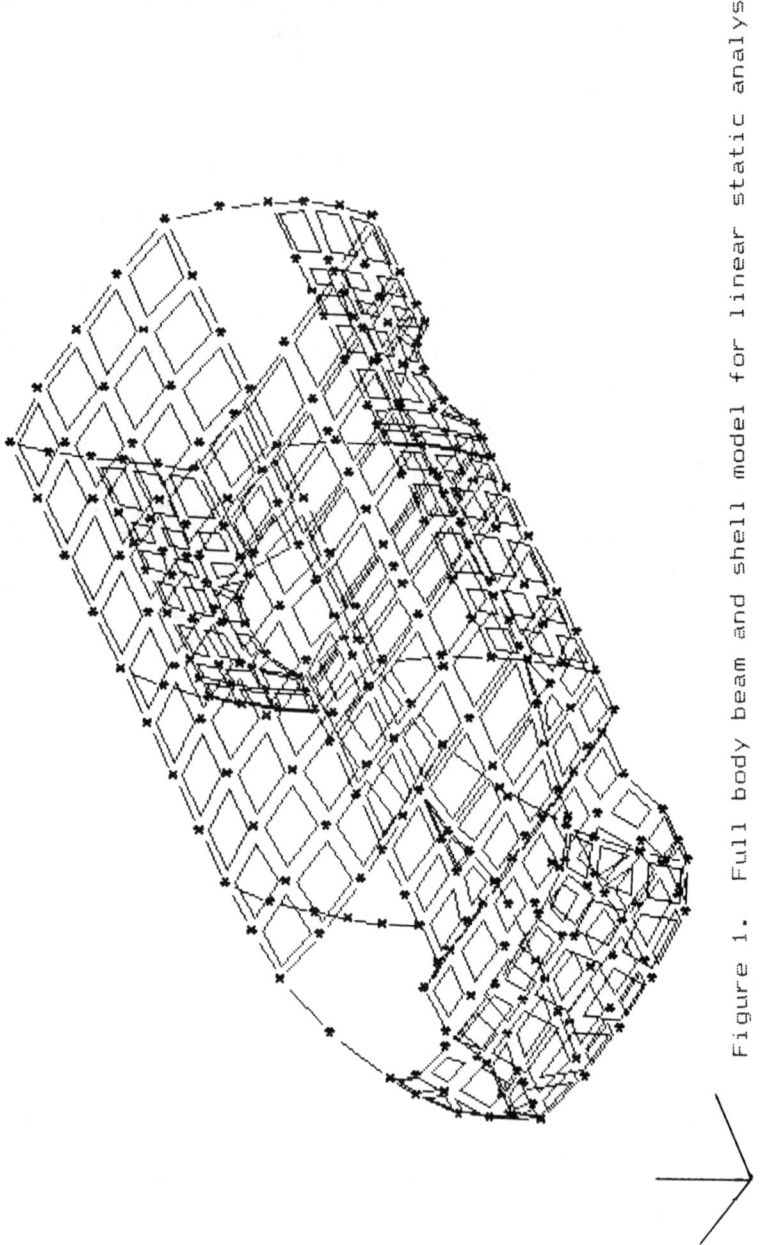

Figure 1. Full body beam and shell model for linear static analysis.

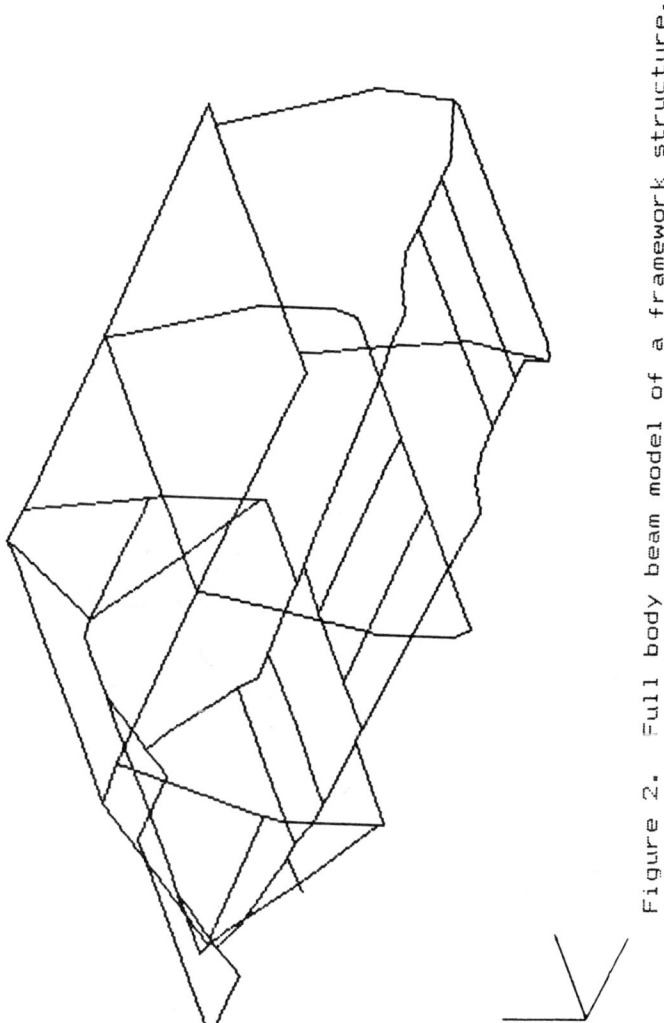

Figure 2. Full body beam model of a framework structure.

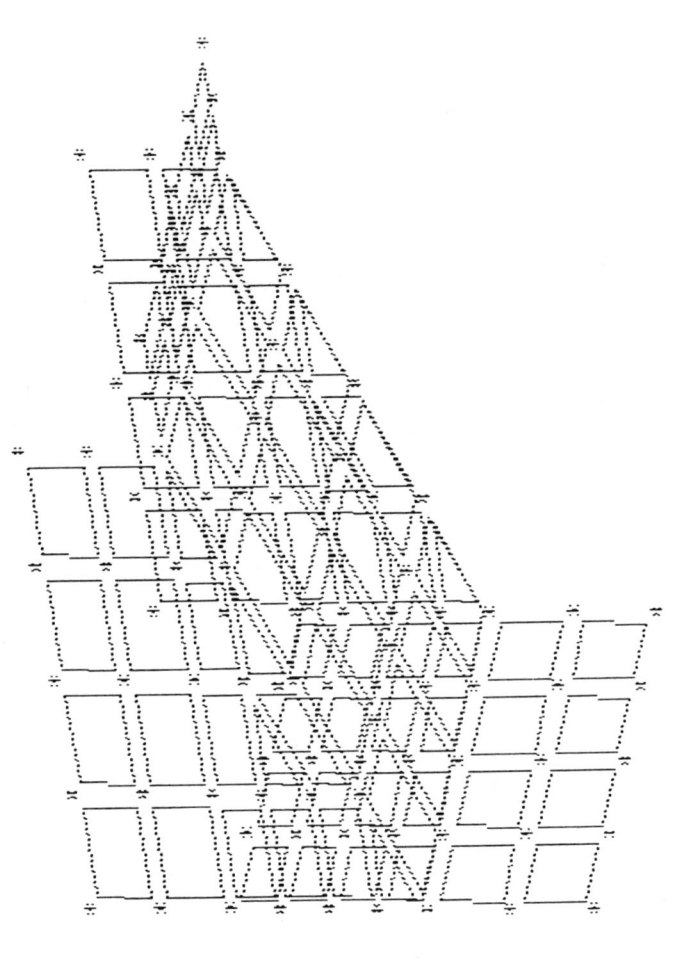

Figure 3. Detailed shell model of a mounting bracket.

For similar reasons to those highlighted in discussion of linear static analysis, Nastran is also a good choice for this type of analysis.

Processes of validating the model must be similar in this case to the linear static case by nature of the two types of investigation. Any validation of the model must be based on joint and component stiffness data, preferably derived experimentally once again.

Dynamic analysis of components or sub-assemblies in relation to particular concerns such as noise and vibration isolation is better carried out in more detail.

As with linear static analyses, most of the dynamic work carried out, consisting largely of N.V.H. development, is targeted by client standards with a view to increased ride comfort and minimisation of noise and vibration, rather than by legal requirements.

NON-LINEAR STATIC ANALYSIS

This category of analysis is particularly challenging. It can be used to model for many requirements of both European and Federal automotive markets, largely in terms of safety engineering. Legislative requirements of the Federal market in particular are stringent where safety standards are concerned. Typical areas of analysis in this field are: roof crush; side door intrusion and occupant restraint systems. The majority of regulations specify static or quasi-static loading conditions representing dynamic situations. These conditions can very often be successfully modelled using large displacement finite element analysis. Abaqus as an analysis package is suited to modelling this type of condition and can produce workable solutions in most instances.

Detailed approach

Non-linear analysis of this nature invariably requires an incremental approach. This iterative solution method by necessity requires a powerful processing unit for models of even moderate size and is often very expensive in terms of central processor usage. In achieving a workable solution this aspect must be considered and will ultimately dictate allowable model size. However, by nature of the large displacement algorithms involved, solution accuracy is also highly dependent on model size. If the computing facility available restricts effective modelling to such an extent that the resulting model is too coarse to represent the modelled condition with any degree of correctness, then the approach is not viable. This poses an interesting problem for a growing bureau. A compromise solution must be sought in order that analysis of this nature may ultimately be carried out satisfactorily.

Whereas approximations and assumptions can be made with a good degree of confidence in linear static and dynamic analysis to reduce model size and job time as already discussed, greater care still is required when attempting to minimize model size for non-linear analysis. Discrepancies introduced as a result of poor assumptions in the first instance can be magnified with each iteration to the extent that the final solution is meaningless. In addition, over-reduction of mesh size to reduce run times can instigate solution convergence difficulties well before the natural finish of a large displacement analysis such as roof crush over five inches or side door intrusion over eighteen inches. Coarse meshes can result in high individual element strains locally and the structural element formulations determine that in order to achieve convergence at these levels in the hope of completing the analysis, unrealistically wide tolerance bands must sometimes be specified.

Bearing these limitations in mind, both individual components and complete substructures can be successfully modelled with care.

Modelling of complete substructures   Considering roof crush as an example, simple respresentation of Pillars, Headers and Cant rails with beam elements and body panels with shell elements in a similar manner to the linear static and dynamic approaches discussed earlier can provide a useful solution. A roof crush model generated in this way is shown in fig 4. The criteria for economising assumptions are largely different for collapse analysis though. Collapse properties of sections have to be carefully established to ensure correct representation as beams. This may be achieved ideally by test procedures or, in the absence of test data, by detailed section analysis. Joint conditions must be fully understood to establish whether mid-section or joint failure will signal the mode of collapse.

COMPUTER OPTIMISATION OF VEHICLE STRUCTURES 181

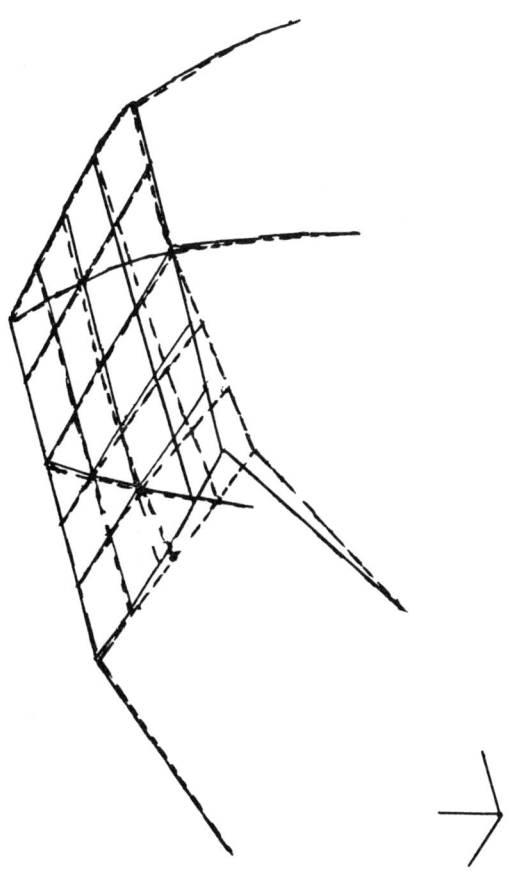

Figure 4. Beam and shell roof crush model showing deformed shape.

A similar approach can be adopted to model side door intrusion, although the lower door sections, if of sheet steel construction, do not usually lend themselves to beam representation as readily. For the purpose of collapse though, section analysis and test procedures provide sufficient data to establish equivalent beam properties. An example of this type of model is shown in fig 5.

Models of this nature of around 300-500 degrees of freedom have been found to give best results on the in-house computer system at I.A.D.. Whilst the use of a multi-noded or intensely powerful machine is obviously preferable, placing far less restriction on model detail, usable results can be obtained on other systems within limited time and budget constraints with the techniques discussed.

Component modelling for absolute performance and for input to further analyses Non-linear static analysis of components or small sub-assemblies can be undertaken in more detail than the larger regions discussed above whilst remaining within the bounds of the machine capabilities. Collapse behaviour of local sections can usually be determined with a good degree of confidence in this way.

Results obtained from these analyses may be useful in their own right, depending on the component being analysed, or can form the basis of input for further investigation. Where component testing is not possible for reasons of time or budget, small sub-assemblies can be investigated for collapse in this way. For example, a section of a longitudinal member may be modelled completely with shell elements to determine it's static collapse properties (fig 6) as a basis for complete vehicle crash simulation using a mathematical mass/spring/damper modelling approach described further on. This is not ideal on two counts in that physical testing will always instil a higher degree of confidence and more critically that crash simulation must consider the dynamic collapse behaviour of the individual sections comprising the whole vehicle if final representation is to be faithful.

For simple static crush of a longitudinal as in this case, the bulk of local dynamic considerations can generally be attributed to strain rate hardening effects. In this event, existing experimental data provides a fairly stable means of

COMPUTER OPTIMISATION OF VEHICLE STRUCTURES 183

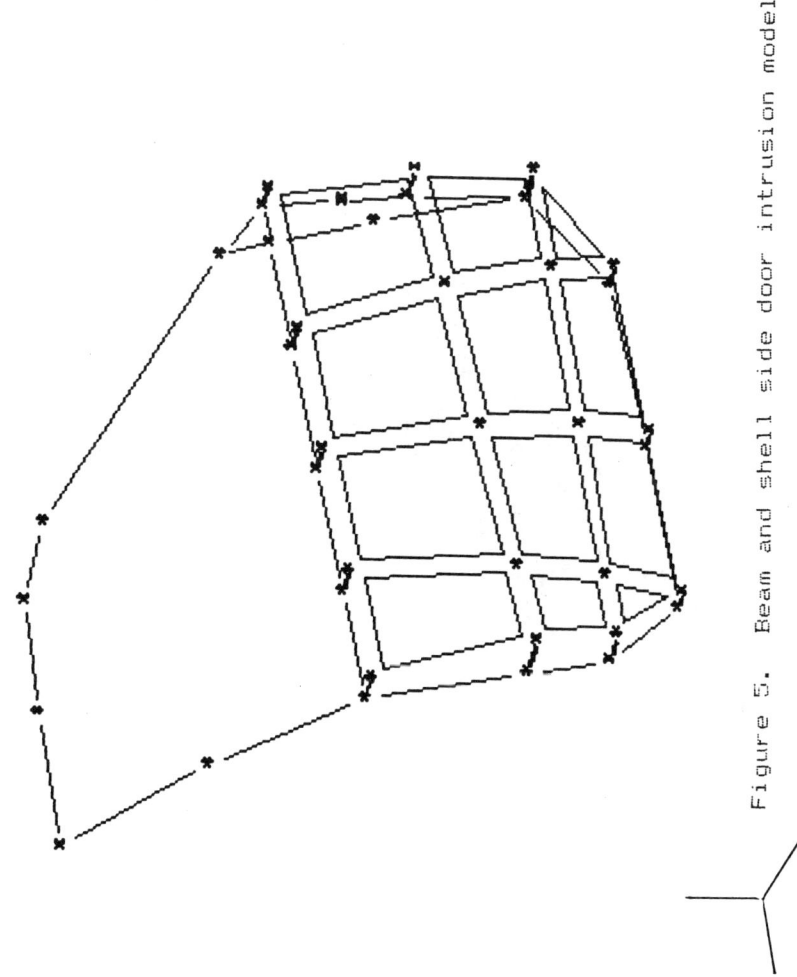

Figure 5. Beam and shell side door intrusion model.

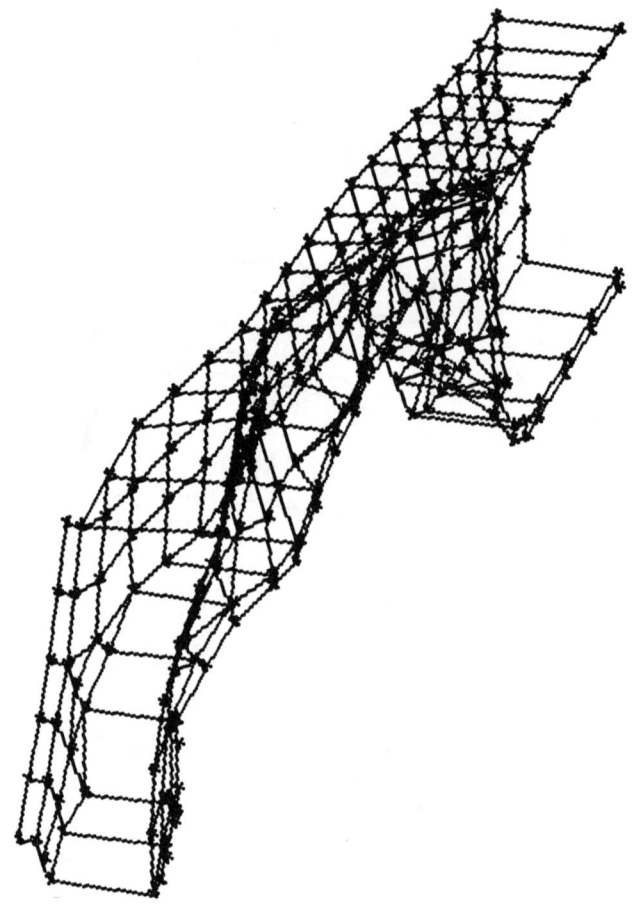

Figure 6. Detailed shell model of a front longitudinal.

COMPUTER OPTIMISATION OF VEHICLE STRUCTURES

factoring for this phenomena, giving rise to a usable approach in general terms.

NON-LINEAR DYNAMIC ANALYSIS

In concept, full vehicle dynamic crash analysis can be representatively modelled with this approach. This is probably the most relevant application of this type of analysis to the automotive work undertaken by the Structural Engineering Group at I.A.D.. Abaqus in particular is ideally suited to setting up structural models for this purpose with initial conditions of velocity and mass distribution and analysis conditions of constraint and accelerations precisely represented. However, as with the non-linear static approach, machine size places strict limitations on model size. The modelling considerations of the static case still apply and the limitations of element formulations are usually prohibitive in terms of crash behaviour of a complete vehicle over a full crash pulse. A more effective means of complete vehicle crash behaviour prediction within the current confines of this bureau has been established and is discussed in later sections.

Component modelling
As with the non-linear static analysis of body components, non-linear dynamic analysis can also be used to model components and small sub-assemblies to establish collapse characteristics in the absence of the facility to test. Relatively detailed models can be constructed and run on the in-house system as an alternative to static analysis. This approach allows exact input of kinematic conditions and can take account of dynamic effects more precisely, provided that they can be quantified in terms of component part behaviour in the whole vehicle. It is not always a simple matter to define precisely the dynamic loading conditions imposed on a front longitudinal rail for example during a barrier impact. In many instances factored non-linear static component analysis is of more practical use, but for a well specified dynamic condition this approach would be prefered.

MATHEMATICAL MODELLING

Vehicle crash simulation
Crash simulation is an increasingly important area of automotive analysis as the emphasis on vehicle safety continues to grow. It is also one of the

most difficult areas of analysis in the general field of automotive structures. As discussed in the previous sections, representation of full vehicles with structural elements for kinematic finite element analysis is generally impractical and out of reach of a growing contract design bureau.

As an extremely economical alternative in terms of computing and contract time, a lumped mass/spring/damper model can be generated and analysed using a differential equation solver package. Several systems are available at a fraction of the cost of large commercial finite element packages such as Abaqus and Nastran. The particular system used at I.A.D. for this analysis is A.C.S.L. (Advanced Continuous Simulations language). Being developed expressly for the purpose of modelling systems described by time dependent, non-linear differential equations and/or transfer functions, it is well suited to this application and particularly attractive in that it can be run on a desk-top micro computer system.

In establishing input data for component non-linear spring behaviour, test procedures are essential. Dynamic, or more usually static, crush tests of components or sub-assemblies, longitudinal members for example, provide the spring data necessary to build a picture of the whole vehicle. Where test data is unattainable, detailed non-linear modelling of important regions can be undertaken to obtain characteristics using the methods described earlier.

With the use of this approach, structures can be theoretically optimized for impact behaviour by iterative investigations, hopefully giving rise to good crash behaviour in initial prototype tests. Information output from A.C.S.L can be displayed visually in the form of displacement, velocity and acceleration verses time plots for individual or combined specified vehicle components. A schematic representation of a model for front end barrier impact is shown in fig 7 and typical output traces are shown in figs 8,9 and 10.

In the event of further analysis of initially tested vehicles, data collected from test vehicle instrumentation is invaluable in assuring that secondary analysis and subsequent testing follow a convergent path.

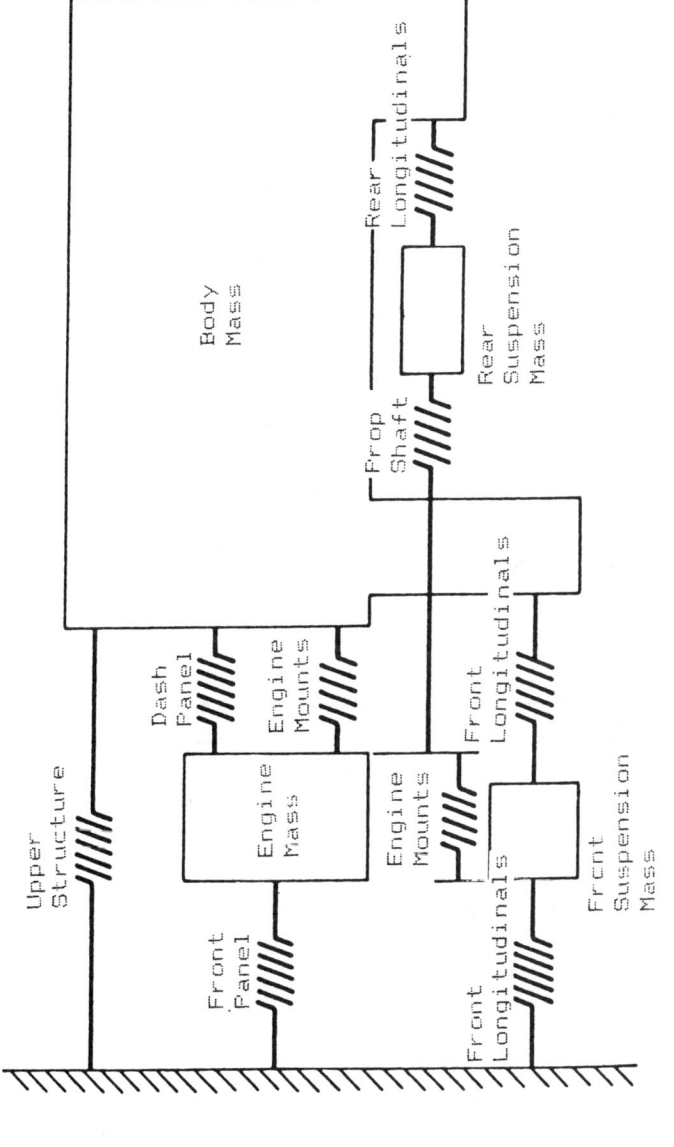

Figure 7. Schematic layout of mass/spring/damper crash simulation model.

188 COMPUTER OPTIMISATION OF VEHICLE STRUCTURES

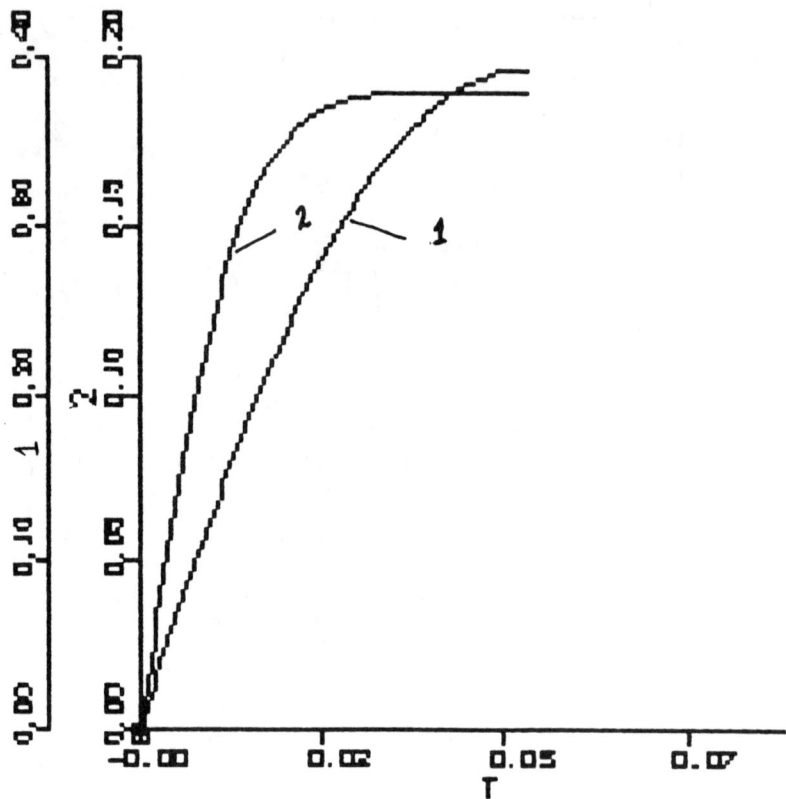

FRONT CRASH SIMULATION

Displacement - time

1 = Body Displacement

2 = Engine Displacement

Velocity, V = 30 mph (13.4 M/S)

Figure 8. Displacement v time output from A.C.S.L.

COMPUTER OPTIMISATION OF VEHICLE STRUCTURES 189

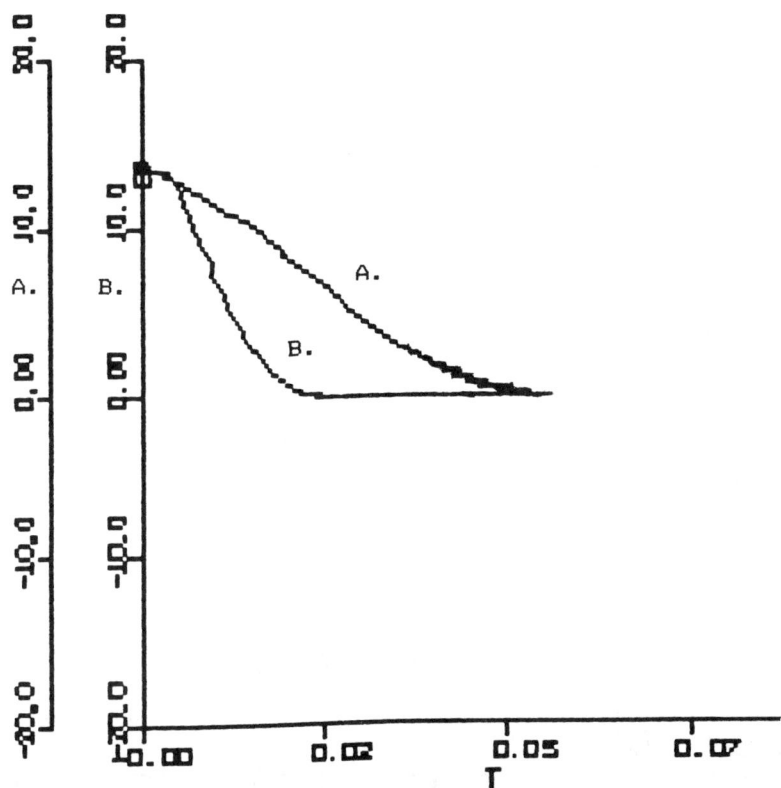

FRONT CRASH SIMULATION

Velocity - time (M/SEC - SEC)

A. = Body velocity

B. = Engine Velocity

Velocity, V = 30 mph (13.4 m/s)

Figure 9. Velocity v time output from A.C.S.L.

COMPUTER OPTIMISATION OF VEHICLE STRUCTURES

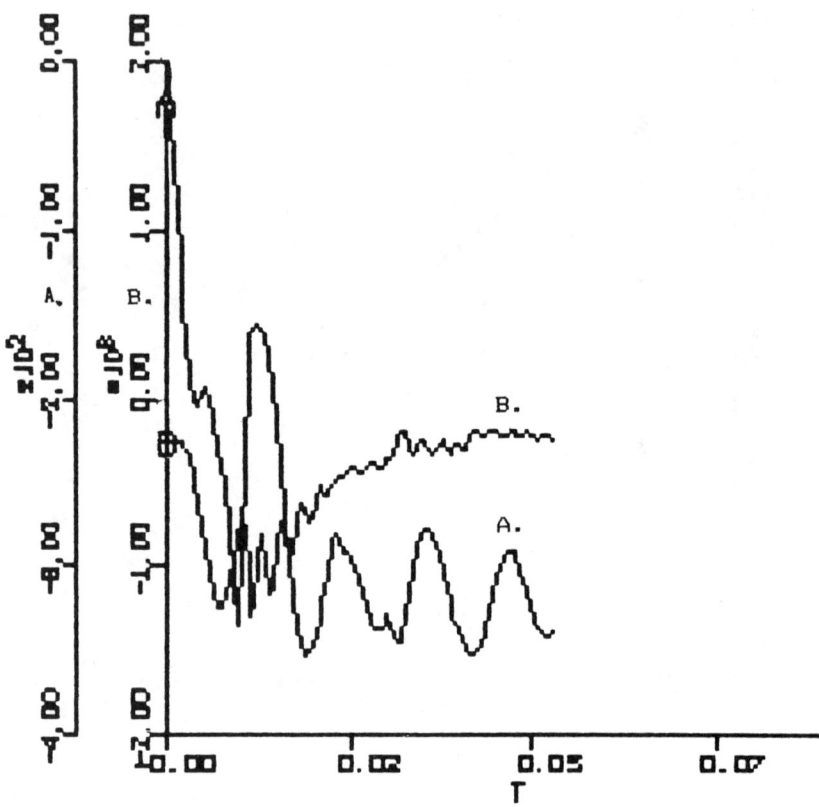

FRONT CRASH SIMULATION

Acceleration - time (M/SEC^2 - SEC)

A. = Body Acceleration

B. - Engine Acceleration

Velocity, V = 30 mph (13.4 m/s)

Figure 10. Acceleration v time output from A.C.S.L.

OVERVIEW

For a contract design bureau to remain competitive it must be flexible in it's activities. Although the accent of this paper is on optimization of structural activities to achieve the best compromise between prefered analysis techniques and time and budget constraints, this criterion must not govern all work undertaken. For particular client requirements of detailed investigation rather than basic production vehicle analysis, facilities and expertise must be accessible. The opportunity to undertake detailed investigative analysis provides an excellent means of increasing knowledge and expertise within the bureau and of embellishing the central core of information for subsequent analyses along the lines discussed here.

The P-Version of the Finite Element Method in Gear Teeth Stress Analysis

A. Pidello(*), F.A. Raffa(**), P.P. Strona(*)
(*) *Centro Ricerche Fiat, Orbassano (Torino), Italy*
(**) *Dipartimento di Meccanica, Politecnico di Torino, Italy*

INTRODUCTION

The aim of this paper is the evaluation of the capabilities of the p-version of the Finite Element Method with hierarchical shape functions, in order to calculate the maximum tensile stress in helical gear teeth by utilizing 3D models.

Firstly a general review of numerical methods applied to gear teeth calculations is presented: the Boundary Element Method (BEM), the h-version and the p-version of the Finite Element Method (FEM) are considered. A comparison of their capabilities is carried out in the case of the analysis of a spur gear tooth; the mathematical models requirements and the results accuracy are investigated. The main features of the p-version of the Finite Element Method and their implications in the analysis procedures are explained.

Following the above general considerations the paper is focused on the problem of the calculation of the maximum tensile stress in a helical gear tooth by utilizing the FIESTA code. A 3D model of a single helical gear tooth is presented and the results of the analysis performed in several load conditions are shown.

GENERAL CONSIDERATIONS

In the static stress analysis of a gear tooth the main objective is the determination of the maximum tensile stress in the bottom land. This value is particularly important in order to obtain both correct design and reliable fatigue life prediction.

Conventional methods, originally conceived to perform hand or desk calculator computations, are still applied for the solution of this problem, but generally they do not lead to a proper simulation of the elastic behaviour of the gear tooth, mainly because of the simplifying hypotheses on which they are based and of the impossibility of taking into account the actual load distribution among several teeth simultaneously in contact.

Nowadays, due to the great development of numerical methods and corresponding computer codes, the stress analysis of a gear tooth can be favourably dealt with, there being no need to introduce limiting, simplifying hypotheses.

Except for the case of a spur gear, the stress analysis of a gear tooth requires the definition of a 3D model. The 3D modelling using the classical finite elements is quite a demanding task. However, a great research effort has been produced in recent years, which has lead to both better utilization of existing codes, through the use of suitable pre and post-processor programs and development of new numerical techniques in order to eliminate the shortcomings of the usual finite elements. As for the latter factor, the main alternatives available are BEM[1] and the p-version of FEM[2].

The BEM valuation in gear teeth stress analysis was performed mainly in 2D applications and some of the most significant results are presented in previous works; the suitability and the advantages of the BEM in gear teeth calculations were proved in comparison with both conventional methods[3] and the h-version of FEM[4,5]. In Figs. 1 and 2 a thick and regular FEM mesh of the transverse section of a spur gear tooth and the corresponding BEM mesh are shown; the results obtained are compared in Fig. 3. It is worth noticing that NASTRAN values must be extrapolated in order to determine the peak stress value, while the BEM code can compute it directly.

Successively, the stress analysis of helical gear teeth was faced and the BEM approach was firstly adopted, due to the reliability of the results obtained in 2D analysis. From a theoretical point of view, the BEM shows in 3D problems the same advantages as in 2D analysis. However, some computations performed with constant and quadratic elements and information on 3D BEM analysis in similar kinds of problem[6] lead to the consideration that in 3D analysis the importance of full and non-symmetric influence coefficients matrices is more considerable than in 2D applications and can prove to be a very limiting factor, unless substructuring techniques are adopted. As a consequence, the need of more sophisticated software arises, which is not widely available.

On the other side, in a 3D analysis of gear stress peak, the h-version of FEM is less efficient than in the 2D problem. The use of 20 nodes solid elements is requested in order to accurately describe the tooth profile and a thick mesh must be

resulting from a parametric investigation that took into account both geometrical and polynomial selection aspects, is shown.

From the geometrical point of view, the tooth profile model entails the description of both a trochoid and an involute curve. The trochoid region of the tooth profile was described according to successive approximations; in Fig. 5 the approximation obtained with a single parabola is presented, which proved to be not acceptable. In Figs. 6a-b and 7a-b the transverse section and the corresponding bottom land shapes are shown, which were obtained by utilizing 2 and 4 quadratic elements respectively. The judgement of the computations results obtained with the above models, also considering that the precision of the bottom land approximation must be of the same order as the tooling tolerance of the gear, lead to the choice of the model of Fig. 7a. As far as the involute profile is concerned, the use of two quadratic curves, as shown in both Figs. 6a and 7a, proved satisfactory.

After describing the geometrical shape of the gear tooth, the problem was tackled of selecting the optimal polynomial distribution on the elements. This was done by taking into account six different polynomial patterns, according to the criterion of increasing the number of degrees of freedom in the bottom land region. In Table 1 the data relevant to the six models are presented; models A1 and A2 correspond to uniform polynomial distribution and were used as starting points for the successive meshes; models B1 and B2 correspond to improved polynomial distributions, the difference between them being the maximum polynomial level on the element (3 for B1 and 4 for B2); the same difference exists between models C1 and C2. The transverse section of models B1, B2 and C1, C2 are given in Figs. 8 and 9 respectively.

Results
The results of the 3D analysis are shown in Table 2 and compared with the BEM results obtained in the corresponding 2D analysis of the same gear tooth. The comparison is carried out in terms of both components of the stress field (σ_x, σ_y) and principal tensile stress (σ_1); σ_{xmax}, σ_{ymax} and σ_{1max}^* refer to the maximum stress values in the whole bottom land region, their occurrence points being therefore independent of each other. As a result of the above comparison, model B2 proved to be the best one. However, in order to reduce the dimension of the problem, still obtaining accurate results, models C1 and C2 were considered, which lead to both good agreement with BEM results and considerably smaller number of degrees of freedom. Model C2 was finally chosen as the standard 3D model of the gear tooth. Isostress curves for B2 and C2 models are shown in Fig. 10.

defined in the bottom land region to achieve good results. Moreover, due to the load inclination along the tooth flank, nodes must be placed in particular positions and this makes heavier and more complicated the definition of a proper mesh.

Another methodology, theoretically suitable to 3D analysis, is the p-version of FEM, whose more interesting features can be summarized as follows[7-9]:

- the interpolation functions, which describe the displacement field, are polynomials of hierarchically increasing order;

- the number of the interpolation functions in each element can be progressively increased (this process is called p-convergence process);

- p-convergent finite elements are intrinsecally suited to adaptive procedure, i.e. they have an "a posteriori" error valuation capability.

From the practical point of view, the above considerations imply that the p-version FEM mesh is fixed, no need arising to change it in order to obtain more reliable results. The user's effort can be therefore focused only on the correct geometrical approximation of the component; moreover, it becomes possible to control the results precision by performing a few successive analyses with polynomials of increasing order. These properties make the p-version FEM particularly interesting in the study of 3D problems. In fact, convergence analysis utilizing either BEM or h-version FEM would require the definition of models with successively increased number of elements. On the contrary, p-convergent FEM allows the performance of successive computations without demanding any further user's effort.

The validation of the p-version FEM in 3D gear teeth analysis was carried out through a 3D spur gear model; in this case, the stress field can be compared with the corresponding results of the 2D analysis previously performed by using BEM. By means of a parametric investigation, a standard mesh was defined and successively applied to the helical gear tooth.

The computations were performed by utilizing the FIESTA code, developed by ISMES. Details on the main capabilities of this code can be found in literature[10,11].

SPUR GEAR TOOTH ANALYSIS

Models description
A spur gear tooth subjected to normal forces uniformly distributed along its flank was considered, the total applied load being equal to 100 Kg. In Fig. 4, the final 3D model,

HELICAL GEAR TOOTH

In the analysis of a helical gear tooth, as a consequence of the previous investigation on the spur gear tooth, the component discretization was carried out in quite a straightforward way.

Three load conditions were considered, corresponding to different load application curves and therefore to different positions on the arc of contact. A total load of 100 Kg, uniformly distributed on each load line, was applied.

A 3D model having the same number of degrees of freedom and the same polynomial distribution as model C2 was defined. The three models corresponding to the different load cases and the relevant isostress curves in the bottom land region are shown in Figs. 11, 12 and 13.

CONCLUSIONS

From the above analysis and from the comparison of the results obtained by utilizing the p-version of FEM and the BEM, the conclusion can be drawn that the p-version of FEM and in particular FIESTA code are suitable to determine the stress distribution in the gear teeth bottom land by means of 3D models.

It is worth stressing the point that in the 3D model of a single tooth few elements are sufficient in order to calculate quite exactly the peak stress value in the bottom land. It would therefore be possible to build a complete 3D model with two, three or four pinion and gear teeth simultaneously in contact. In this way the actual load distribution among the teeth and the corresponding stress field would be determined for any position in the arc of contact.

The p-version FEM approach presented in this paper is general, so that it is possible to analyse mechanical components of different solid geometrical shape, by means of the same procedure.

REFERENCES

1. Brebbia C.A. Telles J.F.C. and Wrobel L.C. (1984). Boundary Element Techniques, Springer-Verlag. Berlin and New York.

2. Zienkiewicz O.C. and Morgan K. (1983). Finite Elements and Approximation, John Wiley & Sons. Toronto and New York.

3. Alemanni M. Bertoglio S. and Strona P.P. (1981). B.E.M. in Gear Teeth Stress Analysis: Comparison with Classical Methods, pp. II-177 to II-182, Proceedings of the Int. Symp. on Gearing & Power Transmission, Tokio, Japan, 1981.

4. Strona P.P. (1984). The Boundary Element Method in the Optimization Procedures of Transmissions, Proceedings of the Int. Meeting on Optimization Problems in Engineering, Cassino, Italy, 1984 (in Italian).

5. Wanderlingh A.I. (1985). Comparison of Boundary Element and Finite Element Methods for Linear Stress Analysis-Technical Program Results, pp. 7-33 to 7-52, Proceedings of the 7th Int. Conf. on Boundary Element Methods, Como, Italy, 1985.

6. Bauer W. and Svoboda M. (1985). Industrial Application of the Three Dimensional Boundary Element Method (BEM) Exemplified Through the BE-Programmsystem DBETSY-3D, pp. 14-3 to 14-20, Proceedings of the 7th Int. Conf. on the Boundary Element Methods, Como, Italy, 1985.

7. Peano A.G. (1976). Hierarchies of Conforming Finite Elements for Plane Elasticity and Plate Bending, Comp. Maths. with Appls., Vol.2, pp. 211-224.

8. Peano et al. (1979). Adaptive Approximations in Finite Element Structural Analysis, Computers and Structures, Vol.10, pp. 333-342.

9. Peano A.G. (1978). Energy Gradient Technique for Adaptive Finite Element Analysis, Proceedings of the 15th Annual Meeting of the Soc. of Engng. Science, Gainesville, USA, 1978.

10. FIESTA User Manual, Vols. I-II, ISMES-Istituto Sperimentale Modelli e Strutture, Bergamo, Italy.

11. Angeloni P. et al. (1985). Accuracy Assessment by Finite Element p-Version Software, Proceedings of the 4th Int. Conf. on Engineering Software, London, U.K., 1985.

GEAR TEETH STRESS ANALYSIS 199

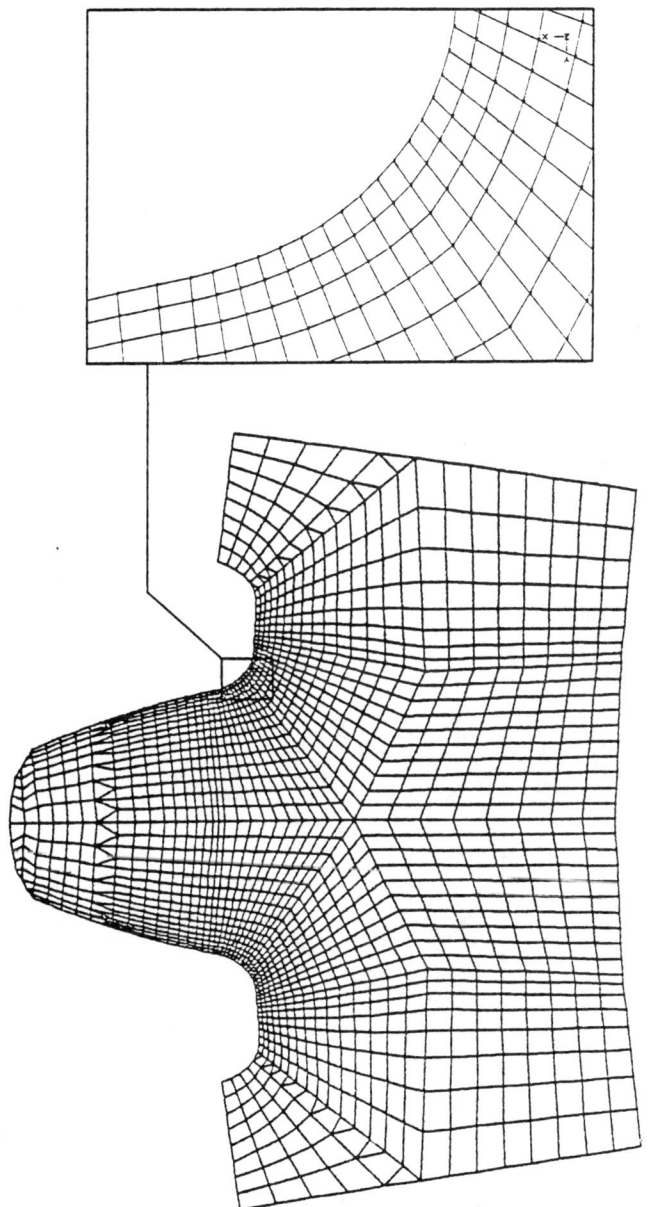

Figure 1 - Spur Gear NASTRAN Model (FEM)

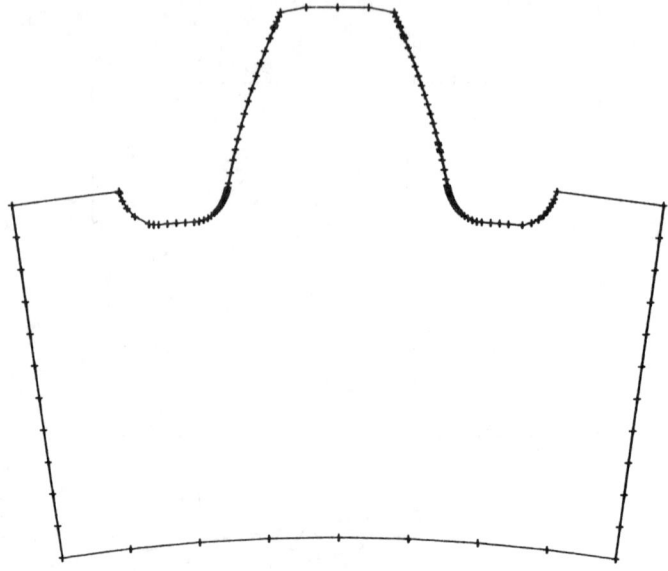

Figure 2 - Spur Gear BEM Model

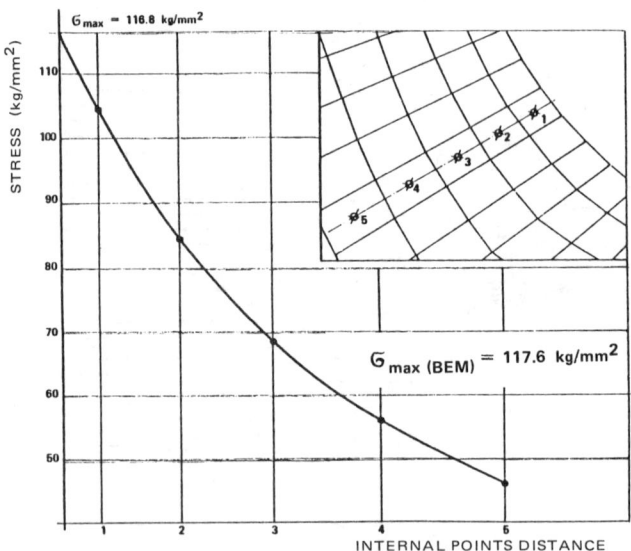

Figure 3 - Spur Gear Stress Results

GEAR TEETH STRESS ANALYSIS 201

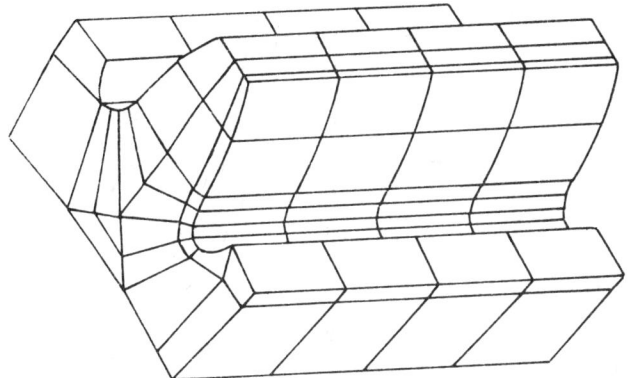

Figure 4 - Spur Gear FIESTA 3D Model   (FEM p-version)

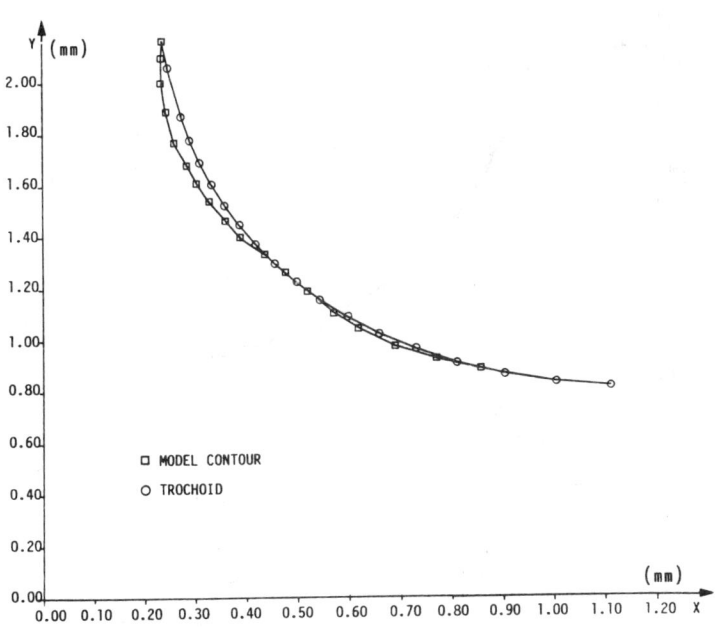

Figure 5 - Bottom Land Geometrical Shape Approximation

202 GEAR TEETH STRESS ANALYSIS

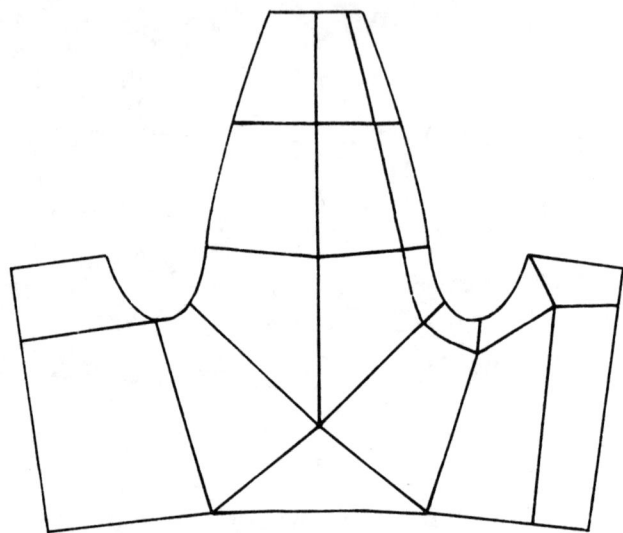

Figure 6a - Transverse Section Mesh 1

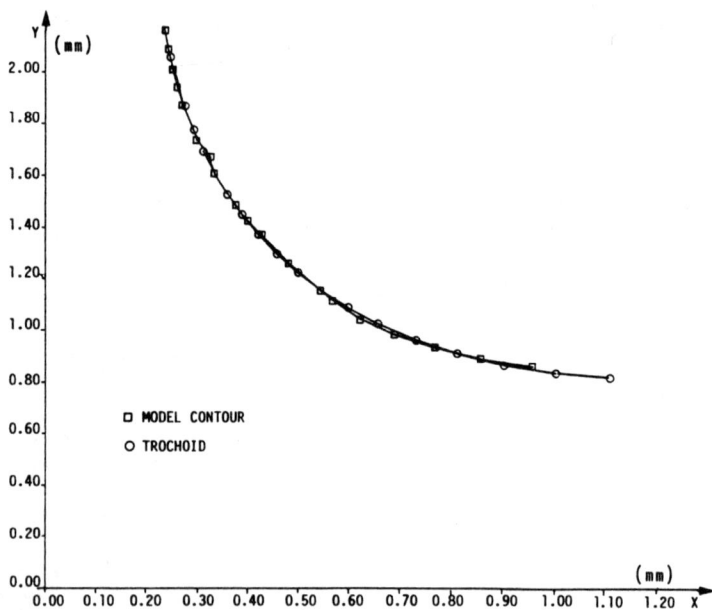

Figure 6b - Bottom Land Geometrical Shape Approximation (Mesh 1)

GEAR TEETH STRESS ANALYSIS 203

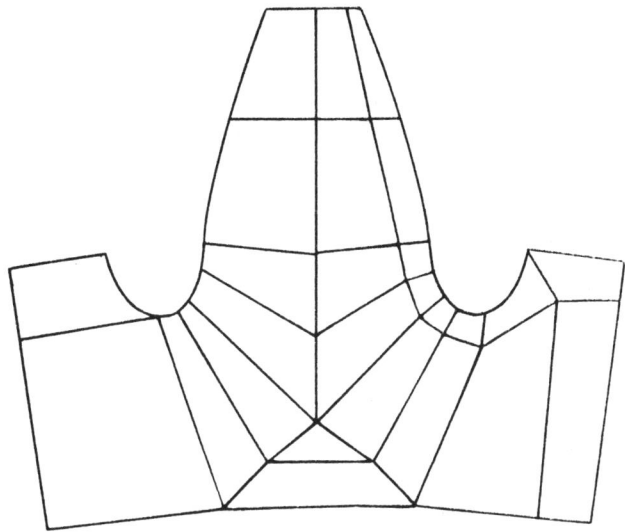

Figure 7a - Transverse Section Mesh 2

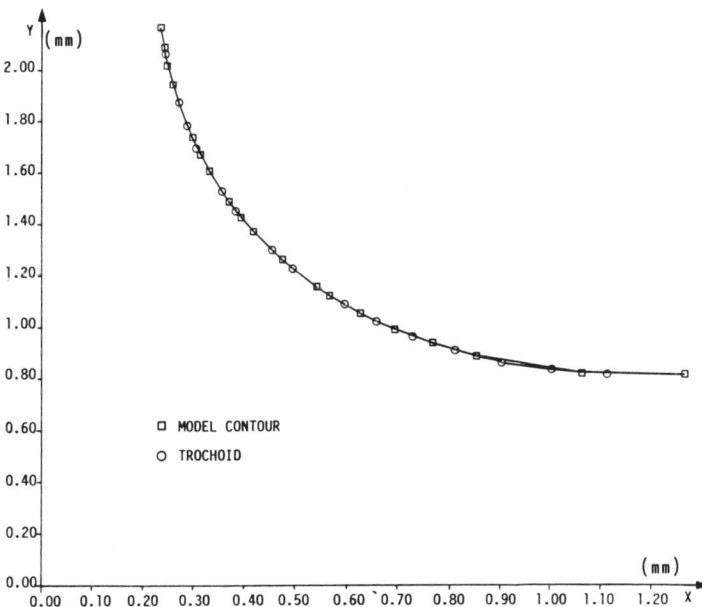

Figure 7b - Bottom Land Geometrical Shape Approximation (Mesh 2)

Model	D.o.f.	Polynomial distribution
A1	501	p-level 1 in the whole model
A2	1667	p-level 2 in the whole model
B1	3140	p-level max = 3 fig. 8
B2	4289	p-level max = 4 fig. 8
C1	2567	p-level max = 3 fig. 9
C2	2996	p-level max = 4 fig. 9

Table 1

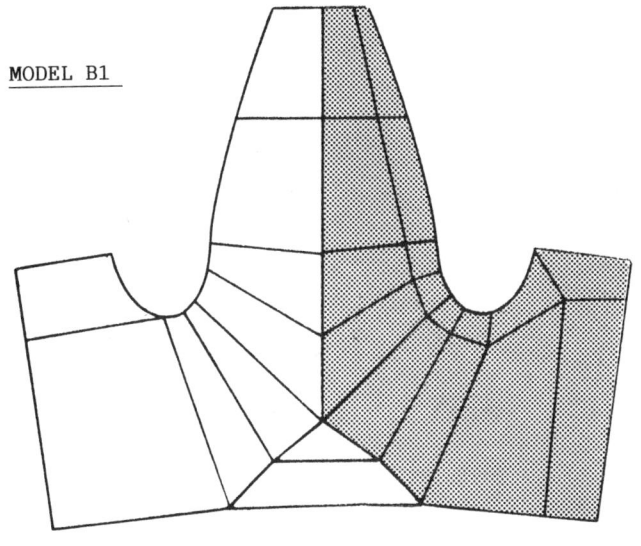

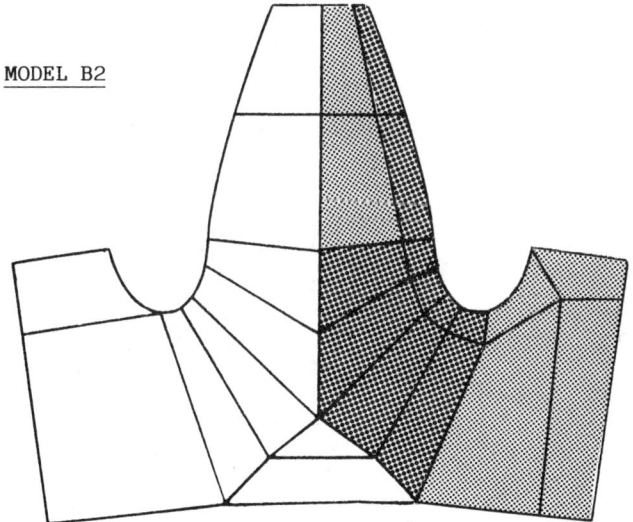

Figure 8 – Selected Polynomial Distributions

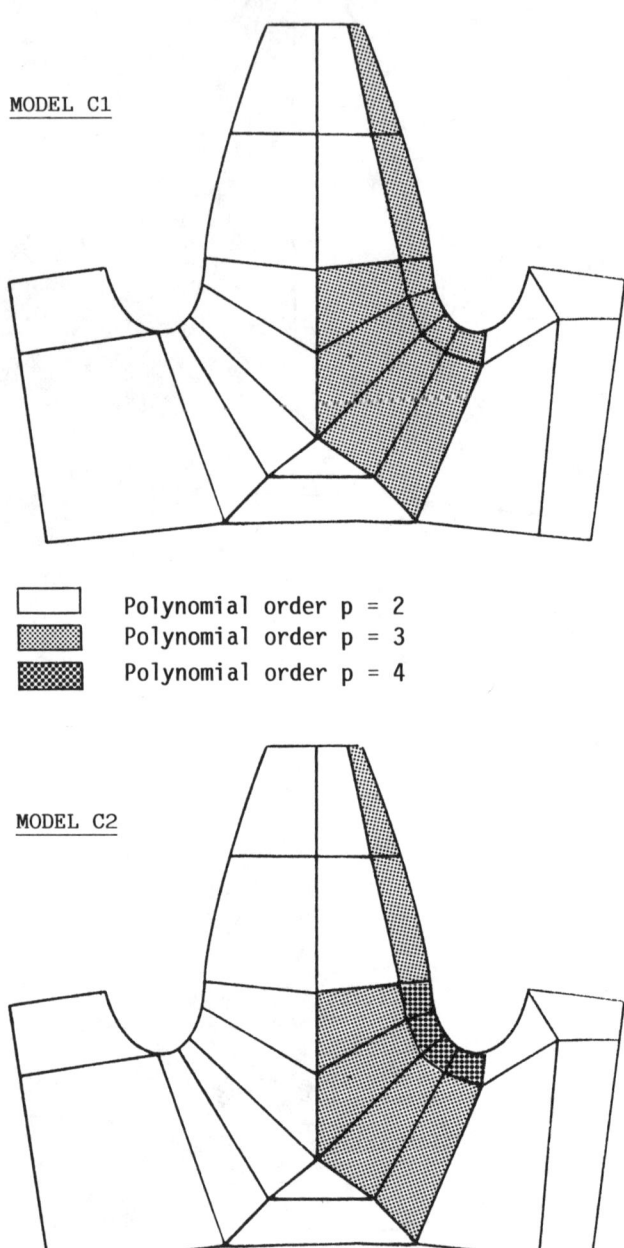

Figure 9 - Selected Polynomial Distributions

GEAR TEETH STRESS ANALYSIS 207

	σ_x max	$\Delta\sigma_x$ %	σ_y max	$\Delta\sigma_y$ %	σ_1^* max	$\Delta\sigma_1^*$ %	σ_x^*	$\Delta\sigma_x^*$ %	σ_y^*	$\Delta\sigma_y^*$ %
A1	67.4	-5.0 %	43.2	-20.7 %	82.0	-5.4 %	62.0	4.2 %	38.0	5.5 %
A2	76.2	7.5 %	50.0	-8.2 %	90.2	4.0 %	64.0	7.5 %	33.5	-7.0 %
B1	71.0	<0.5 %	53.5	-1.8 %	90.0	3.8 %	59.5	<0.1 %	37.0	3.0 %
B2	70.8	<0.1 %	54.0	-1.0 %	86.5	-0.2 %	59.5	<0.1 %	35.9	-0.3 %
C1	72.0	1.6 %	50.5	-7.3 %	91.0	5.0 %	60.0	1.0 %	37.5	4.2 %
C2	70.0	-1.2 %	52.2	-4.2 %	90.0	3.8 %	59.5	0.1 %	35.7	-0.8 %
BEM	70.8	---	54.5	---	86.7	---	59.5	---	36.0	---

$$\Delta\sigma_x \% = \frac{\sigma_x - \sigma_{x\,BEM}}{\sigma_{x\,BEM}} \times 100 \qquad \Delta\sigma_y \% = \frac{\sigma_y - \sigma_{y\,BEM}}{\sigma_{y\,BEM}} \times 100 \qquad \Delta\sigma_1^* \% = \frac{\sigma_1 - \sigma_{1\,BEM}}{\sigma_{1\,BEM}} \times 100$$

$$\Delta\sigma_x^* \% = \frac{\sigma_x^* - \sigma_{x\,BEM}^*}{\sigma_{x\,BEM}^*} \times 100 \qquad \Delta\sigma_y^* \% = \frac{\sigma_y^* - \sigma_{y\,BEM}^*}{\sigma_{y\,BEM}^*} \times 100$$

$\sigma_x^* = \sigma_x$ in the point where $\sigma_1 = \sigma_1^*$ max
$\sigma_y^* = \sigma_y$ in the point where $\sigma_1 = \sigma_1^*$ max

Table 2 - Stress Results

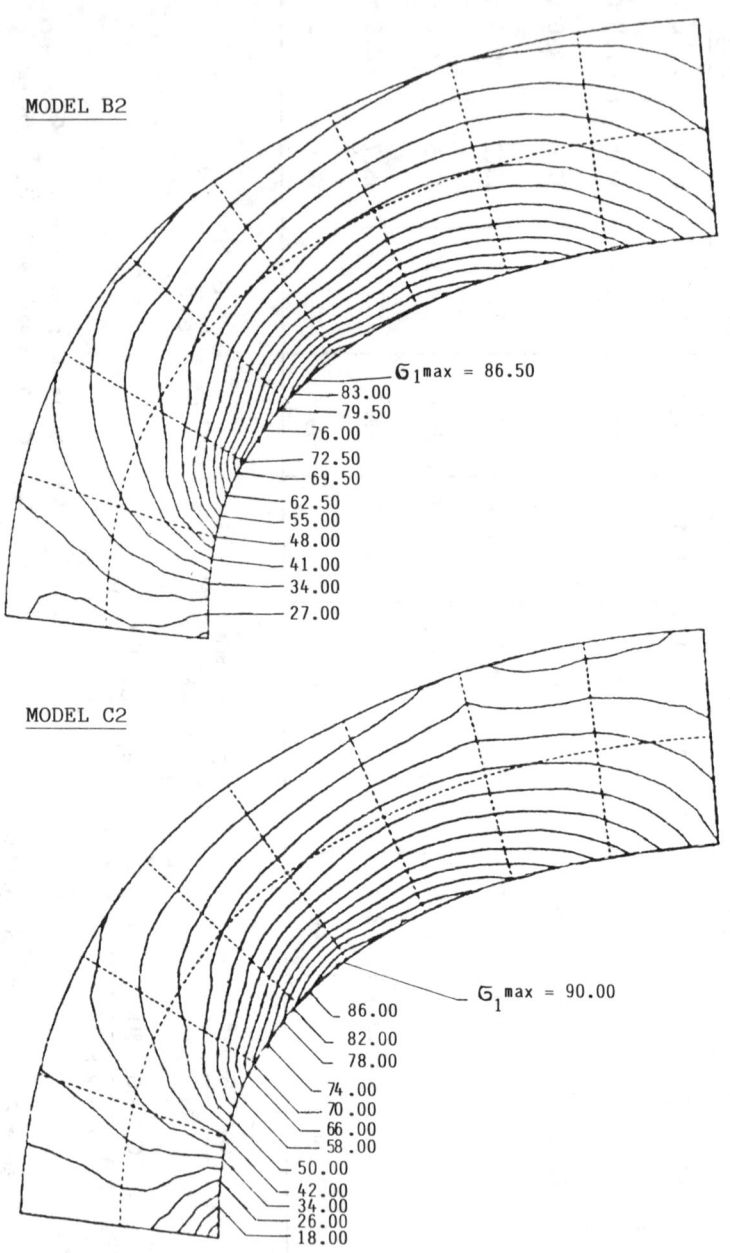

Figure 10 – Spur Gear Middle Transverse Section
Bottom Land Detail: σ_1 Isostress (kg/mm^2)

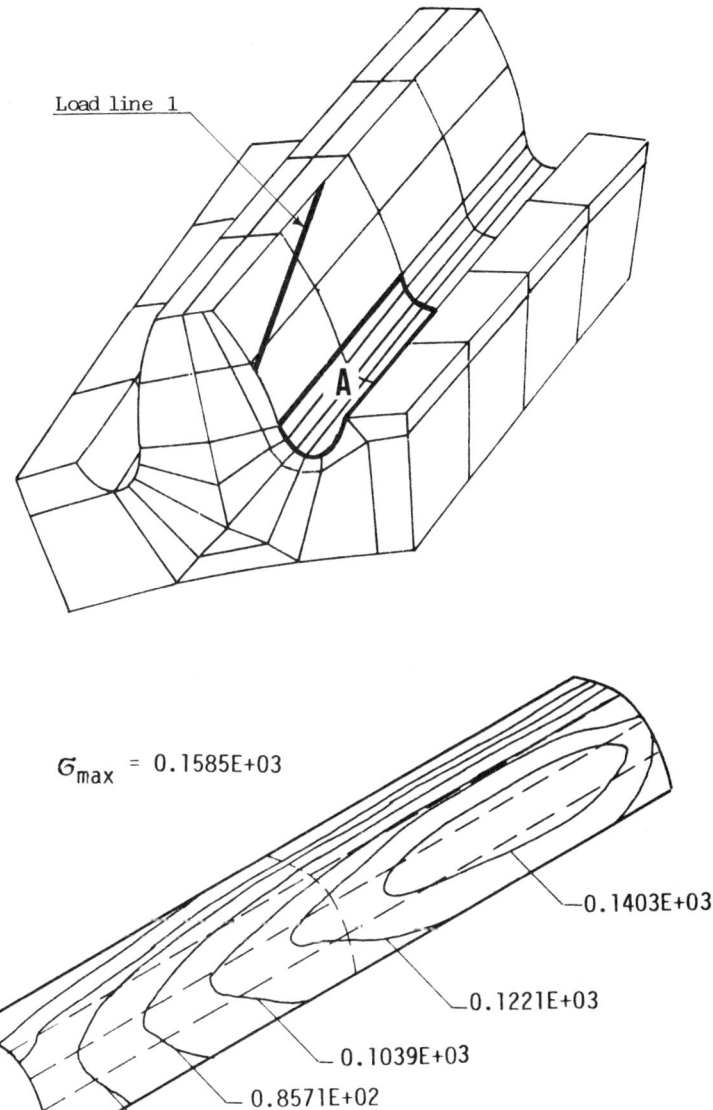

Figure 11 - Helical Gear FIESTA 3D Model
σ_1 Isostress (kg/mm^2) in Region A
Load condition: 1

210 GEAR TEETH STRESS ANALYSIS

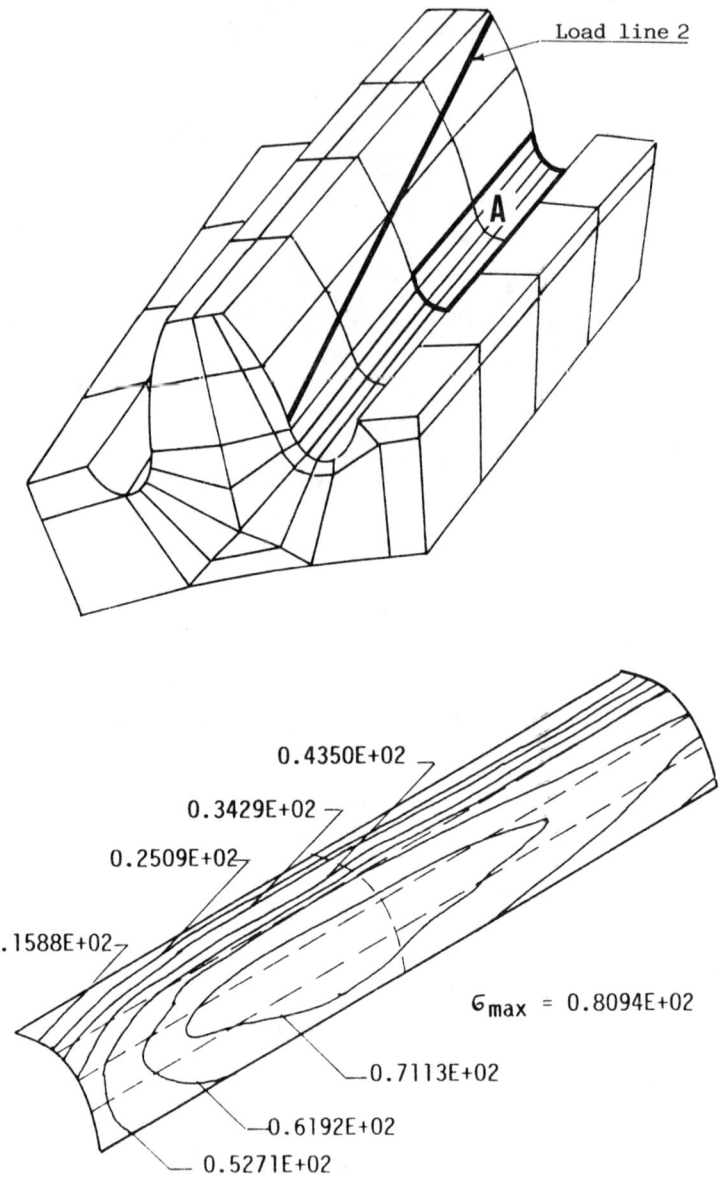

Figure 12 - Helical Gear FIESTA 3D Model
σ_1 Isostress (kg/mm^2) in Region A
Load condition: 2

GEAR TEETH STRESS ANALYSIS 211

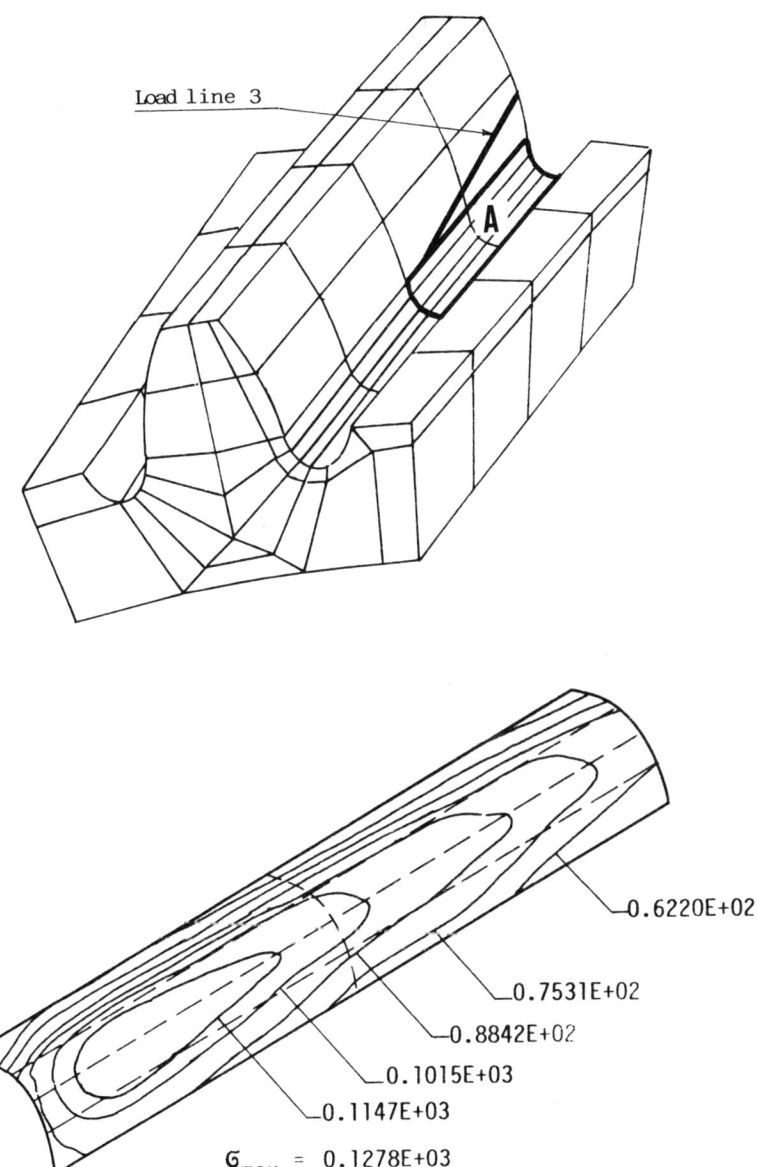

Figure 13 - Helical Gear FIESTA 3D Model
σ_1 Isostress (kg/mm^2) in Region A
Load condition: 3

The Integrated use of Supercomputers and Engineering Workstations to Maximise Productivity

R.A. Parris
Senior Consultant, Boeing Computer Services (Europe) Limited

ABSTRACT

This paper presents a discussion on the integrated use of supercomputers and engineering workstations for the finite element modelling and analysis of complex geometries.

The paper will explore the benefits of dividing the task between supercomputers to solve both large linear and non-linear structural analysis problems, and engineering workstations for finite element modelling and post processing.

Particular reference will be made to the role of the analyst and to design office productivity.

INTRODUCTION

The world of 'computer technology' continues to expand at an ever increasing rate and is becoming one the of the most important influences within today's engineering environment. To realise its full potential it is necessary to constantly review the way we work, the equipment we use, and perhaps more importantly how we manage our resources to optimise productivity and quality.

The key feature of the computers advancement in the world of commerce is the steady increase in processing power coupled with a fall in the cost per processing unit. Today's supercomputers, like the Cray 2, are at least ten times more powerful than the state-of-the-art machines in 1975. By 1995 it is expected that their performance will further increase by perhaps 100 times with a marked decrease in cost. Workstations as we know them today did not even exist in 1977, and will also rapidly grow in performance to rival today's mainframes while costs steadily reduce (Figure 1).

214 SUPERCOMPUTERS AND ENGINEERING WORKSTATIONS

These developments offer real promise of a workstation on every desk and a supercomputer in every major company. To maximise the benefits of such installations it is necessary to understand how these devices function, how they can be efficiently interfaced, and how existing working practices can be optimised. This paper seeks to explore these subjects, to propose how productivity in the field of finite element modelling and analysis may be improved and to invite discussion as to the direction of future structural analysis techniques.

SUPERCOMPUTERS

What is a Supercomputer

The generic term "Supercomputer" is applied to the "Worlds largest and fastest" computers. In particular, it is customarily used to describe the fastest vector processors, capable of executing many arithmetrical operations simultaneously. This gives a great increase in speed over conventional machines which can only execute operations sequentially. Additionally they all have a large in-core memory, exceeding 1 million words (MW), each word normally being expressed to a very high precision using 64 bits.

Today's supercomputers include the Cray family of computers, the Cyber 205, the Japanese Fujitsu and Hitachi machines, and there is now emerging a range of machines dubbed 'mini-supercomputer". The most powerful of these machines generally available is the Cray X-MP/4800; the Cray-2, which has just started to enter commercial service, is of similar capacity. A detailed description of the Cray X-MP computer and its capabilities follow in the next section.

More on the Cray X-MP

The Cray X/MP is one of the latest in a line of supercomputers from Cray Research Incorporated, of the United States. One such machine (Fig 2) was installed by Boeing Computer Services (BCS), at their Seattle Data Centre (Fig 3), early in 1985. This replaced two earlier generation Cray 1-S machines which had been in service for some time.

The BCS model is a Cray X/MP-2400 (Fig 4) which includes two parallel central processing units offering a total of 4 million words of in-core memory. These processors can each handle up to 140 million floating point multiply/add operations a second (Mflops). It also incorporates an optional Solid State Storage Device (Fig 4) SSD, which provides an additional 128 million words of storage (this is equivalent to 1000 Megabytes in 'IBM' terminology). This SSD is connected by ultra high speed parallel connections to the main processors and can read and write data 250 times faster than would be possible using conventional disk drives. To further enhance the speed of the main processors the chore of data distribution to physical disks is undertaken by the I/O subsystem which provides an additional 1 million words of storage. The combined effect of all these features is to provide a very powerful sledge hammer to crack the proverbial nut, or, more usefully, to solve previously unapproachable problems.

The Solid-State-Storage Device (SSD) Explained

Many large structural analysis problems exceed the in-core capacity of even the X-MP and consequently many large scratch files have to be written out of core during execution. Whilst these files are being written from core, the central processing units (CPUs) cannot progress the analysis and execution is temporarily suspended (Fig 6). Unfortunately whilst the CPUs are exceedingly fast even the best, conventional disk drives are, comparatively, very slow and the I/O time to read and write from core becomes the dominant feature of the run time of the analysis. This has a corresponding impact on the cost of the job.

Some methods to reduce this cost are listed in Figs. 5 and 6. However the SSD can reduce the time to read and write files by a factor of up to 250. This dramatically reduces the run time and execution costs of previously I/O bound jobs (Figs. 8 and 9). In one extreme example an oil field simulation analysis which required 10^{12} floating point operations ran for an elapsed time of 23.8 hours on the X/MP-2400 without SSD yet with SSD the analysis was complete in only 3.6 hours and represented a cost saving of many thousands of dollars.

Why use a Supercomputer

Three reasons for using a supercomputer are:

1) To save money
2) To save time
3) To execute an otherwise impossible analysis.

These points are discussed below:

1) To save money
Table 1 lists independently derived performance figures for different computers. This table gives a price performance ratio of 14 when comparing a Cray X/MP-2400 to a VAX 11/780. Clearly in a commercial environment this saving must result in a savings to the end user. For small jobs this saving is offset by the higher overhead costs of initially accessing the Cray. However as the jobs become larger the savings increase. It is often possible to demonstrate that large jobs, which require tens of hours of execution time on small in-house machines, can be run at a real cost saving on a remote supercomputer.

As discussed above the SSD can result in significant time saving and hence costs when large scratch files are required for out of core solutions.

Savings in mantime costs may be made by executing analyses in hours when days or weeks of elapsed time would alternatively be required. Significant savings may also be made in situations when an in-house generated analysis model, which may have taken weeks to construct, is found to exceed the capacity of the in-house machine. The cost of transferring this data to a supercomputer and executing the job may well be less than the cost of remodelling to fit the in-house resources, and, of course, given a better analysis.

2) To Save Time
The value of saving this time will vary from project to project. Sometimes time constraints are purely commercial whilst on other occasions they are important from a practical standpoint.

It may be considered impractical to run a large job in-house when its execution cannot be completed during a single night shift, and if the job is resumed over several shifts there is always the danger of a machine outage aborting the job or the possibility of insufficient disk space to save scratch files. In any case, if several runs are required to correct data or to modify loadcases, a project which would only require a few Cray hours may actually take several weeks to complete on a conventional machine.

The time savings which can be achieved on the Cray X/MP may be considered in two categories. There are the time savings due to the speed of the main processors, which can result in time savings for processing of up to 15 times when compared to a CDC Cyber 760 machine (Fig 9). Secondly there are time savings due to the I/O performance increase resulting from the use of the SSD (Fig 8) and I/O subsystem. Some structural analysis programs such as MSC/NASTRAN report a reduction in I/O time of up to 25 times when the SSD is used (Figs 7 and 8).

3) To execute otherwise impossible jobs
Because of its large memory and SSD the Cray X/MP is able to solve problems which are physically too large to solve on smaller machines. In finite element analysis an important parameter which determines the required machine capacity is the maximum bandwidth or front size of the stiffness matrix. This is the maximum number of degrees of freedom which the computer must store in-core at any one time.

For a virtual memory machine such as a VAX the physical machine memory is augmented by available disk space. However the penalty for extending the machine memory in this way is the I/O time to transfer the data to and from disk. The physical limitation in such cases is the amount of disk space available for scratch files. Even if sufficient disk space is available a practical consideration is the amount of I/O time which would be required. This is because the out-of-core storage and hence data transfer time increases with the square of the bandwidth, eventually locking up the computer with I/O operations. The result is great inconvenience to other in-house users or significant costs if running on a computer bureau's conventional machine.

For non-linear analysis these problems are further multiplied by the number of iterations required. These problems can generally be avoided by using the extra in-core memory of the X/MP-2400 which permits in-core solution of matrices with bandwidths of up to around 1800 degrees of freedom, several times larger than that available on other machines. In addition out of core solutions of larger bandwidths are feasible using the fast access SSD. In any event the SSD provides a rapidly accessible storage device for all other data blocks not required in-core at a particular time.

ENGINEERING WORKSTATION

What is an Engineering Workstation

The term 'engineering workstation' as described in this paper is defined as a single processor with associated peripherals dedicated to a single user. However, much of the following discussion may be equally applied to small clusters of graphics terminals locally networked into a single but more powerful processor dedicated to a common application.

Depending on the application area the workstation may range from an IBM compatible 16 bit Personal Computer to the very much more powerful 32 bit workstations such as those based on DEC's Micro Vax II or Apollo's DOMAIN range of processors.

Why use a workstation

In the early days of computer applications, the high cost of computer installations placed the emphasis for development with economy of scale. Therefore computers were large and were accessed by timesharing users often spread over a large geographic area. In the 1970's the advent of the mini-computer lead to a prolification of the number of individual installations. However, these smaller machines were generally inadequate for CAE and CADCAM applications and the role of the mainframes remained predominant.

At the end of the decade a new generation of superminis such as the VAX 11/780, with virtual memory operating systems began to offer a real opportunity to decentralise engineering applications. This was particularly attractive to CAD/CAM engineers, for whom timesharing on a single machine was never an effective way of undertaking interactive graphics operations, requiring the intensive bursts of computational power and large in-core memory.

At around this time the needs and requirements of the CAD/CAM engineer and the finite element analyst begin to diverge. For CADCAM applications, relatively powerful local interactive processing is paramount, with special emphasis being placed on the speed of graphical operations. However, the FE analyst, whilst requiring interactive graphics for model generation, is frequently far more interested in the ability of the central processor to 'number crunch' large matrices. Indeed, he is even prepared to accept degraded interactive access, in order to get a share of a larger machine to solve progressively larger problems.

We are currently in the situation where the graphical demands of the CADCAM community are driving up the power of the engineering workstations, also with this power comes the ability to use the workstation itself for solving analysis problems. However, the enhanced power of these workstations also enables the engineer to build more sophisticated models which still can only be solved on a remote supercomputer. In anycase it is probably more cost efficient to reserve the top-end workstations for design and solid modelling applications where graphical visualisation is all important, whilst enabling the finite element engineer to access the same database using a quality lower-end device.

INTERFACING

Why interface a supercomputer with a workstation

In an ideal world all engineers would have a personal desk top graphical workstation with the power of the latest supercomputer. These machines would only require networking together in order to facilitate data transfer for large shared projects. However, in reality, compromises must be sought if cost efficiency is to be optimised. This is best achieved by chosing the best machine for the job. Workstations are ideal for interactive graphics and finite element mesh generation, whilst supercomputers are at their most powerful when 'number crunching' large matrices in batch mode. Networked together they make an unbeatable combination.

How can Supercomputers and Workstations be Networked Together

Essentially there are two means of linking supercomputers with workstations. Firstly, they can be linked by a local area network. This would usually be across a single site and is currently only possible within those major organisations that can afford the large investment required to support a supercomputer installation. Secondly, they can be linked by RJE communications, if necessary over intercontinental distances to remote installations. For many finite element applications an RJE connection is usually quite adequate for launching the analysis phase of a project. The finite element model can be generated in-house using a workstation, an analysis deck can be written in the required format, including all necessary job control instructions and the complete deck can be transmitted to the mainframe or supercomputer. After analysis the post processing data files may by transferred back to the in-house workstation for results display.

PRODUCTIVITY

Productivity in finite element analysis is of interest for two reasons: firstly to minimise the cost of constructing a model, and secondly and more importantly, to reduce the design cycle of the finished product. It is an unfortunate state of affairs that all too often the finite element analysis of a complex component or assembly can take so long to complete that it is reduced to a backfitting exercise on a final design. This clearly under-utilises the benefits that are to be gained from the finite element techniques and reduces the opportunity to optimise the design before the prototype phase is reached.

SUPERCOMPUTERS AND ENGINEERING WORKSTATIONS

In this section I will attempt to identify the areas where productivity can be immediately improved and to propose longer term targets for software and hardware developments. Some of these objectives require tangible product development whilst others will pose more philosophical issues.

Where is the bottleneck

For the purposes of this paper we do not seek to discuss the productivity of the CADCAM process itself and we shall assume that our starting point is a completed CAD database. Our experience at Boeing suggests that large supercomputers such as the Cray X-MP can compute the solution of the largest problems within a working day. However we find that by far the most time consuming part of the process is the generation of the finite element model. A typical finite element model of a car body, containing say 15000 elements, may require up to a man-year to generate whilst the subsequent computer analysis many be completed within a month. I make the suggestion therefore, that the bottleneck in productivity is no longer in the solution phase but in the geometry definition and mesh generation phase.

Transfer of data from the CAD database to the FE Modelling Package

As a major finite element modelling consultancy group we find that most major organisations still prefer to transfer geometric data via third angle projection engineering drawings. This is despite their in-house CADCAM databases and IGES Interfaces and is due to reasons ranging from the practical to the political. However on the occasions when we are presented with IGES databases, for example of an engine block, we find that they contain so many superfluous details that they are often unusable. Therefore, for 90% of our work the analyst must sit at a terminal and initially recreate the basis geometry before he can commence generating a mesh for analysis. This double handling of geometry is of course inefficient and necessarily increases the duration of the modelling phase.

The remedy to this situation must depend on the hardware and software resources of all the involved parties. Clearly the ideal situation is to use a single database. In such an arrangement the CADCAM technician would create his basic database including even the finest geometric details. The engineer could then pickup this model using the same database and software, delete superfluous detail and then start generating the finite element mesh using a different module within the same software package. The current flaw in this approach is that the specialist CADCAM terminals and workstations tend to be expensive and whilst they are cost effective for production drafting work they are less attractive if tied up full time for finite element modelling and analysis. Also the finite element meshing capabilities of the currently available CADCAM systems tend to be less powerful then the specialist FE meshing packages. However, it is to be expected that this position will quickly change over the coming years and that fully integrated CADCAM and CAE will become a realistic expectation.

Automatic Mesh Generation

It is perhaps the dream of many an engineer to have fully automatic mesh generation. He dreams that all he has to do is ask the computer for a mesh on a given solid model and a few CPU seconds later the task is complete. Indeed some software suppliers already market so called so called enhanced mesh generators. Of course in reality these matters are rarely so straightforward. However, I propose that with careful management and development of existing packages, practical automatic mesh generation can become a reality.

There are perhaps three major areas which require developing in order to assist this process. Firstly, the existing software packages require enhancing, particularly in the area of generating solid finite element models. These programs must produce meshes which are consistent with good engineering practice. Secondly more work needs to be undertaken in validating and developing finite element formulations for triangular shell and tetrahedral solids in order to allow these elements, which are frequently generated by automatic meshing packages alongside the more widely used quadrilaterals, to be used with more confidence than currently exists. Thirdly, automatic interfacing options in the analysis program between differently meshed adjacent regions can greatly reduce the time required to ensure consistent meshing across a complex, multicomponented structure. This is particularly useful if several engineers are responsible for modelling different areas. Such facilities already exist in programs such as DYNA3D and NIKE3D and their introduction into programs such as MSC/NASTRAN would be most welcome.

In the longer term we can probably look forward to programs which will initially generate a mesh and then optimise it by iterating through an analysis phase adaptively refining the mesh with each iteration. Such routines will undoubtedly require the large throughput capabilities of a supercomputer and the role of the workstation may then be reduced to that of a graphical interrogater.

Are finite elements the best way forward

Much has been written in recent years about the benefits of boundary elements for stress analysis. When used correctly they can can greatly simplify the task of preparing a model for analysis. Complex shell structures can be represented with a few judiciously chosen lines, solid models can be modelled using skin of shells reducing the dimension of the geometric modelling problem. I would suggest there is a potential order of magnitude saving in modelling mantime. Of course there is a penalty. Whereas finite element problems require the numerical solution of sparsely populated matrices the matrices generated by boundary element techniques are fully populated. Hence even small problems require considerable computer resources in order to obtain a solution. There again, the only practical solution is the coupling of modelling workstation with a supercomputer.

Of course finite elements will always have their place in the engineers tool box but we should not blind ourselves to other options in the search for more productive working practices.

SUPERCOMPUTERS AND ENGINEERING WORKSTATIONS 221

A few notes on managing for productivity

Before embarking on a long journey it is advisable to know not only the starting point and destination but also all intermediate stopping off points. To be given an ad-hoc list of stops in mid-journey will result in a considerable amount of back tracking and an extension in travel time. So it is when planning a finite element analysis project.

All too often there is inadequate planning before the project starts, objectives are poorly defined, and internal discussions between interested departments in the same company are incomplete or non-existent. This frequently results in many changes of course, not in response to design changes, but to overcome poor project management. The outcome is projects overrun with consequent impact on product development. However, such shortcomings have long been recognised in many other aspects of general management.

I therefore suggest that management techniques can make as significant a contribution to productivity as new equipment. Certainly the best workstation and supercomputer in the world can produce very expensive mistakes in the hands of inadequate management.

The finite element modelling philosophy - a turning point?

Ever since the introduction of structural analysis techniques, engineers have continued to strive to analyse progressively more complex structures. Central to this process has been the necessity to use engineering judgment to simplify the structures to their essential form. Such idealisation has always been required in order to permit structural behaviour to be calculated and understood.

The arrival of the computer, and finite element techniques in particular, presented enormous leaps forward in the complexity of structure that could be analysed. However, the difficulty of preparing large error free models, and the limitations of the computer hardware have continued to encourage the engineer to make gross idealisations in his search for a cost effective solution. Broadly this has been welcomed, because it enables the engineer to succeed in interpreting the results, by keeping the volume of output under some control. Nevertheless, with todays model sizes it is already essential to utilise comprehensive post-processing to achieve that interpretation, and also to validate the original model.

I would now suggest that the technological advances described in this paper, coupled with the need to increase productivity, will present the engineer with a constructive approach for the future. The pivot for this philosophy will be the fact that constantly updated CADCAM computer databases, containing precise geometry, will exist for major products. Advanced finite element meshing packages will be able to mesh individual components in detail with comparative ease, using the new generation of workstation. These components can then be assembled into, for instance, a complete car body model for analysis. If this model contains, say, 20,000 finite elements then a solution can be attempted on the in-house mini-supercomputer or if it contains 100,000 elements you will find it handled effortlessly in a couple of years time by the next offering from Cray. The post processing of results can then be completed back on the workstation.

Why do I propose this apparently sledgehammer approach? Firstly, I believe CAD databases do not readily lend themselves to idealisation. Secondly, competent structural idealisation on a complex structure is a time consuming process. Thirdly, design modifications can be tested as soon as the designer modifies his database. Finally, I believe that by using the computer to carry the burden of data preparation and analysis the engineer is released to use his imagination, engineering judgment and expertise to help produce better products in a shorter, more cost effective way.

SUMMARY

A supercomputer such as a Cray X/MP may provide cost efficient solutions for

1) Very large structural models.
2) Non-linear or dynamic analysis.
3) Programs generating large quantities of data and results.

Workstations such as a MicroVaxII provides the ability to:

1) Undertake interactive graphical operations.
2) Generate and manipulate geometry databases.
3) Generate complex finite element models.
4) Analyse simple structures.
5) Interface with supercomputers.

Jointly, an interfaced or networked, supercomputer and workstation provide the ability to:

1) Generate and analyse highly complex finite element models.
2) To bridge between CADCAM databases and structural analysis.
3) To open up new advances in finite element modelling productivity.
4) As a result of (3) above to introduce the benefits of structural analysis at at earlier stage in the design process.

TABLES

Boeing Computer Services   Computer Comparisons   XMP/SSD

System		Price ($M)	Mflop	Price/Mflop
VAX11/780		0.25	0.13	1,900,000
CONVEX C-1	(scalar)	0.485	0.80	610,000
Cyber205	(scalar)	6.0	6.00	1,000,000
	(vector)	6.0	27.40	219,000
CrayX-MP	(scalar)	10.0	20.0	500,000
	(vector)	10.0	73.6	136,000

How does X-MP compare in FORTRAN performance?*

	System	Price($M)	Performance
*Based on number of	VAX 11/780	0.3	1
times faster than	VAX+AP	0.6	8-14
VAX 11/780 to execute	IBM 3081	3.0	10-30
benchmark FORTRAN	Cyber 875	4.0	35-100
programs	Cray X-MP24	9.0	90-270

Source: Sandia National Laboratories

Table 1

TECHNOLOGY TRENDS
Hardware
Workstations

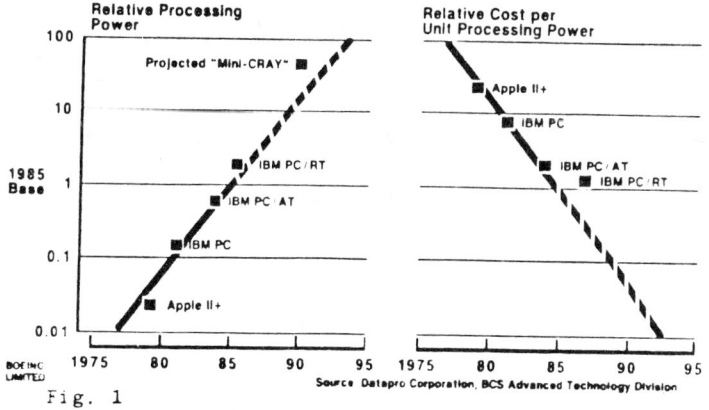

Fig. 1

224 SUPERCOMPUTERS AND ENGINEERING WORKSTATIONS

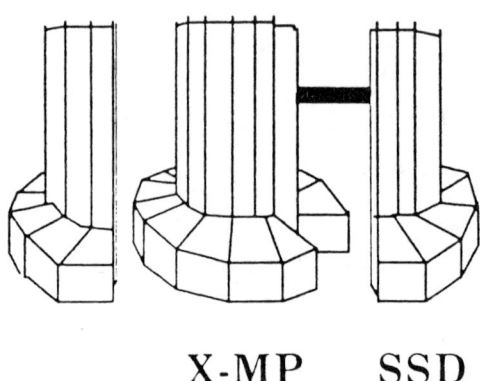

Fig 2

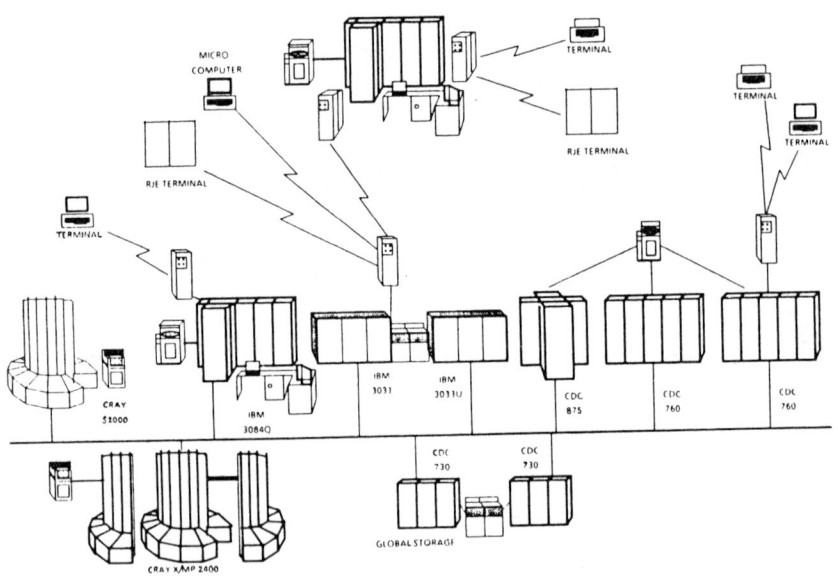

Figure 3

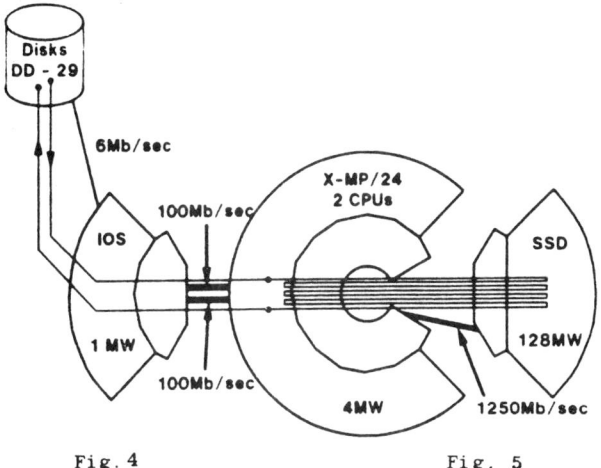

Fig. 4   Fig. 5

I/O   OPTIONS

☐ I/O BUFFER SIZE
  • BUFFSIZE OPTION ON NASTRAN CARD

☐ DOUBLE BUFFERING
  • NEW NASTRAN VERSION 63 FEATURE

☐ SSD
  • SOLIDSTATE STORAGE DEVICE (CRAY HARDWARE)

☐ STRIPED DISK
  • NEW CRAY RESEARCH SOFTWARE

Fig.6

CPU AND I/O TIME

BUFFSIZE AND DOUBLE BUFFERING

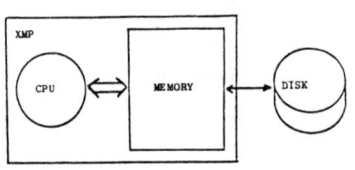

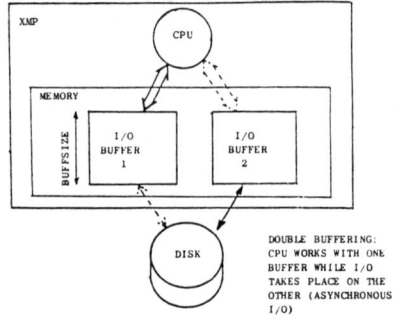

ONCE THE CPU HAS FILLED MEMORY I/O OCCURS TO TRANSFER DATA TO DISK

DOUBLE BUFFERING: CPU WORKS WITH ONE BUFFER WHILE I/O TAKES PLACE ON THE OTHER (ASYNCHRONOUS I/O)

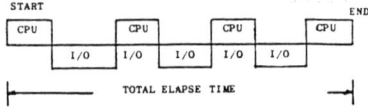

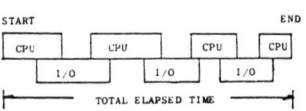

Figure 7

SSD AND DOUBLE BUFFERING OPTIONS

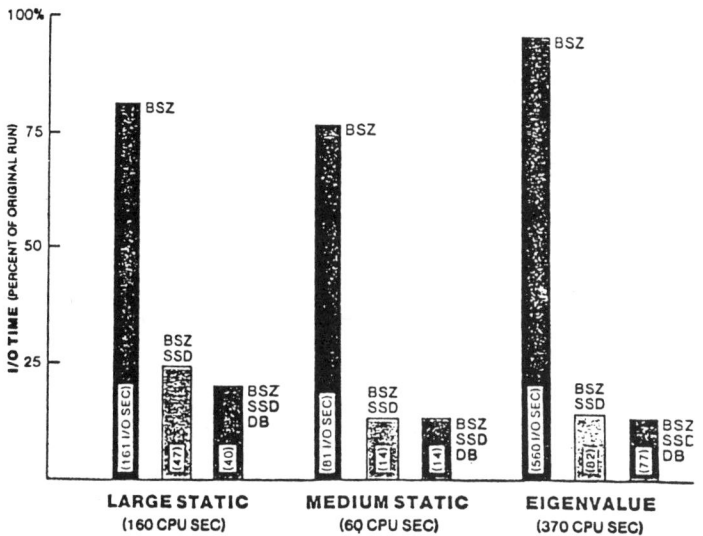

To demonstrate the effect the various options have on the performance of MSC/NASTRAN on the CRAY, three example problems were run using the options. The three models consisted of:

PROBLEM 1 - Large Static Analysis (SOL 24)
PROBLEM 2 - Medium Static Analysis (SOL 24)
PROBLEM 3 - Medium Eigenvalue Analysis (SOL 3, Modified Givens Method)

These are real world production models which provide a reasonable sample with which the MSC/NASTRAN performance can be demonstrated. A brief description of the models is given in Table 1.

Table 1. Summary of Example Problems

	DOF	ACTIVE COL.	RMS COL.	ELEMENTS	
Large Static	12308	889	480	2444	1 load case
Medium Static	6128	585	298	1232	1 load case
Medium Eigen	6411	436	310	1389	35 modes

OPTIONS KEY

Abbreviation	Definition
ORIG	Original data which uses default devices
BSZ	BUFFSIZE = 9217
DB	Double buffering was used
SSD	Scratch files written to the SSD
STRP	Scratch files written to striped disk

Figure 8

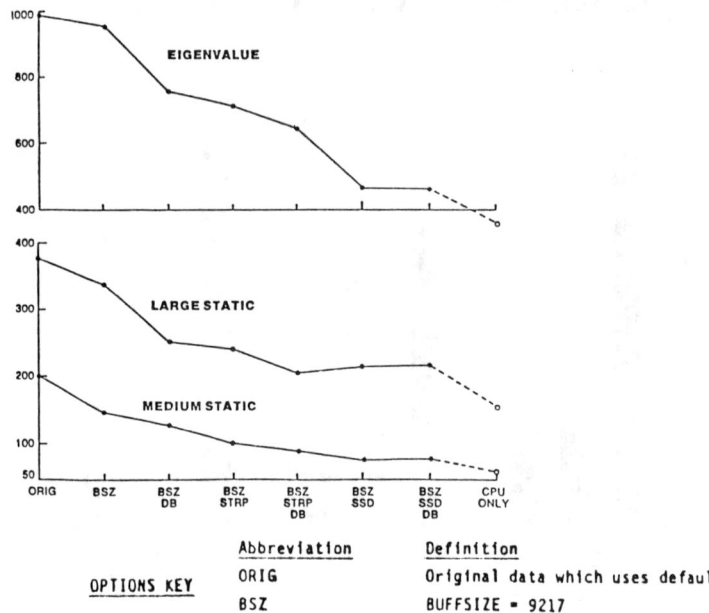

OPTIONS KEY	Abbreviation	Definition
	ORIG	Original data which uses default devices
	BSZ	BUFFSIZE = 9217
	DB	Double buffering was used
	SSD	Scratch files written to the SSD
	STRP	Scratch files written to striped disk

Figure 9

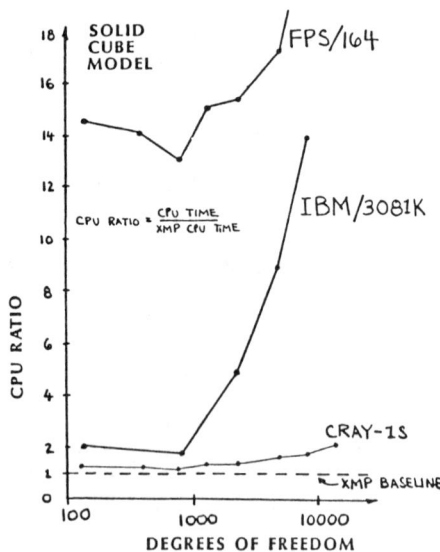

Figure 10

The NISA II Family of Finite Element Programs for Linear and Nonlinear Analysis on PC, Mini, Supermini, Mainframe and Supercomputers

K.S. Kothawala
Engineering Mechanics Research Group, 1707 W. Big Beaver Road, Troy, MI 480084, U.S.A.

INTRODUCTION

The NISA family of programs are well known as powerful, state of the art, finite element programs for all computer environments (CRAY Supercomputers to IBM PC/AT, XT and compatibles). The NISA program has been available commercially since 1974. Beginning in 1982, the NISA program was entirely rewritten and thoroughly upgraded, and NISA II was released in 1985.

The NISA II family of programs encompasses an assortment of general and special purpose programs for the design and analysis of structural and non-structural problems. NISA II includes linear and nonlinear Static, Dynamic, Heat Transfer and Composite analysis modules, and special purpose programs such as ENDURE - a fatigue and fracture analysis program, NISA II/3D-Fluid Flow - a three dimensional fluid flow program, NISAOPT - a shape and structural optimization program, DISPLAY II - an interactive color graphics pre- and post-processing program with geometry data base which directly interfaces with major CAD/CAM programs, and NISA/PCB - a program for finite element design/analysis of printed circuit boards.

NISA II FAMILY OF PROGRAMS

NISA II/STATIC
A 2D and 3D finite element analysis program designed to be operational on mini, supermini and mainframe computers, as well as the IBM PC/XT, AT and compatibles. The NISA II/Static program on the IBM PC is virtually identical to the NISA II/Static program on the CRAY Supercomputer.

Element Library
- Linear & Parabolic isoparametric elements
- Plane stress, plane strain
- Axisymmetric shell and solid with unsymmetric loading
- 3D beam, 3D curved beam
- Very thin shell, general shell and thick shell
- Layered composite shell, sandwich shells
- 3D solid (6, 8, 15, 20 noded)
- 3D solid composite with interlaminar shear stress and edge effect
- 3D spring, axial spring, spar, torsion and cable elements
- Gaps, rigid elements, Multipoint constraint, Point mass
- AISC members and code checking

Loading NISA II/STATIC allows the user a large variety of loading conditions as shown in the figure below.

Output
- Displacements and stresses by elements and nodes
- Sorted result summaries
- Principal stresses, directions
- von Mises, maximum shear and octahedral stresses
- Reaction forces
- Averaged nodal stresses
- Gauss point stresses
- Stresses at element centroid

NISA II FAMILY OF FE PROGRAMS

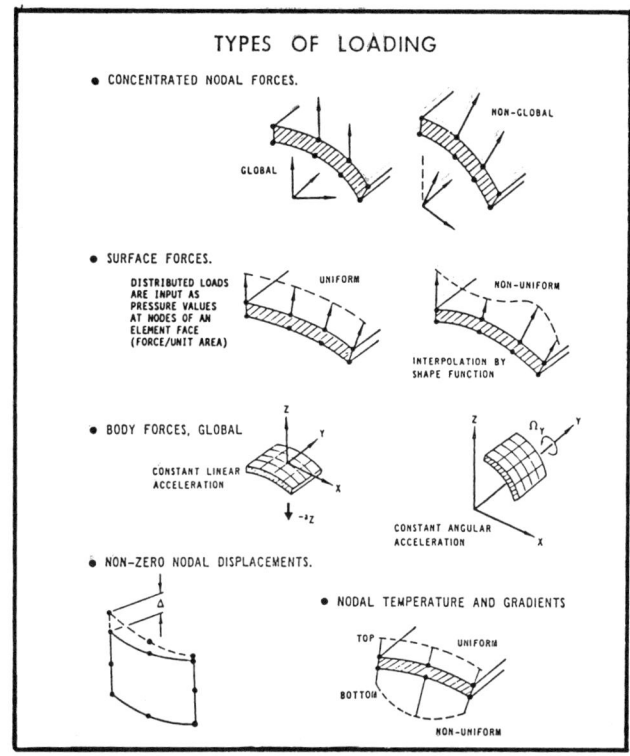

Model description:
Rear knuckle (20 noded solid + rigid elements)
Total number of elements: 620
Total number of DOF: 10854

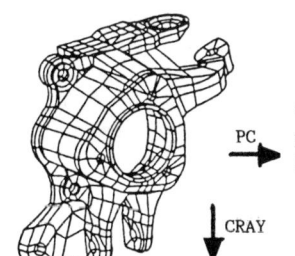

	NISA2 Prime 9955	NISA2 ELXSI	NISA2 CRAY-1S	NASTRAN(64) CRAY-1S
Total CPU :		3078.027	147.3402	465.5740
Average Memory used:			0.355	0.502
IO blocks moved :			31263	131810
IO request :			4317	8250
SSU :			596.50	3322.69
Priority :			5	5

Nonlinear Analysis

NISA II can be used to solve a wide variety of geometrically nonlinear and materially nonlinear problems. The geometrically nonlinear capability includes stress-stiffening effect, large deflections, finite rotations and nonlinear strain-displacement relationships. Surface tractions or forces may be of fixed direction in space or deformation dependent or follower-forces. The program employs a referential formulation and the user has the option to choose from a fixed reference configuration, so that Total Lagrangian Formulation (TLF) will be in effect, or an updated reference configuration, so that Updated Lagranian Formulation (ULF) will be in effect. The user also has the choice of stress measure, either Cauchy, second Piola-Kirchhoff or both, for results printout.

In the material nonlinearity, elastic-perfectly plastic material or elastic-plastic work hardening (isotropic or kinematic work hardening) material can be analyzed. The Von-Mises, Tresca, Drucker-Prager and Mohr-Coulomb yield criterion can be used to model the yield surface. The nonlinear stress-strain data can be given in terms of explicit properties, as a piecewise linear stress-strain curve or as a Ramburg-Osgood representation of the material. The integration algorithms used in the above plasticity models are the generalized trapezoidal and the generalized mid-point rules combined with the subincremention method. The radial return, mean normal and closest point procedures are contained as special cases in the implemented generalized algorithm.

The solution of nonlinear equations is obtained by an incremental and iterative scheme. User can choose modified Newton-Raphson or full Newton-Raphson iterative technique. The convergence is checked by combined displacement, force and energy criterion and Euclidean norms using user-defined tolerances. Both automatic and user-defined stepping may be used.

Temperature dependent material properties can be used in the analysis. Properties can be given in the form of table of temperature vs. properties or in the form of polynomial function of the temperature. Anisotropic material properties can be used in the geometrically nonlinear analysis.

NISA II has been very successful in predicting nonlinear response of a system in a complex situation. Very frequently NISA II is used to predict energy absorbtion, residual stresses, permanent distortion and other quantities which require nonlinear analysis. The demonstration and verification problems are designed to show the user many useful capabilities like work hardening, loading-unloading type load history, snap-through type response, static crash worthiness analysis, failure prediction, pre- and post-buckling analysis, progressive yielding and automatic load stepping.

Nonlinear NISA II Highlights
- Material Nonlinearity
- von-Mises and other yield criteria
- Prandtl-Reuss potential function
- Work hardening
  1. Perfect plasticity (no hardening)
  2. Isotropic hardening
  3. Kinematic hardening

- Uniaxial Stress-Strain Data
- Explicit properties: initial yield stress and work hardening parameter
- Ramburg-Osgood curve: initial yield stress, secant modulus and hardening index
- Multiple piecewise linear stress-strain data, up to 6 pair points
- Multiple two point curves at different temperatures.

- Geometric Nonlinearity
- Reference Configuration Update Key
  Each iteration
  Each load step
- Surface Tractions
  Follower forces
  Non follower forces
- Formulation method
  Total Lagrangian (TLF)
  Updated Lagrangian (ULF)
- Stress Stiffening

- Load History
- Individually at each step
- 'N' increments with equal steps
- Automatic step size selection

- Iterative Scheme
- Modified Newton-Raphson
- Full Newton-Raphson

- Convergence Schemes
- Displacement, force and energy criteria
- Line search for speeding convergence

- Selective Output
- Output at each load step or at every 'N' load steps
- Output for selected elements and nodes
- Files for displacement and stress contours
- Nodal or Gauss point stress-strain contours
- Displacement-force history curve at specified DOF
- Summary of highest Gauss point and nodal stresses.
- Choice of stress measure

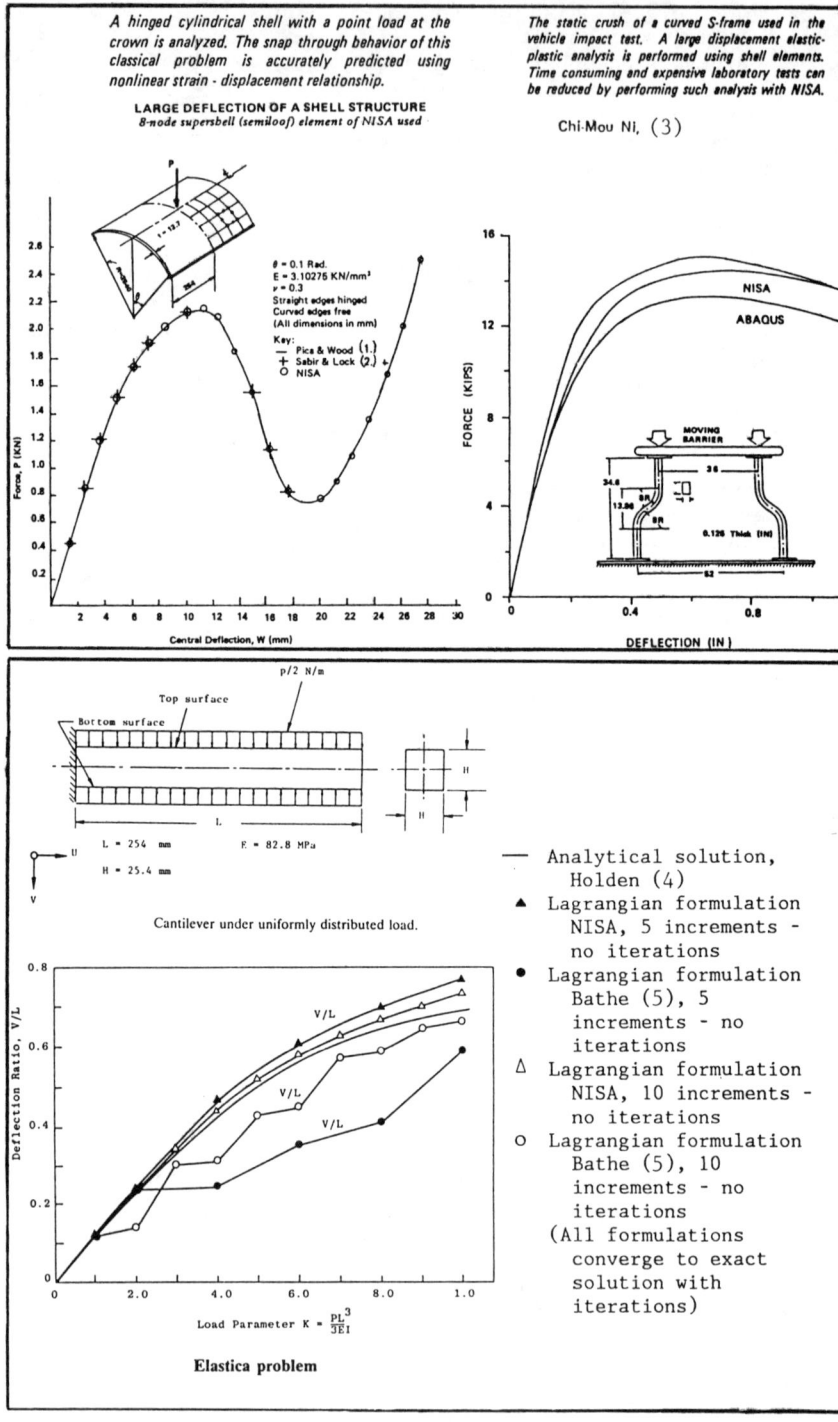

NISA II FAMILY OF FE PROGRAMS 235

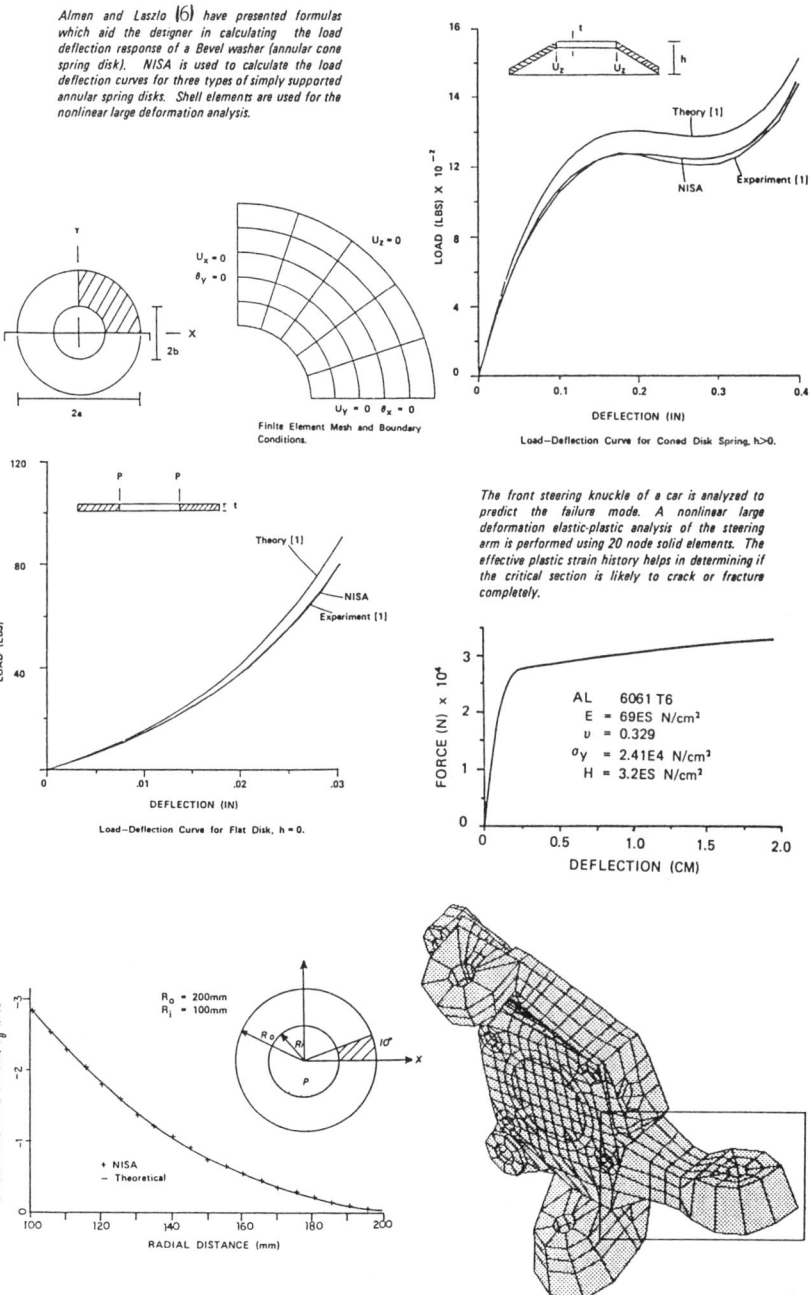

NISA II/DYNAMIC

NISA II/DYNAMIC has outstanding capabilities to solve a wide variety of problems encountered in dynamic analysis. It uses the wavefront technique with the obvious advantage that it can handle large problems efficiently and accurately. Modal solution methods as well as direct integration used can be used for any dynamic analysis. The following features are available:

Steady State Dynamics
- Natural frequency
- Mode shape (Eigenvector)
- Modal stress analysis
- Buckling load

Eigenvalue Extraction Techniques
- Subspace iteration
- Guyan reduction
- QR Householder
- Inverse iteration
- Lanczos method

Transient Dynamic
- Transient dynamics by modal superposition (time dependent loading)
- Viscous, proportional damping
- Direct integration
- Stress, displacement at any time step
- Displacement, velocity and acceleration time history

Shock Spectrum
- Shock spectrum generation from time history records
- Maximum response due to shock input

Frequency Response
- Steady state response of structure to harmonic loads
- Amplitude, phase spectra of displacements, velocity and acceleration determined
- Displacement and stress

Random Vibration
- Power spectral density obtained for random loading
- Cross spectral densities of displacement, velocity and acceleration are determined
- Mean square values of stress and velocity are determined

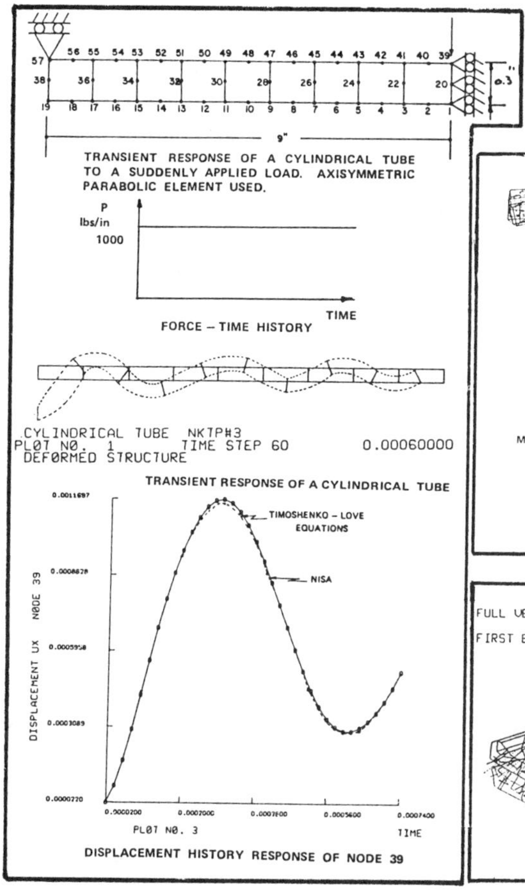

NISA II FAMILY OF FE PROGRAMS 237

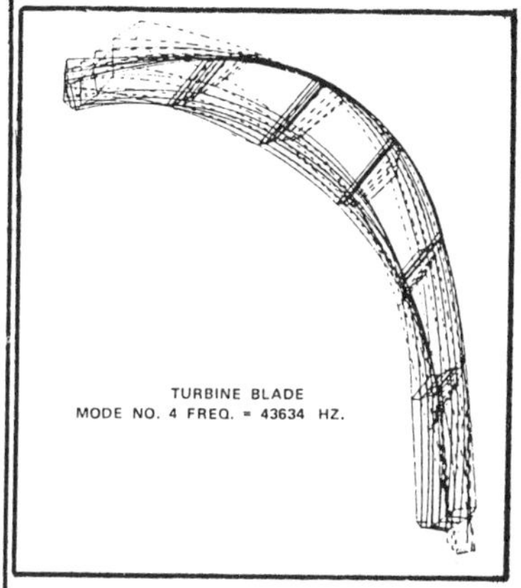

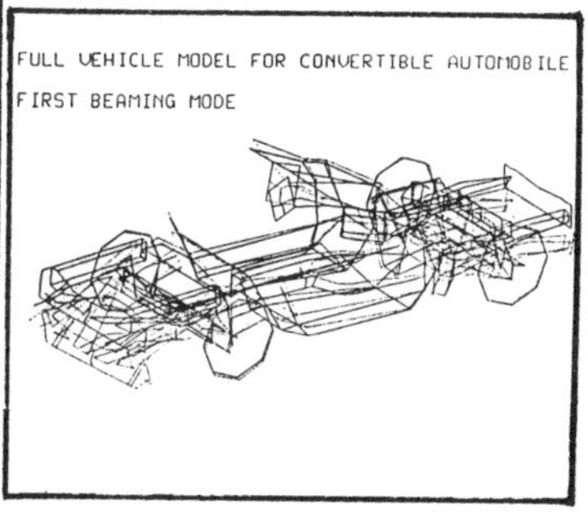

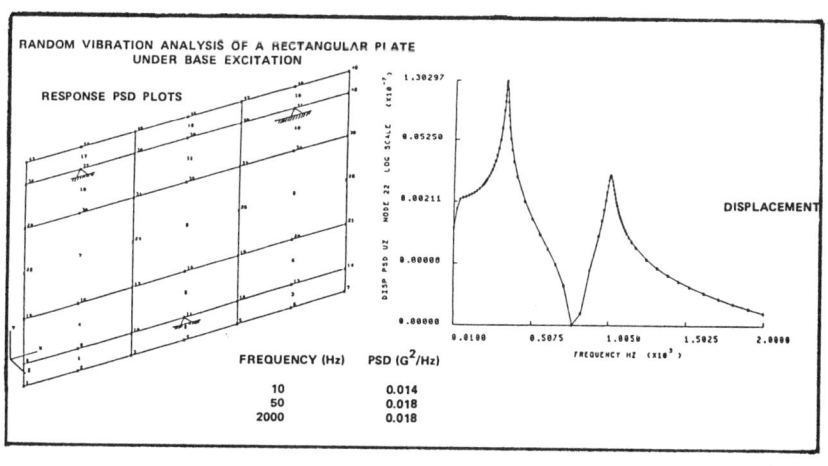

NISA II/HEAT

A 2D and 3D linear and nonlinear, steady state and transient heat transfer finite element analysis program. NISA II/HEAT can be used as a stand-alone program. Also, the output temperature can be stored for thermal stress analysis for NISA II/STATIC directly and the same finite element model may be used for static and heat transfer analysis.

Pre-Processing   The entire data deck including 2D and 3D automatic mesh generation, hidden line removal, distortion index check, wavefront optimization and check, loading and boundary conditions, multiple window display, zooming capabilities, etc. are all available using the color interactive graphics program DISPLAY II.

Solution Techniques   NISA II/HEAT uses the wavefront (frontal) method of equation solving for steady state and transient heat transfer analysis. In the wavefront method, node numbers are entirely arbitrary and the computation expense of assembling global matrix is avoided. NISA II/HEAT can check and/or optimize the wavefront before executing the job. The resequencing of the elements is done internal to NISA and is transparent to the users.

Transient heat transfer problems are solved by using one parameter family of time integration techniques. The user may select any of the following unconditionally stable schemes.
- Forward Difference (Explicit Euler)
- Trapezoidal (Crank-Nicholson)
- Galerkin
- Backward Difference (Implicit Euler)

Choice of Coordinate System   Nodal coordinates can be described in the cartesian, cylindrical or spherical system. Also, the user specified local orthogonal system can be used.
- Material properties: may be temperature dependent. Temperature dependent properties can be a polynomial funtion or a piecewise linear interpolation.
- Thermal conductivity can be isotropic or orthotropic. Direction of the orthotropy may coincide with global coordinates or be specified for each node or element.

Other Useful Features
- Concentrated heat flows can be time dependent
- Distributed heat flux, variables as defined by nodal intensities, can be time and/or temperature dependent.
- Convective and/or radiative heat exchange at heat surfaces. Film heat transfer coefficient and surface emissivity may be temperature and/or time dependent. Ambient temperature may be time dependent.
- Internal heat generation (average or distributed) can vary with time and/or temperature.
- Specified nodal temperature can be time dependent.

- In transient analysis, the user may use automatic variable time step size or define his own time step sizes.

Output Features The NISA II/HEAT element library contains a comprehensive set of elements to provide total flexibility and capability for the analysis of real-life heat transfer problems. Elements included are:
- 2D Planar (thickness input)
- 2D Planar (unit thickness)
- 2D Axisymmetric solid
- 3D General shell
- 3D Thick shell
- 3D Solid
- Radiation and convection link (through boundary conditions)

In general shell heat flux and/or convection coefficient can be specified independently on the top and/or bottom surface of the shell as well as on any of the in-plane edges. The shell theory allows a linear temperature gradient through the thickness, as well as isoparametric variation of temperature in plane direction.

Output Features
- Nodal temperature-time history plots and temperature contour plots at specified time steps can be obtained.
- Nodal temperature - average value at the midsurface of the shell elements.
- Linear temperature gradients at the nodes of shell elements.
- Heat values at the element nodes.
- Heat values at the nodes with specified nodal temperatures.
- Convective heat calculations for the element faces. Positive values indicate heat into the structure.
- Isothermal contour plots.
- Nodal temperatures at selected time intervals
- Isothermal contour plots at selected time intervals.
- Temperature vs. Time plots for selected nodes.
- Also available is ASCII output files containing all nodal temperature and heat flow values for further post-processing.

Plots of all the above output features can be obtained in color graphics form from DISPLAY II as post-processing features.

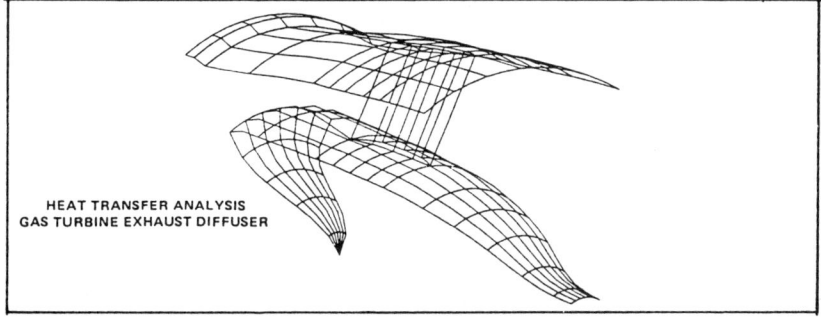

HEAT TRANSFER ANALYSIS
GAS TURBINE EXHAUST DIFFUSER

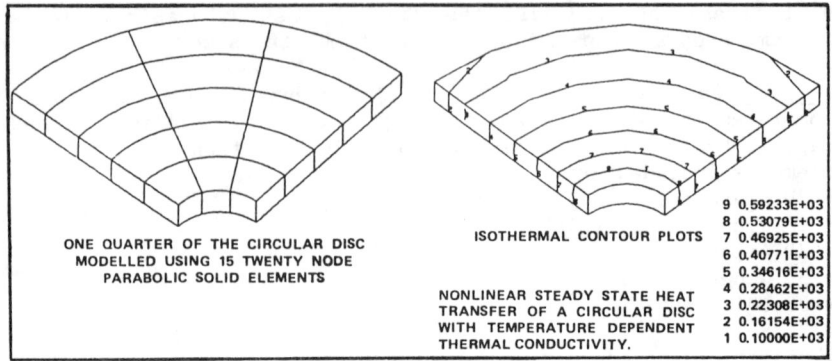

NISA II/COMPOSITE

NISA II/COMPOSITE has the most outstanding capabilities for the simulation of structures made of layered or sandwich composite material. An excellent element library is available.

<u>Laminated, Orthotropic, Linear and Parabolic Shell Elements</u>
These elements have no restriction on the number of layers, and each layer may have different thickness, orientation and material properties. Transverse (interlaminar) shear deformation and bending extensional coupling are included in these elements. The Tsai-Wu and Hill-Mises failure theories are included for these elements.

<u>3D Solid Isoparametric Element</u> Both hexahedra (brick) and pentahedra (wedge) elements are available with either linear or parabolic shape functions. The temperature dependent orthotropic material properties can be defined. Directions of orthotropy may be specified as constant within each element or they may be continously varying through out the structure.

<u>New 3D Solid Overlay Element</u> In this element solid is assumed to be composed of several lamina, each lamina may have different properties or lamination angle with respect to global axes. Each group of lamina is considered as a solid element. The normal stress and interlaminar shear stress are most accurately determined on any desired location. The new element is capable of predicting displacement and stress variations, including 'Edge Effects' accurately.

<u>Composite Element</u> The composite elements account for the effects of transverse (interlaminar) shear deformation, material anisotropy and all possible bending - extensional - twist - shear couplings. Unlike in most plate and shell analysis, which assumes that lines of material points normal to the neutral surface before deformation remain normal to it after deformation, the NISA II composite shell elements allow these normals to rotate relative to the deformed neutral surface giving more accurate transverse shear effects.

Sandwich Shell   In sandwich composite elements, the face sheets are thin which resist extensional and inplane shear deformation and a thick core material which resists only transverse shear. The face sheets themselves can be made of laminated composites and the core may be orthotropic. Multiple cores of more than two face sheets are allowed and the sandwich construction need not be symmetrical.

Modelling Features for Composite Structures   One of the special problems of composite analysis which arises in modelling curved surfaces is specifying fiber orientations. Most programs give users the option to define fiber orientations data for each element. NISA II has this option as well as six others. These options simplify the modelling of singly or doubly curved structures by defining lines on the shell surface which are projections of the global axes. Rotations are in every case about the shell normal and measured from these well defined reference lines. Fiber orientation can be defined at element or node level in either local or global coordinate system.

Failure Theories
- Maximum stress
- Modified Hill-von Mises
- Tsai-Wu
- Delamination

All theories are applied on a ply-by-ply basis, in the layer's principal material coordinate system. Delamination failures are predicted on the basis of interlaminar shear stress exceeding a specified allowable value.

Output Features for Composite Structures
- Plots of original and/or deformed geometry
- Contour plots of displacements, stress components, and stress resultants, in any layer
- Filtered stress output
- Stress survey plots
- Largest magnitudes of the displacement vector
- Highest stress resultants in descending order of magnitude

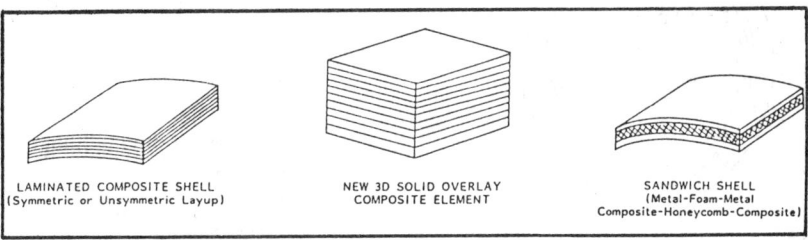

LAMINATED COMPOSITE SHELL
(Symmetric or Unsymmetric Layup)

NEW 3D SOLID OVERLAY
COMPOSITE ELEMENT

SANDWICH SHELL
(Metal-Foam-Metal
Composite-Honeycomb-Composite)

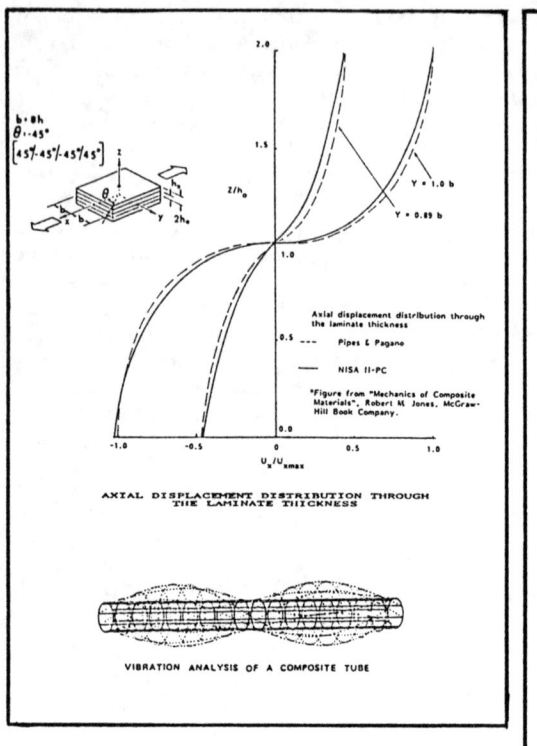

AXIAL DISPLACEMENT DISTRIBUTION THROUGH THE LAMINATE THICKNESS

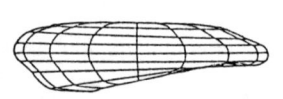

VIBRATION ANALYSIS OF A COMPOSITE TUBE

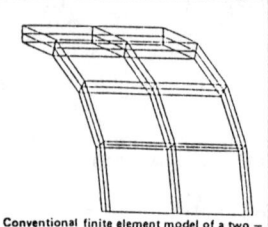

Conventional finite element model of a two-layer composite torque tube. A fine mesh must be used since the directions of orthotropy cannot vary within an element.

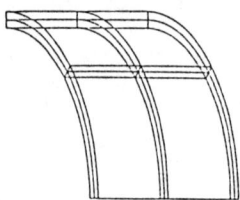

NISA - Composites model using isoparametric thick shells. Geometry and material properties vary continuously.

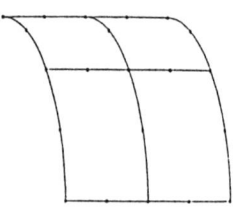

NISA - Composites model using isoparametric general composite shells. Only the shell midsurface is discretized.

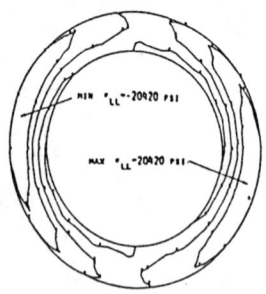

NISA includes comprehensive plot output, including deformed geometry (above) and layer stress contours (below).

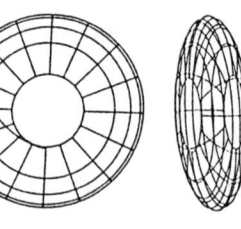

Some composite structures, as this fiber wound helicopter driveshaft coupling, have fibers whose orientation changes rapidly. Exactly modelling complex fiber paths will also be useful in molded composites where fiber angle and layer thickness are changed due to molding pressures.

NISAOPT

NISAOPT is a family of programs for optimum structural design. These programs are specialized for use in a variety of design environments.
- STROPT is a program for optimum design of structures of fixed geometry. The total material volume or the weight of the structure is optimized by resizing the parameters related to the design of the structure.
- SHAPE is a program for shape optimum design of two- or three-dimensional continuum structures. The shape of the design can be changed both at the boundaries and internally by appropriate removal of material.
- SECOPT is a program for optimum design of beam cross-sections of any prescribed shape. The cross-sectional dimensions are changed appropriately to minimize area of the cross-section.

STROPT and SHAPE programs yield optimized designs which satisfy constraints on response as well as on the design variables. The necessary finite element analyses are performed through NISA II into which the programs are integrated. SECOPT allows constraints on the cross-sectional properties and on the cross-sectional dimensions.

STROPT

STROPT is a general purpose, integrated finite element analysis/optimization program of NISA II for the optimum design of structures with prescribed geometry. It is a user friendly program employing the NISA II analysis package and state-of-the-art optimization techniques including design sensitivity computation.

The optimization process involves appropriately resizing the cross-sectional parameters that describe the design, while simultaneously satisfying prescribed limits on the structural response, in order to find the design with the minimum possible material volume or weight.

Prescribed limits (constraints) on the response may refer to the nodal displacements and element stresses under static loading as well as to the eigenvalues for free vibration or for stability. Additional limits may be placed on the cross-sectional parameters that are used as the design variables.

The design variables can be grouped and linked in many possible ways. This facility is especially useful for uniformity of design in certain regions of the structure, for creating a symmetrical design under unsymmetrical loading conditions, and for satisfying certain design specifications.

Optimization can be done for multiple load cases as well as for different associated boundary conditions. The given chart shows the general flow of the program.

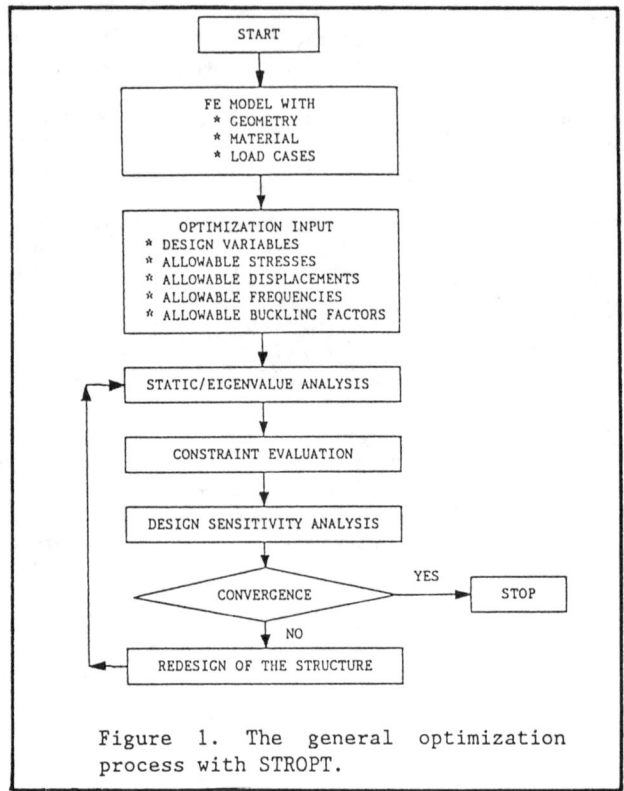

Figure 1. The general optimization process with STROPT.

Currently, the following types of structures can be optimized using STROPT:
- general shells
- layered composite shells or solids
- axisymmetric shell
- plates
- plane stress systems
- beams and frames of any arbitrary cross-section
- trusses
- any combination of the above types.

In addition, rigid elements can also be included in the model to simulate welds or for distribution of loads.

The SMC automobile hood shown on the accompanying figure is representative of the large scale problems that can be treated by STROPT.

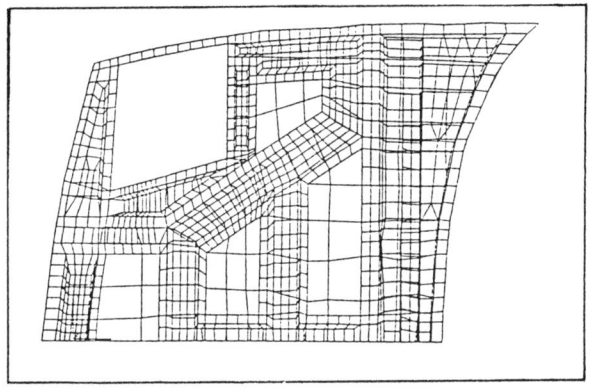

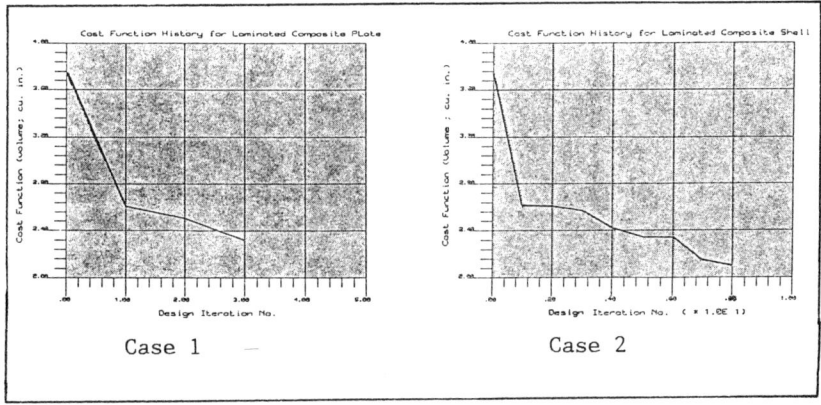

Optimum design of Laminated Composite Shell

The application of optimization procedures to the efficient design of laminates is presented. The problem is posed as the optimum weight of laminates in which the thicknesses and orientation angles of layers are treated as the design variables. Minimum weight designs are obtained considering various types of stress and displacement constraints under multiple load cases. In addition, optimum number of plies can be determined from the final design and the basic ply thickness. A simple example problem is solved to illustrate that the program STROPT offers an efficient and practical design tool of laminates. It should be noted, however, that when orientation angles are treated as design variables the designer may encounter various local minima, since the weight of the structure is independent of these variables. Nevertheless, it should be possible to change orientation angles to achieve better design.

Example: **Simply Supported Square Composite Plate** A simply supported square plate, ten inches on each side is subjected to uniform pressure. The plate has 9 layers, altering at 0 and 90 degrees with respect to the global x-axis.

Case 1 The design objective is to choose the layer thicknesses so that the plate is as light as possible, while satisfying constraints on stresses in fiber direction and layer thicknesses.

Case 2 The design objective is to choose the layer thicknesses and orientation angles so that the plate is as light as possible, while satisfying constraints on stresses in fiber direction and layer thicknesses.

Properties Elastic modulus $E_x = 40.E6$ psi
$E_y = 1.0E6$ psi
$G_{xy} = G_{xz} = 0.6E6$ psi
$G_{yz} = 0.5E6$ psi
Poisson's Ratio $V_{xy} = 0.25$
Basic Ply Thickness = 0.005 in.

Design Data No. of Design Variable Groups = 1
No. of Load Cases = 1
No. of Elements = 4
No. of Design Variable = 9 (case 2)
18 (case 2)
No. of Constraints = 144
Stress Limit = 100. ksi (S_{xx} in fiber direction)

Design Variable Limits

Type of Element	Design Variables	
	Lower Limit	Upper Limit
SHELL	0.005 in.	0.500 in.

Load Data Uniform normal pressure force of 10 psi on surface

Results for Laminated Composite Shell

Case 1 Only layer thickness is design variable

	Initial Design		Optimum Design	
	T_i (in.)	No. of plies	T_i (in.)	No. of plies
Summation	0.150	30	0.0926	19

Volume of total structure	15.000	9.276
No. of Active Constraints	0	2
Max. Constraint Violation	0.0000	0.00042

Case 2 Both layer thickness and angle are design variables

	Initial Design		Optimum Design	
	Ti (in.)	No. of plies	Ti (in.)	No. of plies
Summation	0.150	30	0.0838	17

Volume of total structure	15.000	8.380
No. of Active Constraints	0	2
Max. Constraint Violation	0.0000	0.00020

SHAPE This program adopts a completely new approach to the shape optimization of two- or three-dimensional continuum structures. The novelty of the approach lies in that the design variation is not limited to the original boundaries. Instead, new boundaries may be created as appropriate by removal of material from inside the system. This is accomplished by the ability to describe the entire structure as being subject to design variation.

Such a general approach has significant advantages, both in terms of modelling and in terms of the final results:
- There is no need to model the boundaries by parametric curves, a process which is rather difficult especially for solids. Instead, the finite element mesh for the structure is sufficient.
- While a shape optimization method based on boundary parameterization requires frequent remeshing of the finite element model since the elements on the boundaries get distorted very quickly, SHAPE can accomplish large design changes without the need for mesh refinement provided the original mesh is sufficiently fine. Higher order shape changes may be accomplished through automatic refinement of the mesh as decided upon by the program.
- Any symmetry condition may be fully exploited in modelling. This is in contrast to the boundary parameterization technique where the use of symmetry conditions would often interfere with the parametric model.
- Allowing for design variation throughout the system will often uncover new and more efficient load paths with drastically different stress distribution.
- Shapes can be derived for new applications by starting from a very general model. This is especially useful in guiding the

design towards the appropriate shape for the required application.

While the capability to change the shape of the entire structure is available, certain parts of the original design may be frozen by the user if so desired.

The most profound advantage of the method is due to the removal of material from inside the original structure. Contrary to an approach in conventional optimization, using boundary parameterization and starting with the initial shape would only yield a tapered shape with no holes.

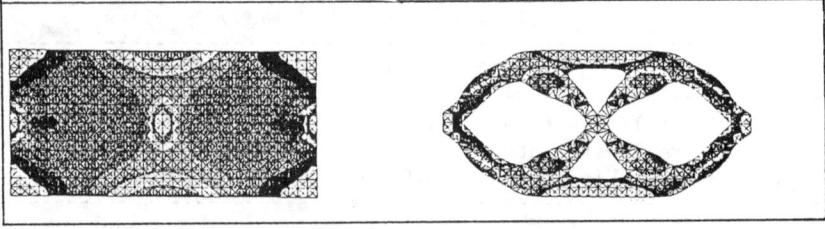

The design at the eighth step is found to be the same as that for the seventh. The material is reduced by 54.3% from the original design. The total CPU time for the eight steps is 285 seconds on an ELXSI-6400 computer.

SECOPT SECOPT is a program for finding the dimensions of a beam section that minimize the beam weight (or area of section) and satisfy a set of constraints on section properties as well as other constraints imposed by code requirements or other practical considerations. At the same time it gives all section properties of the optimum section for input to NISA II or any other similar finite element analysis program. The program is extremely efficient for design of beam cross sections. The user may impose additional constraints to control local buckling of web or flanges and to satisfy any packaging requirements.

NISA/PCB
PCB is a general purpose finite element analysis package for static, dynamic, thermal and stress analysis of printed circuit boards (PCBs). This package has been designed to predict the failure of the PCB or its components using the above mentioned analyses. This program has a built-in graphics pre-processor which allows the user to define a PCB and the different critical components located on the PCB. Once this information is input, the program proceeds to analyze it and automatically generate a finite element mesh for the PCB and all the integrated circuits (ICs). Care has been taken to form a well graded mesh, with a maximum aspect ratio of 5 and adjacent area ratio of 4, to predict reasonably correct answers. Special techniques of grouping several pins (or leads) of an IC are used to reduce the number of elements and nodes.

ENDURE

ENDURE is a general purpose software package for analyzing the fatigue performance of engineering structures. The program is extremely user-friendly and employs state-of-the-art theories to determine crack initiation and crack propagation lives. The propagation phase can be used independently for damage-tolerant structural design. Dynamic and random load effects can also be included in the damage calculations. The program provides various analysis models and allows for different types of load and material data description such as those encountered in aerospace, offshore, and automobile structural design.

Highlights
- Crack-Initiation and Crack-Propagation Analyses
- Low-Cycle and High-Cycle Regimes
- Stress-Life (S-N) and Strain-Life (ε-N) Correlations
- Safe-Life and Damage-Tolerant Analyses
- Choice of Crack-Growth Models
- Library of Standard Crack Configurations
- Variety of Load Descriptions, Including Variable-Amplitude Histories, Peak-Valley Matrices, and Power Spectral Densities
- Single- or Multiple-Point Load Application
- Dynamic Amplification and Random Load Effects
- Variety of Output Options, Including Life-Contour Plots
- Interface with Finite Element Analysis Codes
- Extreme User-Friendliness
- Available in PC, Mini and Mainframe Versions

Interfacing With FEA Codes   ENDURE can be conveniently used as a post processor of finite element analysis codes. It is currently interfaced with the analysis program NISA II and the graphics package DISPLAY II. It can easily be interfaced with other standard software packages such as NASTRAN, PATRAN, etc.

SAE Keyhole Specimen

The fatigue life predictions made by ENDURE are compared to the experimental results [7] generated by the SAE Cumulative Fatigue Damage Test Program. The stresses in the keyhole specimen, particularly near the notch root are determined by a finite element analysis using NISA. The fatigue lives spent in crack initiation and propagation phases under the action of the SAE suspension, transmission, and bracket load histories for two different materials (MANTEN and RQC-100) are shown on the right. The overall agreement is very good (most points lie within the factor-of-three error band) considering that the fatigue life test data is often associated with wide scatter.

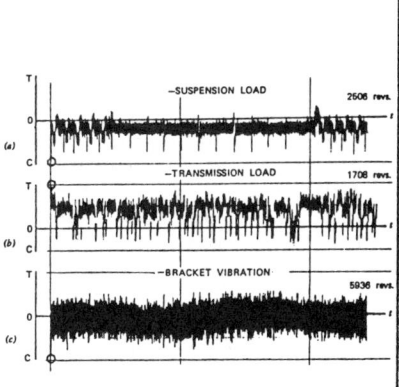

The SAE Load Histories

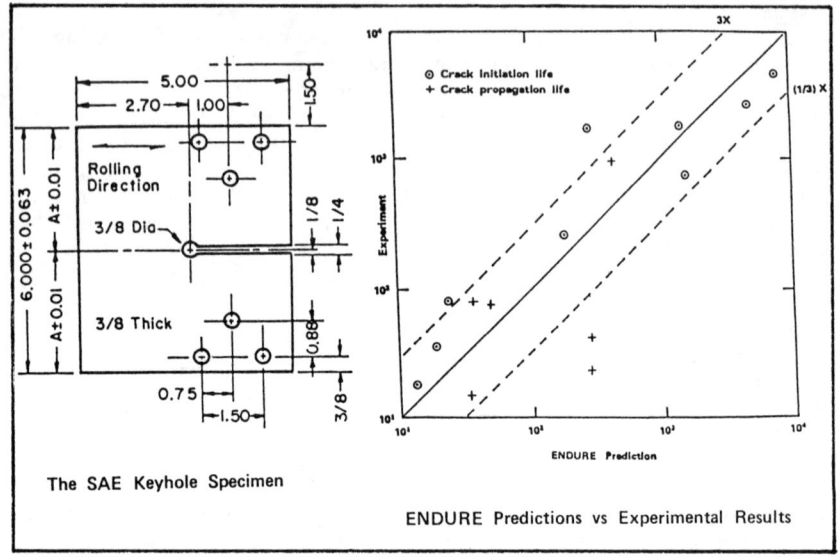

The SAE Keyhole Specimen

ENDURE Predictions vs Experimental Results

NISA/3D-FLUID
NISA/3D-FLUID is a three dimensional and axisymmetric program capable of analyzing a wide range of 2D and 3D incompressible, viscous, laminar and turbulent flow problems, including convective heat transfer problems. It is in a continuous state of development reflecting state-of-the-art techniques.

Element Library:
- Isoparametric linear and parabolic elements for 2D solid and wedge elements for axisymmetric analysis.
- Isoparametric linear and parabolic solid and wedge elements for general 3D problems.

Present Scope of Analysis: NISA/3D-FLUID uses penalty formulation with upwind-scheme for high Reynolds number flow, k-ε turbulence model for turbulent flow and Power-Law equation for Non-Newtonian fluid.

NISA/3D-FLUID can be used for solving a number of different problems in fluid mechanics and convective heat transfer including:
- 2D and axisymmetric steady state flow with heat transfer
- 2D and axisymmetric transient flow
- 3D steady flow with heat transfer
- 3D transient flow with heat transfer
- 2D and 3D turbulent flow
- 2D and 3D Non-Newtonian Fluid

Future Capabilities of NISA/3D-FLUID
- 2D and 3D compressible flow
- Two phase flow
- Combustion/Chemical reaction
- Many other advanced fluid flow capabilities

Practical Applications NISA/3D-FLUID is very user friendly and can be easily used to analyze a number of 2D and 3D practical problems such as:
- Heat transfer in a nuclear reactor
- Flow in pipes and ducts
- Flow through arteries, veins and heart valves, etc.
- Flow past bodies, etc.

Output Features: NISA/3D-FLUID provides output for a comprehensive review of results. The features include:
- Color plots of velocity vector for both 2D and 3D flows
- Color contour plots of pressure distribution
- Color streamline contours
- Color temperature contours
- Color contours of strain rate
- Color contours of shear rate

Sample Problems:
- NISA/3D-FLUID is used to calculate velocity, pressure and temperature of fluid in a 2D channel flow with a plate in the middle. The finite element mesh along with the color plots are shown.
- A 3D cavity flow is also considered to show the capability of the program for 3D fluid flow. Plots of the velocity along with sectional plots of temperature and pressure are shown.
- A transient solution of flow with vortex shedding behind a rectangular cylinder is solved. Plots of the velocity pressure and temperature at different time steps are shown.
- Newtonian and Non-Newtonian Fluid Flow with Reynolds number of 7,573 is shown for an axisymmetric cone (simulating blood flow through a valve).

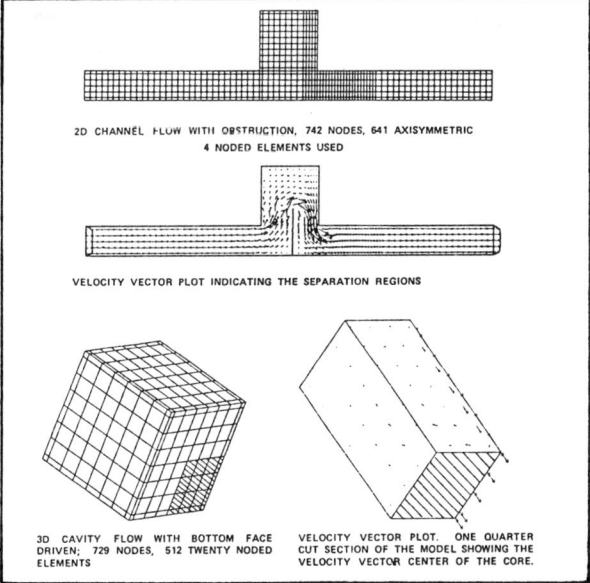

252 NISA II FAMILY OF FE PROGRAMS

THE PRE- AND POST-PROCESSING PROGRAM, DISPLAY II

DISPLAY II is a 3D interactive color graphics program with extensive pre- and post-processing color graphics capabilities. The pre-processing capabilities include preparation of data for finite element analysis compatible with the NISA II program, ANSYS, MSC/NASTRAN and other programs. A wide range of capabilities are offered allowing the user great flexibility and power in modelling any geometry.

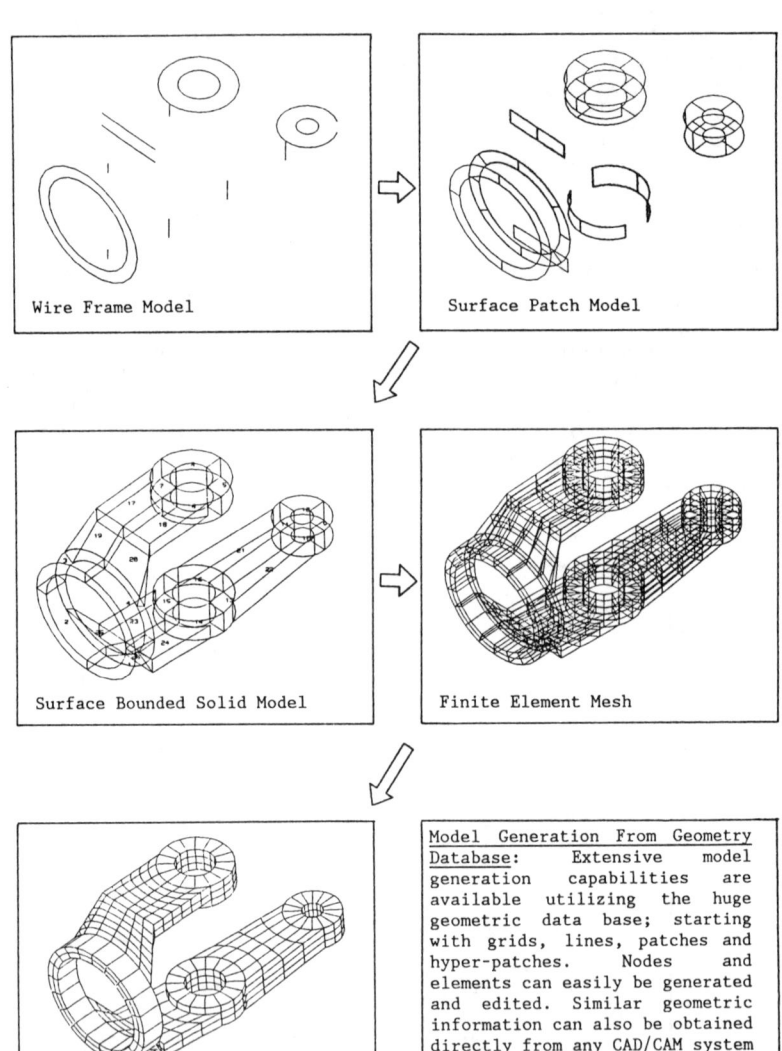

Model Generation From Geometry Database: Extensive model generation capabilities are available utilizing the huge geometric data base; starting with grids, lines, patches and hyper-patches. Nodes and elements can easily be generated and edited. Similar geometric information can also be obtained directly from any CAD/CAM system such as CADKEY, AUTOCAD, and so forth.

NISA II FAMILY OF FE PROGRAMS 253

Model Generation Pre-Processing
- Model any complex geometry using an extensive library of linear and higher order beams, shells, solids, etc.,
- Digitize elements and nodes of a model from drawings, or create the model from geometry data base,
- Merge two views to create a three-dimensional model and define three-dimensional elements,
- Automatically generate a two- or three-dimensional mesh,
- Allows users to generate 3D elements from 2D element mesh with variable thickness,
- Generate mesh by dragging a defined plane along an arbitrary path,
- Generate a symmetric mesh by reflection about a global plane or an arbitrary plane in rectangular or cylindrical coordinates,
- Convert lower order elements into higher order elements and vice versa,
- Allows user to create different parts of the model individually and merges all together to form the whole model,

Display & Editing
- Define and display all NISA data groups interactively, such as, material properties, boundary conditions, coupled displacements, or concentrated nodal forces at any nodes, etc.,
- List interactively a summary of the available options, have online help for any option,
- Interactively edit element and node point data using cursors, digitizing tablet and keyboard,
- Locate element or node numbers from an arbitrary view,
- Allows users to recover the original model after an inappropriate mesh generation,
- Select elements, nodes or element type for plotting,
- Isolate a portion, enlarge it or scale it down, rotate the view and display the model in different views,
- Display shrunk (users specified factor) elements to show element connectivity,
- Draw exact curved boundary of curved structures by using shape functions of higher order elements,
- Automatic hidden line removal,
- Display boundary faces and/or boundary of the structure with or without node numbers,
- Save up to 10 views for later use during a session,
- Checks distortion index for 2D and 3D elements. This allows to detect badly distorted elements,
- Allows users to selectively calculate area and volume for 2D and 3D elements, respectively,
- Check and/or optimize wavefront,
- Captures all user's activities (history of execution) in a file called session file. This file can be resubmitted to DISPLAY to replay the whole execution,
- Allows the user to have a consistent connectivity for shell

elements and solid elements automatically,

Output: Post-Processing The DISPLAY II has extensive interactive 3D color graphics capabilities for post-processing the results of finite element analysis. The ease of use of the program makes it possible for the user to apply the software quickly and without much effort. DISPLAY II also has outstanding color graphics post-processing capabilities for a wide variety of problems. Some of the outstanding and frequently used capabilities are listed below:
- User friendliness
- Speed comparable or faster than rival existing market leaders
- Color or monochrome
- Static or animation
- Contour plotting
  - Lines
  - Color fringes
  - Stresses
  - Displacements
  - Temperatures
- Allows the user to select the color spectrum and/or equal/unequal color bands of his choice for any contour plotting. Also allows the spectrum to be reversed for real interpretation of an entity like fatigue life.
- Light source shading
- Hidden line removal
- Feature line plotting
- Sectioning: Stress, displacements, pressure, velocity, temperature, etc., contour plots can be obtained on any section through solid.
- Several features to limit active plotting set, e.g. constrained volume, selection by element indexes, quantity limits.
- Multiple window plots capability enables plotting of any type of plot simultaneously on the screen. Any number of window plots can be generated on the screen exercising any of the plot options of DISPLAY II.
- Geometry: scaling, rotation, cursor window, symmetric model and results generation.

DISPLAY II can generate the entire data deck, including loading conditions, material properties, etc., for NISA II or NISA II.

For very large jobs, the data prepared by DISPLAY II can be transferred to mini and mainframe computers. For post-processing, files can be transferred to the PC from mini or mainframe computers and vice versa. Interfaces to generate data deck for other programs such as, ANSYS, NASTRAN, ABAQUS, etc., will be released soon.

References

(1) Pica, A. and Wood, R.D. 'Post Buckling Behavior of Plates and Shells using a Mindlin Shallow Shell Formulation'. Computers and Structures, Vol. 12, pp. 759-768, 1980

(2) Sabir, A.B. and Lock, A.C. 'The Application of Finite Elements to the Large Deflection Non-linear Behavior of Cylindrical Shells', 7/66-75, Southampton University Press, 1973.

(3) Chi-Mou Ni, 'Impact Response of Curved Box Beam- Columns with Large Global and Local Defeormations', GMR Publ., GMR-1331, Warren, MI 1973

(4) Holden, J.T. 'On the Finite Deflections of Thin Beams', Int. Journal Solids and Structures, 8 (1972) 1051-5.

(5) Bathe, K.J. and Ozdmir, H. 'Elastic-plastic Large Deformation Static and Dynamic Analysis', Computers and Structures, 6, (1976) 81-92.

(6) Alman, J.O. and Laszlo, A., 'The Uniform Section Disk Springs' Trans. of ASME Research Papers, RP-58-10.

(7) Bussa, S. and Tucker, L. 'The SAE Cumulative Fatigue Damage Test Program', Paper 750038 presented at the SAE Automotive Engineering Congress, Detroit, Michigan, 1975.